TV NEWS 3.0

AN INSIDER'S GUIDE TO LAUNCHING AND
RUNNING NEWS CHANNELS IN THE
DIGITAL AGE

ZAFAR SIDDIQI

**Blue
Magpie**

First published in Great Britain in 2019

By Blue Magpie Books

Paperback ISBN 978-1-912937-05-9

Ebook ISBN 978-1-912937-06-6

Printed in Great Britain by Clays Ltd, Elcograf S.p.A.

Blue Magpie Books

80-83 Long Lane,

London, EC1A 9ET

www.bluemagpiebooks.com

CONTENTS

ABOUT THE AUTHOR

Zafar Siddiqi was an accountant with KPMG for 18 years, initially as a partner and later as the Managing Director of one of its consultancy practices. He left the world of spreadsheets in the mid-1990s, having spotted an opportunity to launch a TV production house in his native Pakistan specialising in providing business programmes to overseas broadcasters.

A few years later, he saw the chance to start a CNBC business network across 18 countries in the Middle East, the first international brand to broadcast in Arabic. This was quickly followed by his establishing similar networks across 39 countries in Africa, and in Pakistan. Later, he started Samaa TV in Karachi, a 24-hour news and current affairs channel.

He still serves as chairman of two of these channels, devoting much of his time to their strategic direction, not least in wrestling with the challenges they face from the digital revolution that this book deals with.

He lives with his family in Dubai, Karachi and London. He can be reached via his website, TVNews3-0.com.

INTRODUCTION

The world of television news is endlessly fascinating. From its origins when the entire family crowded together at a fixed time each evening to watch bulletins from one or two broadcasters to today's intense 24/7, always-connected, multi-screen, multiple-provider world, news has never been more intense or more instant. In such a hyper-competitive environment, the battle to get breaking news on screens first means that the journalists who produce the content are under unremitting pressure.

Managing a TV news business in this day and age has never been more challenging. In its first incarnation, TV news was a comparatively sedate affair; newsrooms were geared up to produce just one or, at most, two 30-minute programmes a day. When Britain's BBC launched its TV news in July 1954, the first bulletin did not even use moving film, consisting of a series of still photographs and maps - with the newsreader heard but not seen on screen. It was only the emergence of a rival service, Independent Television News (ITN), in 1955 that compelled the BBC to rethink its approach.

This cozy situation - where, in every country, a small handful of channels at best had a monopoly on TV news (BBC and ITN in Britain, three big networks, CBS, NBC and ABC, in America, and single, state-controlled channels almost everywhere else) - continued until the 1980s when technological advances in cable and satellite delivery ushered in the world's first 24-hour news channel, Ted Turner's Cable News Network (CNN) in America. At first, CNN was derided as "Chicken Noodle News" for its lack of resources and on-air gaffes, and conventional wisdom said it wouldn't last six months. The then CBS News President, Bill Leonard, asked disdainfully, "Why would anybody choose to watch a patched-together news operation that's just starting against an organization like ours that's been going for 50 years and spends $100 million to $150 million a year?" The smugness began to wear off when, in January 1986, CNN was the only TV network to provide live coverage of the disastrous launch of the Space Shuttle Challenger, which abruptly disintegrated 73 seconds after lift-off, killing all seven crew members, including a female school teacher.

By the late Eighties, 24-hour news channels had sprung up across the world; this was the beginning of the second era of TV news. In this iteration, there was round-the-clock coverage and much more choice for viewers, but all the expensive kit and large numbers of people required by way of resources ensured that TV news remained the play thing of rich businessmen, state broadcasters or established networks. Fifty years on from its first news bulletin, BBC News had grown to comprise 2,000 journalists and 41 overseas newsgathering bureaux, producing more than 45,000 hours of programming a year - an average of 120 hours of news broadcasting for every day of the year. A far cry from one 30-minute programme a day.

Today, new technological advances - principally the ability to stream video over the internet, in the way that Netflix and Amazon Prime operate - has changed TV news again. It is much easier, and much cheaper, to launch a "television" news channel today, to reach audiences and to build a successful business on the back of it. This is the exciting revolution that is TV News 3.0.

My adventure in TV began in the mid-1990s when I launched a production company in Pakistan called Telebiz. I was really a novice who knew nothing about the TV industry - an accountant by profession, I was a partner with KPMG in the Middle East - but had some experience of writing and a deep passion for news.

My only previous foray into the world of screens had come when I saw the 1981 adventure film *Raiders of the Lost Ark* while I was in Buffalo in the US state of New York. We were supposed to have gone on a day visit to Niagara Falls, but it was postponed because of rain and we chose to go to the movies instead. I liked the film so much that I decided to purchase its distribution rights for Pakistan. Ordinarily, foreign films could only be distributed by the state, but United International Pictures (UIP), the owners of the film, invoked a contractual clause declaring the film "special", which effectively gave the power to Steven Spielberg, as the producer, to appoint a consultant (in this case, me) to distribute the film, rather than the government agency.

When released in Pakistan, it ran for more than a year, breaking all the country's box office records. An extra perk for me was that I was invited to the royal premieres of the "Indiana Jones" sequels in London. It was, indeed, a treat to be walking with the stars and royalty.

When launching my first production company, I was fortunate to have good people around who helped on all aspects of the TV business, particularly the systems side. Engineering was never my forte.

When I decided to launch my first TV news station, in the Middle East in 2003 (called CNBC Arabiya), and wanted to know the ins and outs of doing so, I searched in vain for a book that would suffice as a manual. I found publications that covered different aspects - operations, newsrooms, HR etc - but nothing that encompassed all of how to launch and manage a TV station.

The purpose of this book is to try to fill that gap. I hope - indeed, believe - that *TV News 3.0: An insider's guide to launching and running news channels in the digital age* has everything that anyone already in the business, or those seeking to become involved in it, needs to know, from the entrepreneur who wishes to start or invest in a TV station to the media student hoping to work in the industry. I also think it may be of some interest to ordinary viewers seeking to understand more about how the news they see on their screens is put together. I feel that I owe this work to an industry which has been so good to me.

It's been an extremely interesting and rewarding job. There have been joyous occasions over the years, such as when His Highness Sheikh Mohammed, the ruler of Dubai, inaugurated the opening of CNBC Arabiya in 2003, and Pakistan's President Pervez Musharraf launched CNBC Pakistan in 2005. A particular highlight for me was having the good fortune to meet Nelson Mandela just before we launched CNBC Africa in 2007. By that time, he had long retired from frontline politics, but was still mentally very alert and characteristically courteous and humorous. When I told him about our plans, he said: "You have my blessing and it will be good for Africa." I was so lucky to have met him; he radiated warmth and affection, and was such a great man.

Regrettably, there have also been some very sad occasions along the way. Since we launched Samaa, our 24-hour news channel in Pakistan, we have had six members of staff, including three camera operators and a reporter, killed while doing their jobs. These deaths still weigh heavily on my mind. The day when you visit a family whose main breadwinner has died in the line of duty and see his wife and children in shock and bewilderment leaves a lasting impact. These deaths happened in Pakistan between 2010 and 2013, when we endured many bombings, and our brave men and women in the TV industry covered it without fear. Thank God, that terrible period is over but such violence still happens around the world, with terrorism, wars and other forms of human tragedy. When you next watch TV news events of this nature, spare a thought not just for those suffering but also for the reporters and camera operators bringing you the stories and the pictures. They deserve our special prayers and thanks for their dedication and courage.

I have been lucky enough to have ended up in a business about which I am passionate. I have enjoyed every day of my involvement in it. Every day in the TV news business is an exciting new one: you never know what's going to happen next.

The only advice I have ever given to news directors, producers and presenters in the newsroom is to keep their story-telling simple. Don't complicate it for people; the last thing they want to see on their TV is something that does not provide them with understandable explanations and answers about what is happening and why it's happening.

As I did my research for the book and consulted many of my friends and colleagues around the world, I was struck by two main themes. The first was how the digital revolution we are still going through has, alongside a lot of good things, a somewhat darker and more dangerous side. When I was writing the book's final chapter looking at what the future of television news might consist of, I had the light-hearted idea of speaking to some clairvoyants and astrologists to hear their predictions. One forecast, made by a British astrologer, was that in the future someone "bad" will seize control of one or more of the technology giants and use them for nefarious means. She makes a valid point, but given how bad it is already today, I wonder just how much worse it could possibly become?

There has to be something profoundly wrong when we live in a society in which virtually anyone can set themselves up as a purveyor of "news", where click-bait and "fake news" is deliberately concocted to suit political or personal agendas, where anonymous "trolls" can post vile abuse and threats on social media with impunity, and where terrorists can live-stream to the world their slaughter of innocent people. There is an urgent need, in my view, for the creation of an international body to regulate all of this, and for the platforms themselves to be held more responsible for their distribution of such evil material.

The other matter of concern for me is the competition for ratings across the globe. In some countries, this has diluted content to the extent that sensationalism has become the norm, defeating the approach I espouse, which is to calmly present the news in a relatively serious manner. The use of salacious stories to grab people's attention, the use of lurid words to attract and increase viewership, seems to have become a norm. I know that there are exceptions to this "race to the bottom", and, at the end of the day, the viewer now has many choices; he or she can go to a station or a device that suits his or her appetite. But it is a worrying trend seen across both traditional and digital media. Can it be corrected? I doubt it, as the beast is already loose. No longer are there agreed boundaries as to what can and cannot be published. The role of traditional broadcasters and publishers as "gatekeepers" of news has blurred, if it still exists at all. It is troubling. I can only hope that the final prediction from the British astrologer mentioned earlier turns out to be correct: she went on to elaborate that good always defeats evil in the end.

In the TV business, as in all other aspects of life and commerce, it is teamwork that achieves success. A positive attitude in life is a must, as is respect for your colleagues. In writing this book, I was lucky to have some wonderful people helping me, giving guidance and correcting some of my errors. First among those to thank is Richard Ellis, an experienced British newspaper executive who has worked tirelessly in suggesting structures and editing my words as we have moved forward with the project.

There are many others who have given their time and advice. Richard Tait, the former Editor in Chief of Britain's ITN and an ex-BBC governor, graciously agreed to read the whole book and gave some extremely pertinent and useful insights. Another ex-ITN hand, Lesley Everett, the network's former director of operations, shaped and sharpened the operations chapter. Chris Birkett, a former executive editor of Sky News (2006-2013) and managing editor of BBC News 24 (1999-2000), was of particular assistance with the "specials" chapter, while David Hayward, the former head of the BBC Journalism Programme and a BBC editor/reporter, was a great help with the newsroom chapter. Mahim Maher, the head of digital at Samaa TV, was as thorough as ever with her great work on the digital aspects of the book.

Finally, my gratitude goes to the teams at CNBC Africa and Samaa TV, and all my other colleagues and friends who have given their time and advice.

Thank you to all the above. Without them, this book would not have been possible. While I am extremely grateful for their support, it goes without saying that the responsibility for its content - and any errors remaining in it - is mine alone.

I have sought to make the book as accessible as possible by incorporating a few real-life experiences and humorous episodes from my 25 years in the business. I hope that it brings enjoyment and enlightenment to some people somewhere.

London, 2019

To my closest friend and loving wife, Seema, my wonderful children, Saba, Ayesha, Sarah and Bilal, and my first grandchild, Anya, who will be a source of joy for years to come

1

THE TV NEWS INDUSTRY TODAY

"You have brains in your head. You have feet in your shoes. You can steer yourself, any direction you choose." **Dr. Seuss**

So you want to be in the TV news business? Perhaps it's been an ambition since childhood, a dream driven by a desire to tell the world the truth about itself, to right wrongs and fight injustice, to make hard-hitting films and documentaries that change the course of human history. Or perhaps you just love the idea of being on camera, of being "famous", of being fêted and recognised wherever you go.

Whatever your motivation, why not? The lure of a job in the TV industry is a potent one. Television is the most powerful form of mass media in the world. Some nine decades after it first emerged in our world, a small monochrome baby flickering and blinking in the corners of living rooms, it remains a dominant force despite recent challenges to its hegemony. Hundreds of millions of us switch it on every day, to be entertained, informed, educated and amused, and to absorb messages from advertisers keen to promote their wares. Billions of us still tune in at the same time to watch live broadcasts of world-changing events or sporting clashes; on the list of the world's most-watched live events, sports occupies the first 25 places, with the London and Rio Olympics sharing the top spot, each having attracted 3.6 billion viewers.

Television has played a key role in the coverage of the world's most momentous news events over the decades. The assassination of US President John F. Kennedy in 1963. The 2006 capture, trial and execution of Iraq's Saddam Hussein. The fall of the Berlin Wall in 1990. The explosion of the Challenger spacecraft in 1986. The Indian Ocean tsunami of 2004. The 1989 Tiananmen Square protests. The September 11 attacks on the World Trade Center in 2001. Man's first step on the Moon in 1969. Nelson Mandela's walk to freedom from prison in 1990 in South Africa. The tanks rolling in to free Kuwait in 1991. The final Soviet withdrawal from Afghanistan in 1989 and its continuing impact on Pakistan in the form of terrorism. The list is endless. Those of us who were privileged enough to watch those moments as they happened still feel as if we had ringside seats to history; that is the power of television.

The news that broadcasters transmit 24 hours a day, seven days a week continues to have a deep influence on people around the globe, to affect the policies and directions taken by business and political leaders, nationally and internationally, and to shape the destinies of countries. When politicians have something important to say to their people, it is their go-to medium of choice.

Who wouldn't want to be a part of something as important as that? To be even a small cog in the wheel of an industry that affects the course and fortunes of whole peoples and continents is to be part of something monumental. It's a fascinating, captivating industry full of interested, talented individuals doing interesting and talented things, most of them passionate and highly driven by what they do, and by their mission to inform and educate. It is also true that some of them are obsessive, power-hungry narcissists, preoccupied by the way they look on screen and the ratings they attract. When I think about working in TV news, I am sometimes reminded of that passage from the still very watchable 1987 Hollywood movie *Broadcast News*, when the station manager says to a conceited, superstar producer who has challenged his decision, "It must be nice to always believe you know better, to always think you're the smartest person in the room", and she replies in a horrified whisper, without a trace of irony, "No. It's awful."

We live in extremely intriguing and exciting times. Television may still be the world's dominant medium, but is part of a landscape that is being relentlessly challenged by the digital revolution and the changes in the way in which people consume media: no longer just from a fixed-point screen in their homes, but via a small one that travels with them everywhere, always on, always available, and always demanding attention. Each smartphone in our pockets has more computing power than all of Nasa had when it first sent those astronauts to the Moon. And, as others have said, so a part of us have they become, they are like extensions of ourselves.

Although many people still look at a TV when big news events break, if you project 10 or 20 years from now, it will be very different. Print is a (barely) living example of how the digital transformation can cause potentially fatal disruption to traditional media players. Vibrant, forceful and vastly profitable for decades, most newspapers, particularly in the developed world but also a substantial number in the developing world, are now on life-support and fading fast. Many, if not all, are losing money, some are closing down or desperately trying to reinvent themselves as digital brands. Will traditional TV news channels face a similar fate? Perhaps. They certainly need to radically adapt themselves to the new world, if they, too, are to avoid becoming irrelevant. Or, indeed, extinct.

But the broadcast news business has always been adept at evolution. TV news around the world has changed dramatically since the first programmes in the 1940s and 1950s. The changes have been driven by technology, regulation and by audience expectations. For the first 30 years, the bulletin was king - millions tuned in to their favourite channel at the same time every night to see the news. The main newscasters became household names; for many, they were the face of the channel. The bulletin was restricted to 20 minutes or half an hour on a general channel that offered other programming, such as enter-tainment, drama and sport, but the evening news was seen as "an appointment to view" - one of the key moments in the daily schedule. Terrestrial broadcasting technology meant that there were only a few channels to choose from, thus ensuring that audiences were vast.

Revolutionary changes in broadcast technology in the 1970s and 1980s transformed the creation and distribution of television news around the world. Two terms described the revolution in coverage - ENG and SNG. With Electronic News Gathering (ENG), stories could be shot and edited on tape, not film, making the production process much faster. In Satellite News Gathering (SNG), stories could be beamed immediately back to base and presenters could report live into the programme from almost anywhere in the world. Sir David Nicholas, the former Editor in Chief of the UK's Independent Television News (ITN), once described the advent of this (virtually) no-limits technology as "almost every week you could do something new which you couldn't have done the week before".

At the same time, the arrival of cable and satellite distribu-tion systems made room for hundreds of channels, not just a few, dominant, general ones. Enterprising broadcasters realised that there could be a market for specialist channels focusing on one genre - movies, entertainment, sport or news. "Appointment to view" news became "always on" news.

In 1980, Ted Turner, a visionary US broadcast executive, launched the Cable News Network (CNN), the first 24-hour news channel. He boasted: "We won't be signing off till the world ends." Initially, rivals sneered at the low-cost Atlanta-based operation as "Chicken Noodle News" and the White House refused it press credentials. Turner lost $250 million before the channel broke even, and he claimed to have slept on a couch in his office for the first 10 years. But by the time of the first Gulf War in 1990, it was clear that the 24-hour news channel had come of age with its live coverage of the conflict. Its reporters stood on rooftops watching missile battles over Jerusalem and tracked US cruise missiles flying into Baghdad. The White House and politicians and diplomats around the world began to talk about the "CNN Effect" - the ability of images and stories on CNN and other news channels to shift public policy as viewers reacted to what they were seeing.

Turner was joined in not always friendly rivalry by another larger than life character. Rupert Murdoch, an Australian-born newspaper tycoon, launched two very different channels - Sky News in Europe in 1989 and Fox News in the US in 1996. Sky and Fox quickly became household brands, helping Murdoch to build a global broadcast and entertainment empire which, together with his newspapers, gave him enormous political influence on both sides of the Atlantic.

The two interlopers faced fierce competition from one of the traditional broadcasters - NBC - which launched a business channel (CNBC) in 1989, and a general news channel (MSNBC) in 1996. In Europe, the main broadcasters, too, had to react. The BBC launched World Service Television (later BBC World) in 1991, followed by European public service broadcasters launching Euronews in 1993, and a whole host of national channels across the Continent.

In the North American market at least, news channels have become a colossal business. The Pew Research Center estimates that in 2017 the three main news channels - Fox, CNN and MSNBC - had revenues of $5 billion, with more than half of that profit. In contrast, the main evening news programmes on ABC, CBS and NBC, the channels that had once dominated the world of TV news, achieved revenues of less than $600 million. Turner and Murdoch had turned the world upside down.

During the past three decades, there has been enormous growth in the number of news channels available, with more than 300 around the world at last count. And although, as we will see, news channels now face challenges from the digital revolution and the explosive growth of social media, the crucial role of television news in society remains unchanged. For we are now in the third age of television news, driven by the online and social media technologies that are transforming the way it is viewed as well as produced; still always available but now "on demand", streamed over the internet, and with viewers able to choose news tailored to their particular needs and interests.

No one has yet discovered the precise answer as to exactly what form this particular adaptation needs to take. Most broadcasters are experimenting with a variety of initiatives, such as live-streaming over the internet, embracing social media, putting news clips and programmes onto Facebook, YouTube, Instagram and Twitter, or onto new platforms such as Amazon Fire, Apple TV, Sling, Hulu and AT&T's DirecTV. New entrants using only the internet to stream their channels are both a threat and an opportunity. Sling was launched in the US in February 2015, billed as the first multichannel live TV service over the internet. It is giving its subscribers - more than two million at last count - a choice of bundles of channels, including news, entertainment and sport, at less than half the price of cable providers. Its success has spawned more than half a dozen competitors.

The innovation taking place in the industry in America is

fascinating. Ad-supported, free-to-watch streaming news channels are becoming more and more numerous, coming both from
established players and startups. Cheddar, a new media company
launched in 2016 with the goal of becoming the CNBC for
millennials, broadcasts live from the New York Stock Exchange
eight hours a day, is making US$30 million in revenue a year and
was valued at US$160 million in late 2018. Given its aim, and
the fact that I founded three CNBC franchises across the globe,
in Africa, the Middle East and in Pakistan, it is one in which I
take a very personal interest. NBC News was planning to launch
a streaming news channel called Signal aimed at younger audiences in the first half of 2019, while CBS has launched ad-
supported streaming news channels CBSN, CBS Sports HQ, and
ET Live, an entertainment channel. Not to be outdone,
Bloomberg, the American business network, has launched
TicToc, billed as the first and only global news network built for
Twitter. It's unclear which of these initiatives will prosper, but
for the traditional players these are the crucial first steps in trying
to future-proof their businesses; they are good for the brand, and
help build presence and reach.

Many changes have taken place in the markets where I estab-
lished channels. In the Middle East, CNBC Arabiya was the first
Arabic language international brand to launch. In Africa, CNBC
Africa was the continent's first international business brand
name, as CNBC Pakistan was in that country. Since then, in the
Middle East, most international brands have launched in the
Arabic language. In Africa, local news channels have sprung up
in various countries, most prominently in South Africa. In
Pakistan, news channels have sprouted in prodigious numbers.
But, whatever market they are in, all these stations are trying to
cope with the challenging nature of the rise of digital.

Broadcasters need to let go of old certainties, of thinking
about terrestrial, cable and satellite as the go-to ways of transmission, or of the television "set" being the preferred mode of

watching for consumers. These are no longer certainties. TV
bosses need to be less precious and much more relaxed about
where their content appears. In the end, should we really care
about where people watch our content, or on what device? The
importance, surely, is that it's being watched. There has to be a
value in making the content available as widely as possible and
then working out how to monetise it. That may be somewhat
problematical at the moment, but it will become easier with technological advances.

I will deal at length with some of these new ventures and
more on what the future might bring in later chapters. But if we
were to pause briefly to peer into my somewhat cloudy crystal
ball, I would venture three broad predictions here, tempered by
the observation that the accelerating and radical nature of the
change we are caught up in makes it unlikely that anything
written today will remain true the day after.

Firstly, it is far from doom and gloom. News is as important
now as it has ever been - arguably more so. Moving pictures,
video, film, television, whatever you want to term it, remains a
compelling way to tell stories. We traditional broadcasters - most
of us, at least - are alive to the challenges that digital has
brought, and excited by its potential for the work we do, and how
we can use its reach to attract, inform and engage even bigger
audiences. Yes, it is unsettling, daunting, scary - change always
is. But it is also a fascinating and wonderful opportunity for us,
one that we need to embrace wholeheartedly. We are in the midst
of something revolutionary, a seismic shift that will eclipse the
one that terrestrial television wrought to radio from the 1940s
onwards and what cable and then satellite technology did in turn
to the analog world from the 1980s onwards. Our destiny is in
our hands. We need to be bold and seize the opportunities of the
multi-platform world.

Secondly, it seems clear that internet streaming channels and
providers, which include such newcomers as Sling, will

continue to grow and prosper. In the entertainment sector, Netflix's video-on-demand service has proved formidable, causing immense disruption to Hollywood studios and the traditional entertainment networks, driving up production costs and making the small screen the screen of choice for many of the world's most talented and sought-after actors. So, too, Amazon Prime. In America in 2018, an estimated 33 million people ditched their subscriptions to cable and satellite TV in favour of solely using internet streaming services, up 33 per cent on the year before.

There are more questions than answers right now. What will emerge from the foray of the telecoms giants like Verizon and AT&T into the media and entertainment business, particularly following the latter's US$85 billion takeover of Time Warner? Might one of the tech giants - an Amazon, a Google, a Facebook or an Apple - be tempted to set up a Netflix for news, perhaps as an antidote to the growing criticisms of their hosting such material as videos promoting terrorism, white supremacy, child porn and other nefarious activity? Perhaps it will be the initiatives of the traditional news broadcasters, such as those of NBC and CBS, that will crack the secret of the next-generation news network? Or will the big winner emerge from one of the myriad startups?

A cautionary tale from history. I'm old enough to remember, in the year 2000, the US$165 billion takeover of Time Warner by the then king of new media, AoL. It was hailed by the high-fiving chief executives of both companies as the creation of the largest and most powerful media and entertainment conglomerate in the world, bringing together America's leading internet provider with brands such as CNN, HBO, Time, Sports Illustrated and Warner Bros, and was valued at $350 billion. Time Warner's share price soared, and one US media analyst at Bear Stearns told CNN: "Together, they represent an unprecedented powerhouse. If their mantra is content, this alliance is unbeatable. Now they have this great platform they can cross-fertilize with content and redistribute."

A little over a year later, the unbeatable alliance had been floored and was in disarray. That so-called analyst (who had been earning US$4 million a year for dispensing his expert opinion) had given up his career as a media sage to become an artist in New York, and the ill-fated AoL-Time Warner marriage had turned into an unmitigated disaster that signalled the high-water mark of the first dotcom boom. The Time Warner chief executive who brokered the deal, Gerald Levin, was branded by CNBC as one of the "Worst American CEOs of All Time". In 2009, AoL, its subscription business model left for dead by fast-moving competitors like Google, was spun off and was later acquired by Verizon for just US$4.4 billion. Still a lot of money for a somewhat busted flush, in my view, but clearly Verizon's adventurous bosses see some value in it that I don't.

The only certainty we really have is that there is no certainty as to which of today's plays will prevail. Business leaders big and small are making their best calls and rolling the dice. Some will be hailed as visionary heroes, while others will face a similar ignominy as that of Time Warner's former boss. It's an exciting, if somewhat nerve-wracking, time.

My third prediction is that it is going to be increasingly difficult to rely on the traditional advertising-funded model for news channels, at least outside of the United States. As you will learn later in this book, the infrastructure required for a traditional, linear 24-hour news channel is formidably expensive: a studio or two, a dozen well-paid anchors, and contributors and guests who all have to be booked and who, in some countries, are each provided free transportation to the studio. Then there's the required armies of producers, graphic designers, copy writers, reporters, crews and editors, not to mention continually open satellite links, transponders, news feeds etc. And the audiences they attract are generally low, ageing, and, in some cases, numerically declining. TV news can be intoxicating when a genuine news event happens, but when there is not one (which is often), the unlimited and frequent repetition of stories and the endless "two-ways" between bored presenters and weary correspondents with nothing new or interesting to say, but who are compelled to fill the airtime with something - *anything* - makes for very dull viewing. Even a TV news junkie like me often reaches for the off button in those circumstances.

The economics of traditional news channels are not just challenging, but becoming increasingly difficult. Very few are profitable. Many rely on licence revenue, government or taxpayer funding (such as the BBC, Al Jazeera or Russia Today) or subsidies from other parts of their business (such as Sky News). Of course, sometimes news channels have a value beyond their individual profit and loss account. Sky News may not have made money but it gave the fledgling Sky network credibility when it first launched - consumers liked having news as part of the package. And having what the then British Prime Minister Margaret Thatcher once called approvingly "the only unbiased news in the UK" helped its owner Rupert Murdoch persuade her to nod through the takeover deal that gave him a monopoly of satellite broadcasting in Britain. Fox News, on the other hand, is very profitable as well as influential - its enthusiastic espousal of the conservative agenda has given Murdoch a powerful position in US politics, with Fox playing a significant role in the election of, in its owner's words, "my friend, Donald J. Trump".

The future probably involves a combination of revenue approaches. Charging subscriptions plus advertising (the model employed by Sky for its mix of channels) is probably the best answer, but at what stage the economic model will change is unclear. Will people be happy to pay solely for a news channel, as opposed to having it thrown in alongside a package of movies, drama and sport? I think enough might, if we can find ways to bring them closer to the stories we cover, and deliver experiences that they cannot receive elsewhere. Parallels can be drawn from the way that TV sports channels are making the act of watching an immersive experience for audiences by using Virtual Reality (VR) technology.

At some stage, TV news channels will probably have to abandon the traditional approach of linear broadcasting via cable or satellite and follow the example of the Slings and the Cheddars, and start to "broadcast" only over the internet, in a similar way as some newspapers (such as *The Independent* in the UK) have successfully abandoned print to become digital only. Alongside this, we will need to use technology to revolutionise how we cover stories and how our viewers "watch" the news. The future probably lies with digitally streamed news that has VR immersive capacity, and is able to deliver unique and compelling experiences, letting viewers "be there" as stories happen. No longer as mere viewers, but as participants. If we could be virtually transported from our living rooms into a seat next to a President as he or she announces a tearful resignation, or to be (safely) taken into the heart of Syria's war zone, or (again, safely) deposited onto a rooftop in Mozambique as flood waters threaten to tear the building down in the aftermath of a cyclone, these would be experiences worth paying for. To no longer just watch the news, but to be part of it, to explore, as VR pioneer Nonny de la Peña puts it, the "sights and sounds and possibly the feelings and emotions that accompany the news".

But these are just my hunches, my best guesses; in time, perhaps even now, you are almost certainly likely to be a better predictor of the future than me. When I was growing up in Pakistan in the 1960s, we had extremely limited options to satisfy our needs from television news, which was strictly controlled by the state; today, most of us have infinite choices of news channels to watch. You, as part of a lucky generation that has come of age with access to that awe-inspiring variety of content wherever, whenever and on whatever device you want, will have a smarter idea of what tomorrow will bring: tomorrow's television invariably needs tomorrow's people.

Peter Drucker, the father of modern management, once said: "The best way to predict the future is to create it." So this is my challenge to you, the young person who wants to be part of the TV news industry: why settle for just being a small cog, when you could be the wheel? Why not be ambitious and think big? Why not consider the idea of not just working for a television news channel, but of starting, running and owning one?

It may sound far-fetched or fanciful. You may laugh off the idea or put it on a par with my having suggested that you create a startup to launch the first manned flight to Mars (just imagine the ratings that mission would bring!). But almost anything is possible, if you want it badly enough. Who was it who said in 2012: "As I never tire of saying, my chances of becoming prime minister are only slightly better than being decapitated by a frisbee, blinded by a champagne cork, locked in a fridge, finding Elvis on Mars, or being reincarnated as an olive."? Ah, yes, the words of one Boris Johnson, newly installed in July 2019 as Britain's 77th prime minister, neither decapitated, blind, an olive, in a fridge, or accompanied by Elvis.

You may think - and you would be right - that the hurdles you have to overcome to start a television news channel are enormous, despite the digital revolution having made it easier, quicker and many times cheaper than it used to be. You may feel that the task is beyond a novice who's just hoping to get a foothold in the industry. Perhaps. But the hurdles are not - absolutely not - insurmountable. Even the inexperienced hurdler generally manages to clear most of the obstacles. And as you'll learn, I had no experience whatsoever in the television industry when I launched my first production company at the age of 45. Age is, as they say, just a number. Experience? Well, it is often just something too many old people try to hide behind when they want to hang on to their positions of seniority. Don't be put off.

Innovate, plan, believe in your dreams, and you can make it happen.

My foray into television news took place in a different time and landscape. Today's interconnected, always-on, mobile world is vastly different, but there are still valuable lessons to be learned from what's gone before. I hope this book will help you negotiate both the old and the new, and to forge your own path, as I did mine. Alternatively, if you have already made your money and want to start a TV news station in the hope of changing the world, then I suggest you read this book to find the best way to do it, and to save money on the project costs.

So what do you need to achieve all this, you budding media moguls, you next-generation Rupert Murdochs and Ted Turners? You will need certain personal attributes in abundance: a passion for hard work; dedication; tenacity; a dollop or two of personal charm; and a knack of being in the right place, at the right time, with the right people. Always be prepared to follow through on your ambitions, to never give up, and to be honest and positive in everything you do. I have sometimes lost out by putting my trust in people, but that is a price I have been prepared to pay to uphold my values. You will also need to make sacrifices along the road; nothing comes easy. When in doubt - and there will be many moments like this - always rely on your intuition, but surround yourself with smart people whose advice you trust. I'm far from the first to say that. Andrew Carnegie, the legendary steel tycoon who arrived penniless in America in 1848 and half a century later was its richest man, said his epitaph should read: "Here lies a man who was wise enough to bring into his service men who knew more than he." And so it remains.

All such character traits, while essential, are not on their own enough for success. In the next few chapters, we'll look at what are probably the most basic but most crucial other requirements for you to think about: the content for your channel; the team you will need to help you fulfil your dreams; and the money it will be necessary to raise to fund it.

Whatever your ambition, I hope this book will help to give you the motivation and the tools to achieve them. For those of you who still feel daunted and overwhelmed by the notion of starting and running your own TV news channel, or who are pretty certain that they actually wouldn't mind being just one of those small cogs in the industry, thank you very much, Mr Siddiqi, I would say two things. The first is not to be put off from finishing this book because it will help you in your career, whatever job you end up doing. It's always good to know the nuts and bolts of how everything works. The second is that you can always change your mind later. I won't be offended. After all, I worked at KPMG for 16 years before I saw the light and flew towards it; you've got time on your side.

———

How I got into the TV news business

The night I decided I was going to go into television news, the amount I knew about the industry could have been written on the back of an envelope - and even then most of it would have remained blank.

It was 1993, when I was in my mid 40s. I was sitting at home in Karachi, flicking between international channels like the BBC's 24-hour news channel, then just a couple of years old, and America's CNBC business channel. I noticed that some of the business and news programmes were being made for them by production houses in India. The television scene had been liberated from state control in that country, resulting in an explosion of creativity, new channels and privately owned production businesses. I knew a similar liberation was about to get under way in Pakistan, so I decided to make that my future. I would start a production house in Karachi to create programmes on business and finance for the international channels.

The only problem was that I knew nothing about how to actually do it, let alone how to make it a success. I was risking a successful career with KPMG, and putting my family's future financial security in doubt, based on little more than a hunch. But somehow the time and the opportunity felt right.

I had always been interested in news since childhood, when I would listen to the crackling sounds of the radio bulletins reporting on the escalating tensions of the Cuban Missile Crisis in 1962, the Kennedy assassination in 1963 and the landing on the Moon in 1969. After I moved to Britain in the 1970s to pursue my chartered accountancy career, I was fascinated to see how TV news outlets like the BBC and ITN were able to operate independently of the government, so differently from the sanitised fare we were then served up back home by the state-controlled media. I was excited at the thought of being part of a revolution that would bring such freedom to my home country. But as to the mechanics of how to fulfil my ambition, I had no idea. I could write (I edited a monthly economics magazine for KPMG and also had a column on economics in a national newspaper), but I had zero knowledge about TV production.

So the next day, I visited the only person I knew who had a connection to the industry, a friend who was then perhaps the leading advertising man in Pakistan. I told him about my idea of wanting to get into TV news, of producing a weekly business programme for the BBC, and he was kind enough not to send me off and advise me to lie down in a darkened room until the feeling went away. Instead, he spent several hours taking me through his extensive knowledge of the industry, and how my idea might work commercially. He promised to help me as much as he could, including introductions to other people in the TV industry. So, over the next few weeks, I went from expert to expert, learning as much as I could about the different aspects of the business.

My advertising friend ended up taking me to Hong Kong to visit Star TV, and we then made contact with the BBC in London. They sent a scouting team from their business programming unit to see me. They asked me where my production facility was. I told them I did not have one and sheepishly took them round to a small old studio near the main vegetable market, where I would record the programme. They asked where I was going to do the graphics (all business programmes are graphic heavy). I quickly whisked them round to another part of town to a graphics facility. Not surprisingly, they were unimpressed.

That night, I was given some sound advice which started me on my journey. The guys from the BBC told me that NDTV and TV18 had just launched in India and they had both begun with a small production company. (Prannoy Roy and Raghav Bahl were the respective starters of these production companies and both were seasoned journalists.) They advised me to do the same. That's where it all started. I hired some experienced TV people using my own funds, found some premises, and called the new venture Television Business Production Ltd (Telebiz). Luckily, I had investors who agreed to come in even though we had no revenues, nor any contracts.

It took me a year and a half, but I had managed to launch the best-equipped TV production company in Pakistan. Eventually, we landed a deal to produce a weekly business programme for Asia Business News (later taken over by CNBC Asia). A few years later, we got a contract for a weekly series for the BBC called "Question Time Pakistan".

It was an uncertain, but exciting time. I learnt everything on the job. I wrote scripts, anchored interviews, and started to learn how to edit. My new life in television news had begun, and what a ride it was going to be!

2

CONTENT'S NEW GOLDEN AGE

"The world is changing very fast. Big will not beat small anymore. It will be the fast beating the slow." **Rupert Murdoch**

The adage that content is king is probably truer today than perhaps it has ever been. Why has Netflix achieved such global runaway success? Well, the fact that it is priced markedly lower than traditional entertainment offerings from cable and satellite providers is one factor. Its ad-free environment is nice, as is its slick usability, the personalised recommendations and the way it remembers where you're up to with your watching, whatever device you use. But all that would count for little were it not for its great, compelling content - hugely popular series like *House of Cards*, *Orange Is The New Black* and *The Crown*, and its large array of movies, children's shows, comedy etc.

With a worldwide, and growing, subscriber base of 137 million collectively watching more than 125 million hours of movies and shows daily, Netflix is a phenomenal story about how a business can see and seize an opportunity. It started out modestly in 1999 as a mail-order DVD service. When it began streaming video over the internet in 2007, few would have predicted it becoming the giant it is today, with a market capitalisation north of US$150 billion. Disney, stung by its fledgling rival's success, announced it was no longer going to help it succeed. Hence Disney has pulled all its movies from Netflix and started its own direct-to-consumer internet streaming service, joining an increasingly crowded space alongside offerings from HBO, Showtime, CBS, Hulu, Amazon, Sony, Apple, YouTube TV and others. Get ready for *Streaming Wars: The Reckoning*, coming to screens near you soon, and every bit as entertaining and bloody as any of the cinematic dramas on offer.

This is where the big beasts of entertainment and the media will slug it out over the next few years, and where the winners and losers of the worldwide industry will be determined. The entertainment part of the industry, where the really big bucks are, is the one wearing the crown jewels; we, by contrast, in the news industry, are the poor cousins in the diamante; talking, at best, about revenues and valuations in the tens of millions rather than the tens of billions.

But we are also talking about a business that is at the heart of everything that is serious and important in our lives. What the Disneys and the Netflixes do is to entertain us, and that's great. But at the end of the day, it's just good, frivolous fun; an escape from the real world - the world that we in the TV news business occupy. The stories that TV news covers matter enormously, and affect our destinies as individuals, societies and humans. Wars. Famines. Global warming. Economic meltdowns. Terrorism. Corruption.

Content is equally as important to us as it is to the guys in entertainment. Unless we have compelling storytelling and programming, presented in a captivating way, we are extremely unlikely to succeed.

So let's get down to the business of your business. What

subject area of the news will your channel cover? Will it seek to cover everything - "the whole waterfront", as journalists say - like a CNN, a Sky News or a Samaa, or will it become a niche channel specialising in one subject area, such as business or sport or health? Will it be confined to a specific geographical location, or will it be a global news network? Who is its intended audience? Over what platforms will it be distributed? How will it differ from existing TV news outlets - as the marketeers like to say, what's its unique selling proposition?

Three out of the four stations I founded were niche channels, covering business news, and that has somewhat protected them from some of the disruptions that have hammered general news outlets like a digital tsunami. Specialist channels are not immune to the need to change and to embrace digital, of course, but they tend to have more select, more loyal audiences who are avid and obsessive about their interest in the subject. In the case of business, they are generally also wealthy individuals, the sort that advertisers love to reach. As we've seen with the growth in subscription numbers enjoyed by our print equivalents, such as the *Financial Times* and *The Wall Street Journal*, these consumers also have a greater propensity to pay for access to news and information digitally (one factor possibly being that they can claim it as a legitimate business expense, rather than be out of pocket themselves).

There are further opportunities in niche subjects beyond business, in my view, perhaps in science, health or well-being, travel, food, fashion, or music. Or maybe in catering to the wants and needs of other defined, minority audiences, whether it be farmers or rock climbers, or squash players or skateboarders. With the much lower cost of entry afforded by digital, these sorts of channels start to become viable propositions. Could a profitable business be constructed out of an internet-streamed news channel for the followers and participants in electronic sports (esports), for example? The idea of competitive video games becoming popular spectator events to rival existing professional sports in terms of viewership probably baffles most people over the age of 40, but, as I'm sure you know, it shouldn't. It's a reality. There are an estimated 148 million active esports enthusiasts around the world, and the numbers just keep growing. Analysts believe it is the world's next billion-dollar industry, and is on course to eclipse sports such as basketball and American football. Traditional sports moguls are buying esports teams and 2018 saw a host of non-gaming companies, from car manufacturers to telecoms giants, striking deals to sponsor events, leagues and teams. Just one event - the League of Legends World Championship - set a record with 200 million concurrent viewers tuning in to the finals; the Superbowl, historically the most-watched sporting event on TV, had viewership numbers of just over 103 million.

You may already have a germ of an idea for your channel, or you may still be seeking inspiration. Be prepared - it could come at any moment. The seeds of my television news venture were sown in early 1991, when something happened that changed many people's lives and played a pivotal role in transforming mine. The Gulf War - the military action waged by coalition forces led by the United States against Iraq in response to Baghdad's invasion and annexation of Kuwait - was in full swing. For the first time, audiences in the Middle East and elsewhere were viewing CNN in large numbers, to find out what was going on. The coverage was like a breath of fresh air for many people - Pakistanis included - used to a diet of only censored, state-controlled television news. Having worked as a partner in the audit practice of KPMG in the Middle East for more than 14 years, I knew the region very well, and was as fascinated as the next person as to what it would all mean.

Three or four years later, after I had started my small production company, Telebiz, I was sitting in our office in Karachi, working on our weekly programme. In the background, the latest news from CNN was on one of our screens, while another was showing CNBC. All of a sudden, I had an idea: the Middle East (and we in Pakistan) were receiving the American, English-language versions of CNN and CNBC. Why was there no dedicated channel covering business and economics for the Middle East, I thought, broadcasting in Arabic, the language of more than 400 million people? It was an immensely important region in economic and business terms, surely? After all, why had America, Britain, France and a couple of dozen other countries put their troops on the ground to fight if not to protect their strategic economic interests, principally oil, in the region? So I approached CNBC with the proposal of setting up a franchise, and eventually - after a lot of hard work and some setbacks along the way - was successful in launching CNBC Arabiya in 2003, which in turn led to the start of CNBC Pakistan and CNBC Africa. The rest, as they say, is history!

As we are on these subjects, a word or two first on the language your channel might adopt, and then on the business of franchising.

Language

It was central to our strategies with CNBC Arabiya and CNBC Pakistan to broadcast in the principal native language of our audience; we wanted to be different from the international giants broadcasting in English, and we wanted to carve out a niche as the authoritative voice for business in our regions. We broadcast in English across Africa, as that is the best *lingua franca* for most of a continent that speaks more than 1,500 indigenous languages. *Je suis profondément désolé*, my French-speaking friends, but you know it's true.

You will have to choose a language based on what best suits your target audience and your business. Does it then follow that all manifestations of the channel should be in that language? Probably, but some news organisations choose to broadcast in an indigenous language and then have their website and its presence across social media in English. Some do this because they assume this is *de rigueur*; others do it for the "prestige" factor or for more basic business reasons.

The choice of language is a difficult one for news organisations in the Global South and especially if you are in a postcolonial country where English supplanted the native languages. The dilemma today is that search engines such as Google that drive traffic to your websites are in English. While Google has developed searches for the Urdu or Arabic script, the bulk of traffic comes from English searches.

This usually means that television channels that are in an indigenous language (such as Urdu or Hindi or Tamil) may have to go through the painful - and costly - process of erecting an English news website. It is akin to fitting a round peg in a square hole and brings with it an entire host of problems. On the flip side, if you are smart about it, you can develop multiple streams of traffic over several digital properties.

If a television channel's news website is in English but what is being broadcast on the "TV" screen is in another language, an entire team has to be set up to render this content into English. However, staffing the desk with translators, as many people believe, is not the best answer. There are reasons for this.

If your television channel is in one language, a local language, then its short scripts are likely to be further compressed when translated into English. For example, an Urdu or Arabic television package script is already fairly short. But when translated into English, it will yield hardly one paragraph. If the brand or identity of your website is that it delivers short news, or briefs, then this is not a problem. But if you are hoping to provide readers with more full-bodied news, then getting a translator to do the job will not be good enough. This is when you need fluent English-speaking sub-editors, who are generally in short supply in a country where the mother tongue is not

English. So, as you can see, the implications of your choice of language need to be carefully thought through.

Franchising

As I found with CNBC, partnering with an already-established international brand name can sometimes be a relatively painless way to achieve your dreams.

So what do you get when you franchise? Well, access to the parent company's programming, for one. To the look and the feel, the identity of a well-known brand, for another. And the expertise of the parent company's management team.

Is it worth it? Well, that depends on the cost of the deal and the market in which you are operating. Usually, the parent company will demand an upfront payment, which I suppose you can refer to as the brand name cost. When you buy a Mercedes, you pay a premium for the name.

Then there is an annual royalty fee, which is tied to the revenue generated by the franchised station. It can be a lump sum, a flat percentage of total revenue, or one calculated at a graduated scale, such as 1 per cent on the first million of revenues, and 2 per cent on the balance. Sometimes it might be a percentage or a lump sum, whichever is the greater.

Whatever the approach, you need to be realistic about what you can afford to pay while still managing to turn a profit. Get the calculation wrong, and the annual royalty can prove very burdensome indeed. Remember that the infrastructure, talent and recurring costs of the station are all yours and that you will need to pay the royalties whether you make a profit or not.

The franchise agreement should be long term in nature - at least 20 years or more, with an automatic right of renewal - and contractually watertight, so that it is capable of surviving changes in the key personnel. Be careful on the terms and condi-tions. While you may have to, or want to, agree that the commercial terms of the deal are renegotiated every five years (which could work in your favour if, for example, the local economy goes into freefall), the underlying grant of the franchise should be untouchable. The last thing you need is for a new CEO of the parent company to come in with plans to do their own thing in your market. In my case, the people I dealt with originally over the CNBC franchises have long since retired; fortunately, our contracts have continued to be honoured.

Wherever you find the inspiration for your venture, it's all about ideas, creativity and very importantly "passion".

Whatever your preferred route - a niche news channel or a general one - it's my belief that the quality of your content is crucial. I make no apology for repeating myself on this - it's a fundamental issue. Whatever platform you are putting your news out on - on traditional television, on the web, on dead trees, on radio, or just shouting down a tin can connected by some string to another tin can - no one will listen/watch/read unless your content is relevant, different, interesting, useful or entertaining, and is presented slickly and professionally in a timely manner.

In a world where, as I write, there are an estimated four million hours of video content uploaded to YouTube, 4.3 billion Facebook messages posted, 650 million tweets and 22 billion texts sent *every day*, you need to be saying or doing something different or extremely useful to stand out. Unless you have compelling programming and stories, presented in a slick way, you will not succeed in generating the audiences you need; and fewer viewers, of course, equals less revenue.

So spend time crafting and re-crafting your content proposition. It needs to tick at least several of these boxes: to be impactful, effective, engaging, relevant, useful, entertaining. Ask yourself, why would someone tune in to my channel? What will they get from it that makes their day better, informs them about something they need or want in their work or personal life, or simply gives them something interesting to share with their friends?

At our CNBC channels, our mission was simple and straight-forward: our audience needed up-to-date news about what was going on in the business world so that they could run their companies efficiently and well, react to news developments or changing market conditions, or learn something new that gave them a possible advantage or helped them to decide where to make their next investment move. We are - or at least strive to be - useful to them. If we are not, they will switch off and move on. So this is the mission all of our employees keep in their heads on a daily basis, and which is part of our corporate DNA.

There is one other vital ingredient needed for long-term success, and that is trust. Your audience has to be confident that what you are telling them is true, has been checked and verified, and that all sides involved in it have been given a chance to express their viewpoint. If you cannot quickly establish trust, then it is unlikely that you will succeed in the long run; viewers are not stupid. If they feel they are being misled or deceived, they will no longer watch your channel. So endeavour to be impartial and to be seen as such. These days, it is fashionable to deliberately seek to be labelled politically as left, right or centre; some TV stations take a strong view on how they want to be perceived by viewers. It's not wrong to take such a strong posi-tion if that's what you want, however, one should always preserve credibility and integrity.

Today, anyone with a few dollars in his or her pocket can set up channels on the web and on social media and start pumping out made-up "news", hoping to make some quick money or to propagate his or her own political beliefs; and there are too many fools who have already done that. It's part of the reason that the entire media sector has been engulfed in the fake news furore recently. In the old days, the traditional media sector was the gatekeeper of the news, checking, filtering, investigating what was going on. In most countries (ignoring those in which state censorship and/or state ownership of the media remains), a plurality of media covering almost all ends of the political spectrum has ensured that the public is offered a diverse range of news and views, and they are free to choose the one they like and trust most. Where a free media is allowed to exist, and where there is competition and choice, it is my firm belief that citizens generally get the news and the truth they deserve.

We cannot turn the clock back, however. The advent of the internet has dramatically changed the game. It has "democratised" news by lowering the barriers to entry, allowing almost anyone who wishes it to have their own "news channel", or at least a platform or two from which to air their views, however self-indulgent or repugnant. Minority groups, particularly extremists at both ends of the political spectrum who feel that the mainstream media ignores them, have seized their chance and are using every available outlet to push their alternative views, their "take", their propaganda, doing little or no checking, and caring even less about "facts" or the truth. Terrorist groups, white supremacists, and neo-Nazis use Twitter and Facebook to push their aims and brainwash and recruit supporters; sadly, social media generally has become a purveyor of falsity, anger and hatred, polarising opinions and fuelling extremism.

Back in the day, journalists on British newspapers used to talk of the "green ink brigade" to describe the writers of handwritten letters, often penned in that colour ink, sent to their offices, and which were full of obsessive, outlandish and unsubstantiated conspiracy theories, secret plots involving illegitimate royals, or explanations as to why a political leader was actually an alien from another planet. After a cursory perusal, most of these letters would be tossed into the rubbish bin, which is probably where they belonged. These days, no member of the "green ink brigade" needs to write such letters any more; they can simply post their musings on the internet, gain a worldwide audience, and, joy of joys, find other kindred conspiracy theorists around the globe.

Would the Barack Obama "birther" conspiracy - the utterly false allegations that he was born in Kenya and not in Hawaii, thereby making him ineligible to be US President - have been aired at all, let alone have gained so much traction, were it not for the internet age? I very much doubt it. Today's "green inkers" are able to shout it out loud, rinse, repeat and retweet. These things are not just matters of political rivalry, of petty point-scoring, but of life and death. Michelle Obama's 2018 autobiography details how she feared that the birther claims would lead to some "wingnuts and kooks" assassinating her, her husband and their children.

Around the same time, a story on the BBC website revealed how fake news on the internet had fuelled the deaths of a dozen people in Nigeria. Under the headline, "Like. Share. Kill.", the report detailed how a series of horrifying images had circulated on Facebook, allegedly showing the slaughter of Christians by Muslims in Plateau state. One showed a baby with open machete wounds across his head and jaw; another was of a man's skull hacked open. Except they had nothing to do with the recent violence. The photograph of the baby had first appeared on Facebook months earlier. The video of the man's head did not even come from Nigeria; it was recorded in Congo-Brazzaville, nearly a thousand miles away, in 2012. By the time this was discovered, it was too late: enraged Christians had taken their revenge by killing a dozen Muslims. Of course, such ethnic or religious hostility predates the rise of social media. But the police in Nigeria are convinced that the graphic imagery and misinformation circulating on Facebook greatly contributed to the reprisals.

These examples of how false images and outright lies can survive and prosper on social media and cause misery and death in real life, show why our job as news journalists is so important, today more than ever. People are being brainwashed by misinformation circulated as news. When a recent survey in Britain asked 12- to 15-year-olds where they went for their news, Facebook, YouTube and Instagram occupied three of the first five places in the list of top sources, alongside the BBC and ITV. Right across the world, social media musings and the forwarding of messages have become increasingly unreliable. I am sometimes shocked, as I am sure you are, by what's been circulated. And shocked, too, that so many people believe that what they read or receive is true. I am afraid that with all the good things digital brings us, comes the bad.

In such a world, we must be able to trust the source providing the information. The majority of us need - perhaps as never before - someone credible to sift through the day's news, to reject the false and unverifiable, to put the stories in some order of importance, to add some context and analysis, and to serve it up in digestible chunks. Truth matters. Most people are looking for and need trustworthy sources and that is what traditional TV news providers with good brand names continue to provide. Any newcomer to the business should strive to do the same. In my view, Quality + Trust + One's best stab at the truth and impartiality = Success. Thankfully, there is hope: in the same survey I mentioned above, the 12- to 15-year olds scored the traditional TV news providers roughly twice as highly as social media when it came to being trustworthy and accurate.

But you may think differently about the importance of quality, truthfulness and trust. You may reject my beliefs as the orthodoxy of an old and out-of-touch man, and be adamant that there is an opportunity to challenge it and do things differently; that partiality not impartiality, views not news, and he who shouts loudest and most often is the future for news in the 21st century. If so, I wish you - and humanity - good luck. I will stick to my firm belief: that the winners in media at the end of the day will be those who cleave to the principle of seeking to broadcast the truth, and those who have won, and continue to preserve and cherish, the trust of their audience.

————

Why getting your content right matters

Back in 2012, the breakfast programme on my Samaa news channel in Pakistan was extremely popular, and was the highest-rated morning programme in the country. Then, the show decided it would film and air a segment about young unmarried couples who were meeting clandestinely in a public park in Karachi. The female host of the programme was shown running around chasing the young men and women, filming them without their consent, asking about their marital status, and shouting, "Don't deceive your parents!"

It caused an immediate controversy, with complaints pouring in to the station and on to social media, condemning the piece for having violated the young people's privacy, and for being intolerant, unethical and unfair, with some comparing it to the kind of moral policing practised by the Taliban in Afghanistan.

I was travelling in South East Asia at the time, but it was not long before I got to hear about the furore. I immediately asked the host of the show to apologise publicly. Regrettably, she chose to do so in a rather wishy-washy way, more in the manner of what is called a nonpology - saying she was sorry "if" she had offended anyone - which simply served to further enrage people. She also, without the knowledge or permission of the station, chose to give an interview to The New York Times, *defending her actions as merely having been intended to highlight the dangers that youths face in Karachi and rejecting her critics as "an elite class that didn't even watch my show".*

To all liberal-minded persons, the stunt was simply unaccept-able. It also flew in the face of the progressive position adopted by Samaa, which we had carefully nurtured and maintained over the years. There was the very real possibility that our brand, our reputation, and the trust that our viewers and advertisers had in us, was going to be damaged beyond repair by the uproar. It was time for swift and decisive action.

So, despite the show being popular and top of the ratings, I resolved to scrap it by sacking the entire team, including the errant host, and issued an unconditional apology, disavowing the segment's content. It was a draconian measure, perhaps, however I felt I had little option but to stick to our principles. I was gratified when my decision was met with widespread appreciation in the country and Samaa received international support and coverage for its action. It also helped to portray Pakistan as a tolerant society, where narrow-minded bigotry is not to be condoned.

3

MONEY MATTERS

"Genius is one percent inspiration, ninety-nine percent perspiration." **Thomas Edison**

In the world of TV, as in much of business life, nothing much happens without money. So spending time at an early stage considering how you might be able to raise the capital you will require to fulfil your ambition is important. I am making the assumption here that you probably don't have a spare US$20 million lying around ready to be used on this venture; if that's wrong, you can skip this bit, and I am sorry for any offence caused. Alternatively, read on to see how you may raise a substantial portion of it.

We will first of all look at roughly how much money you will need, and then consider the ways in which you might obtain the funds; we'll also go through finances in more detail in the next chapter, *Creating a Winning Business Plan.* But before we do that, a reminder about not allowing yourself to be put off by the challenges that lie ahead, or overawed by the sums we will be considering. Yes, we will be talking about raising millions of dollars, but don't feel intimidated by these numbers. Of course, securing the financing will not be easy - far from it - but if your idea for the channel is good, your management team has gravitas and experience, and the business model underpinning it is exciting and sound, then it can be done. In fact, it is a curious thing in business that raising multiple millions is often easier than raising a few hundred thousand.

So how much will it cost? That, naturally, depends on what it is, and where it is. If you were starting out down the traditional TV news channel route - with the expense of the studios, the well-stocked newsroom, the satellite links, and all the other trappings that go with being a satellite or cable channel - then you would probably need to line up US$75 million if you are in America, about US$28 million in Europe, and somewhere between US$10-17 million in Asia.

It's fairly difficult, however, to raise finance for a traditional news channel now. Most of them struggle to turn a profit. The eye-watering returns made by the big news channels in the US reflect the particular conditions of the North American market, sadly, for us non-American TV owners. And even they face a challenge from the digital newcomers. Many investors are increasingly nervous about putting large amounts of money into a channel that is only ever likely to attract a small audience; getting a return on that investment is risky, and, even if it does pay off in the end, it is likely to take longer than most investors are prepared to wait.

Among the exceptions to this is when a country wishes, for whatever reason, to launch a news channel to help promote itself or its take on the world. The latest examples of this are Beijing's formation of a new global broadcaster called Voice of China to ensure that its views are heard loud and clear, and Russia's version, RT, which is extremely subtle in promoting the Kremlin's point of view. The only other exception is where a very wealthy individual wants to have a trophy asset.

So unless you are extremely well connected to your country's leaders or have a close friendship with an ambitious billionaire or two, I suggest you look at the other less-costly routes afforded by the digital revolution.

Whether you need $5 million or $50 million, credibility is key to raising finance. You will need to assemble a solid management team that has experience and a good track record in the television industry. You don't need to fill every position, but some of the integral ones would be useful, such as a head of news and programming (these might be two different roles), a head of operations, a head of sales and marketing, a top digital person, and an experienced, level-headed finance director. I may be a little biased, being an accountant by profession, but having a heavyweight numbers person adds a good deal of acceptability and reassurance to a project. People with money to invest tend to like people who are careful with, and understand the worth of, money.

It's also helpful to have on your board of directors or on an advisory board some well-connected people from the world of television and business, who are likely to be known to investors and politicians alike. This adds to the authority of the venture, is comforting to those about to put their money into it, and aids in the process of acquiring from the government a licence to run the TV station, if one is required.

Whatever your route and your idea, you will not be able to attract investment, get well-known business leaders on board, or gain a licence (if one is needed), unless the plan for your business is both plausible and persuasive.

Broadly, the likely investors into your media company would be:

Private equity or venture capital firms;

Ultra-high-net-worth individuals;
Corporations wanting to enter the media sector;
Existing media companies.

Private equity firms

These firms are risk-takers, and they look at their investments on a short horizon of about five to six years. They come in only when they are convinced that the idea is solid *and* they can see a clear path and timeline to selling their stake at a markedly higher valuation. We're not just talking here about an uplift of 50 per cent or even 100 per cent: they like to think, talk and dream in terms of 10x. So you will need to set out a plan for how these investors will be able to realise their money and when. We'll go through some of the potential exit strategies during the next chapter on creating a business plan. One of the other issues you face when having a private equity firm on board is that if, or - more likely - when, they decide to sell out you will have no say over who your new partner will be.

It is important that your company is structured so that you not only have control of it now but retain that control in the future, especially when investors sell off their shares. My advice is to divide your equity into "A" and "B" shares. "A" shares will have voting rights, while "B" shares will not. The profits or dividends generated by the company will be divided in the same proportions as the equity put in, but the voting rights will be structured so that control remains with you as the creator and founder. It is a common approach adopted by many businesses - Rupert Murdoch's empire, for example, or Alphabet, Google's parent company.

The other important aspect to consider is the concept of "sweat equity". As the originator of the project and having spent time, energy and money in bringing the project to its current state, you can demand some equity, normally in the range of between 5 per cent and 15 per cent, depending on the size of the capital needed. The valuation placed on your company at this stage is an important element when you are pitching for invest-ment, so that money you have personally invested gets you a higher percentage at the starting gate. To give an example, let's say you have invested US$2 million into the business by the time your potential investor comes in, and the value placed to date on the company is US$5 million. If its overall capital requirements are US$25 million, your startup percentage would be 20 per cent, and the investor coming in would put up US$23 million for an 80 per cent stake.

In addition to this, you may negotiate to get further "sweat equity", based on milestones achieved. "Sweat equity" normally vests over a period of around three to five years. The shares are transferred free of cost to you over the agreed period and there are various clauses drawn up to cover this. These conditions will be tied to certain goals that the business achieves. For example, at launch you might get 1 per cent. If you achieve year one's financial goals, another 1 per cent, and so on until the entire agreed amount is transferred.

Ultra-high-net-worth individuals

These are invariably defined as people with US$50 million or more of investable capital. You should draw up a list of such potential people, then bring it down to five or 10 individuals who you think may be attracted to investing in your business. Why do these people invest? I really have never been able to fathom that one out, but, rationally, it has to be for one or two reasons.

They may just wish to be associated with a news station because it brings glamour, or perhaps opens doors to the corri-dors of power that they desire and which might help them achieve other objectives. The other reason is purely on account of the investable value. Or a combination of both. Be sure that you are going with a clean, well-known name; an association with someone with a reputation for dodgy deals will not reflect well on you or your business, and that is something you should always be conscious of.

Large corporations

There are often companies in other sectors that are on the lookout to invest in feasible projects, again either as a pure investment or because they see synergies that might assist their core business. Many consumer brands in the retail sector have made large investments in creating new media assets, such as some British supermarkets launching their own magazines or gardening websites or food-related online video channels, through which they can encourage sales of their products. Having a strategic partnership with a business full of media specialists can be of great benefit to that sort of strategy.

Existing media companies

Traditional media powerhouses are often interested in buying a stake in attractive new startups in the sector, sometimes purely as an investment and sometimes partly as a strategic move into a genre or market demographic in which they are weak, or that they see as complementary to their main business, or as a hedge for the future. Disney and 21st Century Fox invested hundreds of millions of dollars in Vice, for example, back in the day when it and similar companies were coveted for their cachet with young people. NBC has done the same with Buzzfeed. Newspaper groups may wish to establish a foothold in television news, or in radio or digital groups.

There are many ways to make an approach to all these various sorts of potential investors, but my advice is to avoid doing a cold call. Do some research and try to work out the best tactic. The usual channels are through their bankers, lawyers, accountants or close advisers or friends. Choose your route wisely.

One last thing on seeking investors. Never lose hope. Keep trying. If your idea is good, you will eventually succeed. What you will need in order to achieve that, however, is a killer business plan, so we will go through how to construct one next. Keep believing - this dream is getting closer to reality!

———

Opportunity out of the sky

When I was looking for investors in CNBC Arabiya, it was a very long journey. It almost seemed doomed at one stage. The capital required for the project was substantial, in the range of US$60 million to US$75 million. The first phase required US$5 million, which was used to set up a production company in Dubai Media City. I put that sum up with two of my friends. These original investors had been backers of my private production company in Karachi. One of them was among the richest businessmen in Pakistan and a school friend of mine who now lives on the West Coast of America and we touch base whenever he is visiting Dubai or I am in California. The other one was an expat Pakistani who had a successful asset management business.

We had come to the second round requiring about US$10 million to cover the next six months, which took into account the signing of the franchise agreement with CNBC. In these sorts of franchise operations, once you have the international brand signed up, you have immediately established some credibility and people look at it much more seriously. CNBC had given us three months to find the money or they were going with someone else who was very substantial in the Middle East.

I went from pillar to post to no avail and had virtually given up. It was definitely the most testing time of my life. An accountant who I had hired after he had lost his job in Oman, asked me whether I could see an investment banker who was visiting Oman from the UK. He had dealt with him through his previous employment with one of the richest groups in the Sultanate.

So I went to Oman but could not manage to see him until about 10pm in a hotel lobby, just as he was about to leave for the airport. After a brief discussion, he asked me to come to London and later fixed an appointment with a private banker who was an adviser to a fairly well off person in the Middle East, whom he thought might be interested.

I went to London. I had a few other appointments for the purpose of seeking investment funds, all of which turned out to be disappointing dead ends. My appointment with the private banker was at 5pm. It was a dark and cold March evening with rain pouring down. His office was in Mayfair, in central London, where it is always very difficult to find a parking space. After much time spent driving around looking for somewhere to put the car, I thought of just giving it up; it was bound to be another futile meeting, and I was tired and feeling sorry for myself. I was about to leave when suddenly in front of his office, I saw a car pull out. I immediately pulled in, walked inside the bank and was taken to see the private banker.

As I entered his office, I could see he was going over our business plan and proposal. He looked up, and told me: "Ok, I will give you a shortcut to the gentleman, but only in a few weeks when the weather is better and he will be in Cannes on his yacht." When the man's name was mentioned, my immediate reaction was "Wow!", yes, I have certainly heard of him; he was one of the richest people in the Middle East and needed no introduction. Though everyone was familiar with his name, I had never met him personally.

At the given date and time, I arrived in Cannes. We met the private banker from London and his team for a nice breakfast in *one of the poshest hotels in the town. His investment manager was an astute ex-banker from the UK. He was a bit distracted and agitated that morning, however: his wife had just presented him with a Harley Davidson motorbike as a birthday present and he had been very pleased to ride it to the hotel for the meeting, until someone had taken took off with his helmet!*

It was clear that these were people who routinely dealt with investments in the hundreds of millions of dollars at a time; my requirements were paltry in comparison. After breakfast, we proceeded to the investor's yacht. Actually, you could hardly call it a yacht - it was as big as a cruise ship. To give some idea of how large it was, it could not dock in the port's normal private moorings. But the port of Cannes, of course, had made special arrangements in order to accommodate it; it is not the go-to popular destination for the super rich without good reason.

We were ushered into the investor's presence. He quickly said, "I have seen the papers and I have already decided to come in on the second round but just wanted to see you and meet you face to face." I was elated. After all the fruitless meetings, after all the rebuffs and rejections, we'd finally done it. He was going to put in US$10 million and, if the venture were a success, I would receive a substantial sum as sweat equity.

Just as I thought we'd cracked it, however, there was a twist. The investor's phone rang and some words were exchanged in Arabic, which I didn't understand. He put down the phone and immediately said, "I need to go, sorry. I will not be able to invest." There was no explanation at all. I was stunned. Just minutes after thinking I'd won the jackpot, it had now been snatched away. OMG, I thought, what the hell has happened here? What had gone wrong? Had I done something to change his mind? We were ushered quickly off the boat, just as it abruptly started to sail. I almost fell into the sea jumping off the ship, which was already in motion.

That night, as I sat forlornly at my hotel bemoaning my lot *and wondering what on earth had transpired, the banker from London came to see me to tell me that the phone call had been from his client's senior partner, who had asked him what he was doing, to which he responded that he was about to invest in the CNBC Arabiya channel that was to be launched soon. His partner had instructed him not to invest because he wanted to invest the whole US$75 million! The investment was contingent on my two friends being bought out at a significant premium. I was to be the only other shareholder, with a sweat equity payable on set targets in five years' time, along with a huge premium on my original investment. You could have knocked me down with a feather at that point. From elation to despair and back again in the space of a few hours!*

I flew back to Dubai the next day a very happy man. It took a further five weeks to draw up the legal documents. I have to say that I am really bad at negotiating agreements and one of my very dear friends, who was one of the original investors with me helped in the process. Everything - eventually - turned out well in the end, even though my nerves remained somewhat shredded for months. So, the bottom line is: never, ever give up. Even if you can't find a parking place on a wet March evening in Mayfair, persevere.

4

CREATING A WINNING BUSINESS PLAN

"Success is not final, failure is not fatal: it is the courage to continue that counts." **Winston Churchill**

Your business concept may well be the greatest idea since a chap came up with a plan to quit his Wall Street job in 1993 and launch an online bookstore. But however good it is, it's not enough on its own. Sorry. Even the most excellent idea can turn to nothing if you cannot devise and execute a strategic plan that turns it from a proposal into a successful working venture.

A business plan is a roadmap of how your business will operate in order to succeed. Writing such a plan forces you into disciplined and critical thinking, into checking and stress-testing every aspect of your business and challenging your assumptions. Only when you write down all the details and the numbers associated with the business, will you be able to see whether your great-sounding idea works: whether it stands a chance of being a healthy, profitable business or a costly failure.

There are some entrepreneurs, particularly among millennials, who don't like the concept of business plans, who are reluctant to have their ideas written down or subjected to any sort of checks that they fear might stifle their creativity or slow down their rush to market. They argue that the process is an unnecessary distraction. There are countless articles online proclaiming the death of the business plan - "Why You Should Scrap Writing That Business Plan And Become a Lean Start-Up", "The Secret to a Great Business Plan? Don't Write One", to give just two examples. They maintain that business plans are outdated and irrelevant, some kind of historical artefact akin to a mechanical typewriter, and belonging to the same scrapheap. Even some business schools are no longer teaching students to write business plans, but to instead create PowerPoint-style presentations.

Believe me, they're wrong: the business plan remains an essential, vital tool that is key to the success of any commercial operation. I'm with Benjamin Franklin on this one: "If you fail to plan, you are planning to fail." Oh, and with that chap who quit his Wall Street job in 1993 - that online bookstore he launched now has annual sales of US$178 billion and Jeff Bezos has been named by *Forbes* as the "richest man in modern history" after his net worth increased to $150 billion in 2018. He wrote his business plan for Amazon on a trip from New York to Seattle, flight time 6.5 hours. I can relate to that, since my business plan for Samaa TV, including the programming grid, was sketched out on two napkins in a restaurant in Western Australia, and then completed the next day on a flight from Perth to Dubai (flight time 10.5 hours). Obviously, it was revised and reformed later. In fact, all my finest thoughts have come on flights, including many of the chapters for this book.

Far from being outmoded, a well-thought-through business plan is more important than ever before in today's competitive business environment. It will assist you in raising the money that you need to start your business, and will help you achieve your short- and long-term objectives once it is up and running. And it shows you are serious, that you've put the time and effort in, and have done more than just a quick brainstorm down the pub with your friends.

It doesn't have to be a formal, 250-page bound book, laden with multiple tabs and appendices; few people want that sort of minute detail any more. It also doesn't need to take you days or weeks, as Mr Bezos proved. But it is also going to be one of, if not the, most important documents you will ever write, so it is worth expending some energy on it.

Of course, you should also produce a snazzy PowerPoint presentation that will allow you to wow would-be investors as you pitch your brilliant idea to them. And perhaps a video presentation showing just how slick and compelling your content is going to be. But you will need substance and real numbers underpinning the glitz; you will need answers to satisfy such questions as why you want so many millions to launch the business, and what the return on that investment will be and by when. Even the best "pitch decks" must contain solid, reliable information about target markets, revenues, costs and financial projections.

There are about a billion books out there on how to write a business plan (I exaggerate only a little) and there are templates and other help available online. What I am going to give you here is some general guidance, along with aspects that are specific to the business we are interested in: launching and running a successful TV news station, across whatever platforms you see fit.

The business plan's principal purpose is to check that your concept has a commercial basis and that the business will be profitable. Even in the unlikely event that you never have to show the document to anyone else, wouldn't you want some reassurances that your proposal is actually going to fly before you invest much more of your time, energy and money in to it?

If you want to raise money to fund it, then I maintain that a business plan is essential. Potential investors - whether they are existing media companies, high-net-worth individuals, venture capital or private equity firms, other companies, or commercial lenders such as banks - will want to see that you have got robust business principles and financial numbers underpinning your idea. They require as much reassurance as they can get that the money they put into the business is not just going to be safe, but will deliver them the healthy return they are looking for.

One way to get a sound business plan is to go to a firm of accountants or investment consultants (such as my old employer, KPMG) and ask them to produce it for you. If you choose this route, be warned: it is expensive. The costs will vary considerably depending on the scope of the assignment and the region you are in, but, to give you some idea, you are probably looking at from £50,000 to £75,000 in Europe, £30,00 to £35,000 in the Middle East, £20,000 to £25,000 in Africa, and £25,000 to £35,000 in South Asia.

You need to ensure that any such outfit you use has relevant experience in the media sector and has dealt with similar projects. If you choose a good name to produce a business plan, it will count for a great deal. The trust factor increases as far as would-be investors are concerned: their comfort zone widens when they see an international firm or a well-known brand name giving its stamp of approval.

It can be a minefield, though. I have seen many wealthy individuals losing substantial amounts of money by choosing the wrong advisers. Without mentioning any names, I personally know of two such cases. There was one in the Middle East in which millions of dollars was paid to advisers to draw up detailed plans for a TV channel project. In the end, however, all the plans had to be completely changed because these so-called experts had recommended that the channel be launched in a country that was completely unsuitable for such a venture, because of its political and cultural issues. Just imagine: a simple thing like a location and you are out of pocket by millions of dollars, and having to start again virtually from scratch. The other example was in Africa, where the consultants produced an extremely attractive business plan on paper, and went through phase one of hiring the core team, and buying the land where the TV station would be built, only to discover that a licence would not be granted because the country was preparing for a revision to its broadcasting laws. So beware when putting such projects together by hiring expensive consultants and advisers who charge an arm and a leg - having them on board does not mean that all the most crucial aspects will have been covered.

It is also no automatic guarantee that your fundraising efforts will be successful. Even the most blue-chip of brand names on your plan's front cover will not mean that potential investors will simply walk in and shower you with large amounts of cash. Most investors are, quite rightly, extremely careful with their money and have a rigorous due-diligence process that subjects the business plan to various stress tests and "what-if" scenarios, whatever the name on the label.

The cheaper - and I would argue, best - way to produce the business plan is to do it yourself, with the help of your key colleagues (and this book). You, after all, are the ones who know most about the business, and are passionate about and dedicated to seeing your big idea come to fruition. It helps here if you have the requisite financial know-how among your team; either way, you could do worse than present the financial forecasts that you come up with to an independent financial firm to stress test them with the knowledge and experience they have. They could then produce their own report verifying the projections. It will cost some money, of course, but the reassurance it will give would-be investors may make it worth it.

Let's now look at the structure of a typical business plan. The one we wrote about a decade ago for the proposed launch of CNBC Africa had ten chapters:

Executive Summary
Market Overview
Competition & Positioning
Programming
Distribution
Sales & Marketing
Organisation Structure
Technical
Risk Factors
Financial Overview

You can choose what structure or order you prefer for your business plan, but there are some crucial elements that must be included. Most plans cover the first three to five years of the business (though I will later show you why your financial projections for a TV business should cover 10 years) and generally contain the following:

- A one-page executive summary (usually the last thing to be written, once the rest of the plan is completed);
- An outline of the management team, how the business will operate, its key aims and goals, and how and when these will be achieved;
- An overview of the market that the business will be in, its target customers and what marketing strategies will be used to attract them;
- An assessment of the comparative strengths, weaknesses, opportunities and threats posed by rivals, now and in the future;
- Comprehensive financial projections, including a breakdown of how much money will be required to set up and run the business, costs, revenues, and profit and loss forecasts;
- Risks & Exit Strategy.

Let's go through each of these areas in turn.

THE EXECUTIVE SUMMARY

The executive summary's purpose is to succinctly highlight what your company is and will be, where it is heading and how it plans to be successful. It needs to educate, inform and excite the reader, at a glance. This is the first thing (perhaps the only thing, if it doesn't capture their attention) that external would-be investors will read, so it needs to grab them and convince them of the brilliance of your plan. In television terms, it's like a showreel highlighting you and your business. You should include:

Your vision, or mission statement. This explains to the reader why your company exists. The fashion these days is to call this a mission statement, and that's fine (though all of my businesses have somehow managed to operate successfully for years without one). It seems to me that a good mission statement can inspire and transform your business; while, it goes almost without needing to be said, a bad one does the opposite. It should be a clearly stated purpose of what your company is, what it does, how it benefits customers, and what it aspires to become. It is your vision for the business, summed up in one sentence. Steer clear of anything too general, bland or wishy-washy, and don't make the mistake of assuming that your business will change the fate of the world and its 7.7 billion inhabitants. One step at a time, tiger: your venture may become the next Fox or Sky, or even the next Amazon or Apple, but let's be realistic at this stage. Stating something basic like "XYZ TV exists to bring the most exciting, up-to-the-minute news and information to the world's 300 million esport enthusiasts" will serve you better than trying to come over all schmaltzy and evangelical. You can adopt the tone of a Microsoft (*"Our mission is to empower every person and every organization on the planet to achieve more"*) or a Coca-Cola (*"To refresh the world... To inspire moments of optimism and happiness... To create value and make a difference"*) or a Starbucks ("*To inspire and nurture the human spirit - one person, one cup, and one neighborhood at a time*"), when you're as big as them.

Or maybe not. I always think it's best to describe what you do, in simple, clear language, without hyperbole or being overly sentimental. Compare the three above to the simple, easily understood message from Google (*"To organize the world's information and make it universally accessible and useful"*) and from our friends at Amazon, consistently voted by the public as one of the most well-respected companies in the world: *"Our vision is to be Earth's most customer-centric company; to build a place where people can come to find and discover anything they might want to buy online."* I also like the one from Cheddar, the New York business channel: *"The CNBC for millennials."* Simple, to the point, instantly understandable.

Details of how your company will meet the needs of its target consumers and why those needs and wants are currently unmet. What's the problem you will solve? Reference market data and the marketing strategies that demonstrate how you will take advantage of this.

The projected financial highlights. How the company will make its money (its revenue model); how much investment is required; and the forecast profits and timelines.

Future Projections. Explain the direction in which ownership and management plan to take the business and - crucially - how and when investors will be able to exit from the company and realise their returns.

One of the reasons for saving the writing of the executive summary until last is to give you the chance to include the best parts from each section of your business plan. Write it with your audience in mind. If you are trying to attract investors, you should focus on giving them the information they will be looking for: reasons to invest their money into your company, rather than the scores of other businesses out there looking for cash.

As one Silicon Valley professional investor recently said: "You are selling the investment, not the product. I want to know what the entrepreneur wants (how much funding), why they want it and what the return on the investment will be."

After completing the summary, read it aloud a few times. It should convey your intended message in clear, unequivocal terms that flow easily - without sounding desperate or too much like a sales pitch.

OPERATIONS & MANAGEMENT

This section of the business plan gives a more detailed overview of the company, including its organisational structure, its owners and management, its history, and the product it will offer. The purpose is to give a clear view of the company's goals and how they will be achieved.

You and your colleagues who comprise the core senior team will be the focus here - investors need to know and have confidence in the people who are in charge of the business.

You will need to explain the background of the company, and to create an organisation chart showing the structure of the business and detailing the chain of command, and who does what. This should show the titles, duties and responsibilities of each senior member of the business along with brief biographical information on each of them, setting out the qualifications and expertise they bring to the organisation. What previous successes or failures have they had in business?

If you have advisers or members of the board who are experienced business executives, name them here and briefly set out their relevant background. Explain how they help the business, and whether they have invested or intend to invest their own money into it. Be careful here: if these business-savvy individuals are not taking up the opportunity to make some money from this venture, it will set alarm bells ringing: other would-be investors will wonder why not and may take it as a sign of a lack of confidence in the plan.

If you have hired specific or well-known talent to present or report for your channel, you should mention them here - but I would do so only if you have a firm commitment that they are joining, ideally a signed contract. If you tell investors that you have hired some celebrated name, only for him or her to pull out at a later date, it will reflect badly on you and could affect the success of your fundraising. With this and everything else, only promise what you are 100 per cent sure you can deliver; it's better to "over-deliver" at a later date than to "over-promise" now and subsequently let people down.

I would give an illustration of your "product" here, an example of what the channel will deliver on a daily basis; a sort of day-in-the-life of XYZ TV. Stress what makes it different from competitors and emphasise the attractiveness of the offering to your target consumer, and the problem you will be solving for them - don't worry about duplicating this point, as it is absolutely fundamental and worth repetition.

A word or two more about standing out. There are lots of news channels out there in the marketplace. How will you be different in your product offerings or programmes or your positioning? How you differentiate yourself from other players will be a critical factor in determining your success, in both raising funds and the business.

This positioning could be a combination of content and some other matter, such as the technology you are using. The "look and feel" of your station can also be a differentiating factor, with such elements as the logo, the typesize and font that you use on screen, the music you choose, all being important. Look at how Vice, for example, characterises itself by covering stories and topics that traditional media outlets largely ignore. Aimed at and made by young people, the content of its documentaries can be graphic, edgy and often controversial, and it could never be accused of being boring or another "me too" channel. It's not a guarantee of sustained success, of course. Vice, which started life as a punk music magazine in Montreal, grew into a global media company valued at more than $5 billion in 2015, and was coveted by traditional media companies seeking to maintain relevance with younger generations; in late 2018, however, it was merging websites and put a freeze on hiring as it grappled with a tough environment for digital media. Its US$5 billion valuation now looks absurdly high (and Disney has had to write off some US$157 million of its investment in the company), but that is the way the often strange world of media business works. What's flavour of the month one year, can start leaving a sour taste the next.

As you do your research on existing rivals, you may be tempted to decide "Why reinvent the wheel? Why don't we just replicate what's currently getting the top ratings?". I'd strongly urge you not to fall into this trap. Be original in the thoughts and processes that you establish; your investors will want to see that passion and innovation in you.

List the objectives of the business - its key aims and goals - with estimated but realistic completion dates. When will it hit 10,000 or 100,000 subscribers, for example? When will it secure its first 10 advertisers? When will it be profitable?

You might want to end this chapter by finishing this sentence: "We are the right team to execute this business plan and deliver these goals because…"

THE MARKET

This is where you describe the market into which you are going to launch your channel. You should include an analysis of the marketplace, its size, and the percentage of that market you think you will attract as viewers/subscribers. Is the market growing or declining? What are the potential changes in consumer demand and anticipated trends or cycles that could affect the performance of your channel?

Unless you are going to rely on making money solely from subscribers, you need to look at and give details of two market-places here: one about the consumers you want to attract to watch your channel; and the other explaining the advertiser marketplace.

Give a detailed description of your customers, their demographics and buying habits. Flesh out your ideal customer profile, perhaps giving portraits of three or four of your most likely customers, in order to bring to life the people you are aiming for. Explain - yes, again - the customer need that your channel is going to satisfy. Describe how your channel will have an advantage in the market, what it is that will give it an edge against your competitors.

If you are intending to ask people to pay a subscription to your channel, mention your pricing strategy here. What evidence do you have that they will be willing to pay to watch your channel? And if they are, why will they pay the price you intend to charge? What's the likely churn rate, the number of customers who quit? What's your target ARPU (average revenue per user) and the LTV (lifetime value) of a viewer or subscriber?

If you are also seeking to sell advertising on your channel, explain the size of that pie, what percentage of it you will attract and why, and name the brands who will want to advertise with you. Identify the top 10 companies you expect to be able to attract and give the reasons why. What's their market expenditure on television/digital platforms, where do they currently spend it, and how are you going to get a slice of that and in what proportion? Why is your audience going to be attractive to these companies?

Ideally, you should carry out some proper market research so as to answer these sorts of questions. If you can afford it, hire a reputable firm to do that research for you; it will provide very useful evidential data that can help persuade investors that your target market not only exists, but is also likely to want to watch your channel and subscribe to it. Speak to potential advertisers - and use quotes from them to demonstrate their excitement about your channel and their willingness to be an advertiser on it.

Show what the company's strategy is to market the channel in order to attract its target audience. This should cover initial entry into the market and how the marketing evolves as the channel matures. What is the estimated annual expenditure on marketing and how many viewers/subscribers will that bring? Using these figures, you should work out the average cost of acquiring a customer (known as CAC). Many investors look extremely carefully at a company's LTV/CAC multiple - after all, if you're spending, say, US$250 to acquire a customer, but his or her lifetime value to the business is US$249, it's not going to be a profitable enterprise. Think of how you might increase the LTV of a customer over time, and decrease the CAC. You are bound to be asked, believe me.

COMPETITION

Unless you have an absolutely one-of-a-kind idea for a TV channel, you are likely to be entering a market in which you have some rivals already doing something similar to what you are proposing. Even if your idea - or parts of it - are unique, chances are that it won't stay that way for long; others will see what you're doing, and if it's a good idea, they'll copy you. You won't be novel for long.

So doing a thorough (and ongoing) analysis of your competitors and potential competitors is vital in strategic planning, and essential if you are to persuade people that you have a viable business proposition. Create a list of your current and future competitors, and get as much data and information as you can about them, their customers and their advertisers. Analyse that data and draw up a list of their strengths and weaknesses, and devise strategies to take advantage of their weaknesses while minimising any threats posed by their strengths. Use graphs or venn diagrams to illustrate where they sit in the marketplace, and where you will fit in.

You should also draw up a product feature comparison that allows you to compare your company's channel with channels produced by competitors. What features of the competitors' products do customers like or dislike? Emphasise your differences and explain why your channel will be popular. Do you have any sustainable competitive advantages, such as exclusive relationships or partnerships? In our example of the XYZ TV channel devoted to esports, securing a long-term contract to exclusively screen the official events put on by the esport's governing body would give XYZ a distinct advantage over its existing rivals, and create a significant barrier to entry to newcomers.

FINANCIAL PROJECTIONS

What we will be looking at here are the costs of running your business, the revenues it will make, and how to construct detailed financial forecasts calculating the company's profit or loss from those two, as well as a host of other useful information such as your monthly burn rate (how much more money is being spent each month over the amount that is coming in), and when you will begin to be profitable. These forecasts will also give you an estimate of the capital required to launch and keep your business running until it becomes cash positive - i.e., is taking in more revenue per month than it is spending.

Costs

You will need to think through and put down all the costs associated with starting and running your new venture, including original capital costs.

The vast majority of the annual running costs will undoubtedly be on people. Television news traditionally requires a lot of them, and will probably do so for the foreseeable future, although the recent development of the world's first artificial intelligence news presenter, by China's Xinhua news agency, may in time be a game changer. He - or should that be it? - is so disturbingly lifelike, it's frankly hard to tell which of the two on-screen presenters is the human being and which one's the virtual being. These AI presenters are happy to work 24 hours a day, seven days a week, never moan about their lot and don't need pay, overtime, make-up, or constant reassurance and praise. Now that is novel.

The personnel costs for a traditional news channel work out at about 62 per cent of annual costs and generally break down between departments like this:

Programming 40%
Operations 10%
Research and interactive 3%
Executive office 4%
HR, Admin and finance 7%
Contractual and support staff 18%
Taxes 18%

Among the programming staff are news reporters, producers and presenters, while operations include engineering, master control room, graphics, satellite staff, central apparatus room (CAR) and IT.

The CAR is comprised of servers, routers, transmission

systems, patch panels etc. Research and interactive is a small but important department that deals with data analytics. It provides the metrics for the ratings your programmes receive.

Executive covers the CEO's office.

In contractual and support staff, you may have heavyweight anchors who prefer working on a contract basis, rather than being on staff, so that they can reduce their tax burden.

Taxes comprise various government taxes on employees (not corporate tax on profits) and include pension fund contributions by the company on behalf of staff.

The 62 per cent eaten up in personnel costs is a chunky number, but, in the TV business, where content and star names can be pivotal to success or failure, one would expect them to be high. In small screen entertainment, new entrants such as Netflix and Amazon have upped the ante as far as production quality and costs are concerned. Will news follow a similar pattern? A whole new method of presenting news using VR, integrated with AI and digital drones to closely engage with the audience, would require large investments in technology. Perhaps AI anchors like the one unveiled in China will gradually take over the bog-standard news reading, such as the generally dull overnight shifts, freeing up money to spend on value-added programming presented by humans at other parts of the day? Whatever the future brings, however, it is likely that personnel expenses will remain a significant cost for TV news channels.

The other 38 per cent of expenditure covers operating costs. In traditional 24-hour news channels, it breaks down like this:

Direct costs 20%
Marketing 6%
Distribution 5%
Rent and communications 17%
Utilities 10%
Travel and vehicle operations 11%

Staff expenses 13%
Repairs, maintenance and insurance 5%
Office expenses 13%

Direct expenses comprise the transponder[s], news gathering which includes out-of-station correspondents, outside broadcasts, other live news gathering sources, ENPS (the multi-platform newsroom software system used in the newsroom), and broadcast maintenance costs which include keeping DSNG vans, cameras and other equipment in good working order.

So, personnel (62 per cent) and operating expenses (38 per cent) make up 100 per cent of your station's cost structure. Of course, costs differ from country to country and between developing economies and developed ones, and so you will need to carefully assess the various costs your operation will incur. However, the 62:38 percentage is, in my experience across three different continents and dozens of countries, a pretty standard rule of thumb. It might skew 75:25 in some places, but no more.

These costs are the typical annual operating costs. In addition to these, for the business plan, you need to add capital expenditure, launch costs and a contingency element as well.

Capital costs

Rather than going through a detailed list of equipment you might need, let's look at the macro picture for equipment, infrastructure and bureau equipment and connectivity.

Infrastructure costs (lease or purchase of building) **US$3m**
Equipment (studios/cameras/edit equipment/virtual) **US$8m**
Bureau costs and connectivity (rent/setup/small studio/cabling/antennas) **US$2m**
Sub-total **US$13m**
Launch costs (marketing/training) **US$3m**

Contingency **US$1m**

Total **US$17m**

These costs will vary widely depending on the type of channel you are launching, the platforms it will be delivered on, and where it is based. The figures above are for a regular 24-hour TV news station, in a developed part of Asia. If we were to look at costs in other territories, we need to take a base comparison of say Asia, Europe and the US, then break it down further into developed and developing markets in these continents:

South Asia **US$10m**

Developed Asia **US$17**m

Europe **US$35m**

America **US$75m**

Various arguments can be put forward as to why the above figures are high or low. They will differ depending on the type, size and nature of the channel you intend to launch, and what platforms it will be on, but they are useful illustrations of the sorts of money needed. Of course, all these numbers could be reduced by making savings here and there, such as not having contingencies or reducing launch costs. But I would counsel against skimping too much on these - how you launch, and the way in which you are received by the public, is extremely important in establishing your business.

REVENUES

The revenue buildup is the most crucial part of the business plan exercise. Most traditional news stations derive their revenue from advertising and a small percentage from sharing subscription revenue with cable operators. Your revenue model may include direct subscriptions as well. So let's look at each in turn.

Advertising revenue

This is traditionally based on the ratings a station receives and forecasting this for a news station demands an in-depth study into market conditions and an analysis of what competitors are achieving. Where your station stands in terms of ratings is an imponderable "million-dollar question".

You will, of course, be reasonably confident that your wonderful idea will attract large audiences. The star roster of talented presenters and reporters you are going to have on board, and the great content and shows they will produce, will naturally win a big following. You will make assumptions that you will be able to get X amount of ratings, which will, therefore, attract dollar amount of Y million in advertising per annum. But when it comes to putting revenue forecasts into your financial projections, remember two things: be conservative, and base all your forecasts on data or on logical and plausible extrapolations of that data, not optimistic guesswork. Be prepared to be challenged by investors on this aspect of your plan; it is critical to the success or failure of the business. Putting in inflated revenue numbers that are unlikely to be met is easily done, and a simple way to make the financial projections look promising. Don't. It's also the easiest way to fool yourself and others into launching something that won't work.

The mantra that is frequently, loudly, and some would say boringly, repeated by accountants is: costs are certain, revenues are not. So do not let yourself be carried away by assuming that your station will be the best. Plan and recruit wisely. Spend only where you have evidence that the talent you are buying in will bring in the ratings. Control your costs on other aspects of the business.

There are certain prime advertisers within every country that you must focus on acquiring as clients. They might be consumer-based multinationals, players in the financial sector, domestic consumer companies or various others. As a guide, I would calculate that these constitute about 80 per cent of your advertising market. You will need to look at how these sectors are expected to grow, or not, and factor the results into your revenue calculations.

The pharmaceutical sector is enormous in some markets - for example, in the US, drug companies are substantial advertisers, spending about US$5 billion a year promoting their products. The car industry is also significant in many markets. In essence, a pragmatic and sensible model should be created to assess and project your expected numbers. You might want to state, in percentage and real terms, the amounts you estimate that you will bring in from different sectors.

While assessing your market's key advertisers, you should also think about your proposed programming strategy and schedule. What programmes might attract the larger brands to your channel? Bear in mind that there is a herd instinct when it comes to luring advertising. If you get two or three well-known brands on board, others will follow. Easier said than done, of course, but, if you can achieve the initial breakthrough, it will become easier.

Sometimes ratings are not everything. Some brands may wish to attach themselves to a good name, for example to an anchor who may not be getting the highest ratings but is respected for his or her integrity and prowess. Think of the likes of CNN's Christiane Amanpour, CBS's Dan Rather, BBC's George Alagiah, Lamees Al Hadidi from Egypt, Lojain Omran from Saudi Arabia and Lerato Mbele from South Africa.

Overall you need to show to would-be backers that you have a clear understanding of the advertising market, its integral players, its trajectory and where you see your channel fitting in to attract some of the spending.

History and experience also suggest that you should factor in zero advertising revenues for the first six months of the business.

Not only is there time needed to get your ratings settled, land the deals and persuade the brands to come on board, there is the question of actually receiving the payments from advertisers and media houses. Your costs are on the dot every month, but debtors usually take three months, sometimes longer, to pay. This evens out in the long term, but is a heavy burden initially. So plan on having very little income in the first half year. The six-month rule is very conservative, and it may not apply to your company if you can be proactive and do advertising deals with pitches directly to media agencies and companies before you launch.

Subscription revenue

If you will be selling subscriptions, you need to have a well-thought-through, sophisticated approach. It's not quite enough to simply come up with a monthly price for access, and just stick to that. You should think about how you are going to acquire new customers, increase the value of those customers over time - i.e., drive up that LTV figure, and reduce churn so that you keep more of them.

Some questions to consider: are you going to set a price that changes based on usage, or consumption, or features/access? Is your subscription term monthly, quarterly, annual? Will there be different tiers of access, with different price points? What promotions will you do? Do you intend to offer upgrades, or cross-sell new services? Will any of your content be allowed to be watched for free, with only the most premium content behind the paywall?

The most popular pricing model is pretty simple: the customer pays a fixed price, on a recurring, mostly monthly basis. It's the model Amazon Prime uses. But you will need to think about when you introduce periodic price changes to reflect new value being delivered on the channel - extra programming, new features etc - or to simply keep up with inflation

You also may want to consider giving people free or discounted trials, to get them hooked on your product. When Paul Reuter, the founder of the now global news agency Reuters, first started in the late 19th century and sought to persuade sceptical newspapers that his news and information service over the telegraph - the cutting-edge technology of its day - was faster and cheaper than the available alternatives, he offered to supply his service to them free for two weeks. Several papers took up the offer, but *The Times* refused. It quickly reversed its decision when it saw its rivals breaking far more up-to-date news of important events. Reuter soon enjoyed a monopoly.

Another way to entice consumers is to present them with what is known as a beacon offering. The price of this offering should be relatively low compared to the rest of your packages to generate interest. DISH Network in America, for instance, has pay TV packages starting at just $19.99 per month to position it as an affordable alternative to cable. In reality, few $19.99 packages are sold: DISH's ARPU is north of $80 per month.

DISH carefully fences off its beacon offering in three ways: content, features and sales channels. On the content front, the $19.99 package lacks some popular TV channels like ESPN, USA and Disney, which limits the appeal among sports lovers and families. In terms of features, those who buy the $19.99 package cannot get HD or record programmes. And they can only purchase it if they call a freephone number, when sales reps try to get them into a higher tier. Whether those are techniques you want to employ, is your call.

So, finally, having done all the rigorous research to back up your assumptions, you are now in the happy place of having a robust set of figures for your costs and revenues. You can start putting together your financial projections. Remember that the objective is to arrive at a set of cash-flow forecasts that assess the viability of the project, which work out what the total equity requirement will be, and which demonstrate when and to what extent the venture will be profitable.

You should now produce a 10-year financial plan. A whole decade, I hear you cry? Yes, because media is a long-term business and it's normal to think 10 years ahead as to the value of the "brand" that will be created and the income that will be generated.

Once that's done, set out some variations to your base forecasts, so that you and the potential investors can see what happens if your assumptions are adrift by minus-20 per cent or (unlikely) better off by 20 per cent. It's important to set out several different financial scenarios. These could be revenue-related, where it's projected to be down because of failures to hit sales targets for reasons that could be internal or because the economy unexpectedly hits a downturn, or cost-related, where your spending on people, programmes or marketing is much greater than forecast. Or a combination of both. As with most of the battle plans drawn up by generals, business plans don't often survive for long after their first contact with reality. But that mustn't stop you giving it your best shot, and being prepared to adapt, learn and iterate. Or pivot, as it is fashionable to say in Silicon Valley.

These spreadsheets will show how much money you will require to start and run the business before it becomes profitable, and therefore how much capital you will have to raise from investors. Make sure that the business has adequate capital resources to start off with. This is a golden rule. If you get stuck with financial constraints in year one, and need to cut spending on marketing, programming and people, then these are only likely to exacerbate year on year, as that reduced spending, in turn, leads to lower ratings and lower revenues. Something unexpected - an event or extra costs - will occur that you have not thought of or factored in. So be sure to build in a reasonable buffer for contingencies and nasty surprises.

There is no need to include the whole 10-year outline in the business plan. Have it ready to share with would-be investors if they want it, but otherwise show a summary, or perhaps the period covering launch to profitability.

RISKS

It is essential to include an honest and wide-ranging analysis of the risks facing your business. The entrepreneur who seeks to maintain that there are no perils to worry about and all will be fine is either a fool, will not raise any money, or will lose some gullible people a lot of money.

Research from the Harvard Business School has shown that as many as 75 per cent of startup companies fail, so the chances are stacked against success. We don't hear about most of them because private equity firms and venture capitalists bury their dead very quietly, quickly... and deep. The failures are swiftly erased from the investors' websites, never to be spoken of again. No one wants a reputation for having chosen to sink millions into what turned out to be a turkey.

It's important that you lay out all the potential risks, however small. Your would-be investors will almost certainly do this from their perspective, if they are serious about investing in your venture. If their analysis turns up something you've ignored or glossed-over, it will cause alarm and damage your credibility.

What could possibly go wrong? Well, almost anything.

Perhaps your product - your channel - doesn't turn out to be as good, or as popular, as you think it's going to be. Perhaps it doesn't address a big enough market, or the right opportunity within that market. What if the price you've set for subscriptions is too expensive for your target customers? What if it turns out that all those people who told your market researchers they'd definitely subscribe, were lying?

Perhaps your launch - a potential make or break event - goes wrong, for technical or human reasons. Remember you only get one bite at the cherry. If the first perceptions of the channel is not good or is dodgy, you are in trouble. It takes a Herculean effort to bring back a station that has had a bad beginning.

What if you miss the crucial business milestones and time-lines that you've set yourself and the money starts to run out? What if that star presenter you pinned many of your hopes on gets offered double the money to stay at your rival channel and doesn't end up joining you? Or what if two of your anchors end up brawling on camera? (Not as unlikely as it might seem: it happened in the early days of the UK's Sky News.) Or you face a multi-million dollar libel action from a well-known politician after one of your reporters accuses him of taking bribes, without having the facts to prove it?

Most of these damaging potholes can be avoided provided you do the research for your business plan properly and have a good management team. And a dollop or two of luck doesn't go amiss.

EXIT

There are several ways in which investors can realise the profits they have made from funding your business: a stock market flotation; the sale of the business to another company; selling on their take to another private equity firm; or selling it to one of the other existing investors or the owners of the company. You will need to take a view on which is most likely in your case, and to set out your reasons in this section of the plan.

The stock market flotation is known as an IPO, an initial public offer, of the company. In such a scenario, investors will be able to sell their shares as they start trading on the exchange. Stock market flotation is generally used only for very large companies and can be costly.

A strategic acquisition or trade sale, in which your company is bought by another company, is probably one of the most popular exit routes. The buyer will usually see some strategic advantages in acquiring the business, and will often pay a premium to do so.

In a secondary sale, investors sell their stake in the business to another private equity firm. This can happen for many reasons. The business may require more money than the original investors can or want to afford. Or the business may have progressed to the stage that the original investors wanted it to reach, and other equity investors are needed to take over from there.

Or you, or other investors, may be keen to increase your stake in the company, and are happy to buy the shares of those investors keen to realise their return. This can be an attractive exit option for the investors, and a welcome one for the founders.

Before we move on, a word or two here about valuation. How do you value how much your fledgling business is worth? Determining this is difficult but important - it will, in turn, decide what percentage of the equity you will need to hand over to your investors, and therefore what share is left in your hands and those of your fellow founders.

When a business has been running for a while, and you can see the real revenues, costs and profits that it makes, determining what it is worth is relatively simple. It's normally a multiple of, say, 10x revenues or four or five times profit, with other factors such as long-term viability, the quality of the leadership team, growth prospects, strategic fit, etc, thrown into the equation. But when it is a startup that exists only on paper and is operating only on forecasts, and which has yet to take a dollar, a pound, a rupee or a riyal in revenue, how is the calculation made?

In the end, it comes down to the price someone is willing to pay, how excited they are by your vision, and how convinced they are that the business is going to be a winner. It's a negotiation, and you need to be tough and resolute. Investors, particularly VCs and private equity firms, will seek to get as big a slice as they can get for their buck, and think you should be grateful that they are even considering putting money in to fund your idea. Be grateful, of course, but don't be a pushover: only give them what you consider is fair, and make sure you stay in control of your company and your destiny. I've seen too many entrepreneurs, desperate to obtain the funds they need, give away too much at this stage, and eventually lose jurisdiction over their companies. Don't let this happen to you. I remember reading the sad story of the fate of David Buick, one of America's pioneer car manufacturers at the beginning of the 20th century. For various reasons, he lost control of his business, the Buick Automobile Company, which went on to be a founding part of the giant General Motors. He lost out on a fortune, and his last years were spent in poverty. He died in 1929 in a shabby little flat in Detroit, and could not even afford a telephone, much less a car, though thousands of them bearing his name drove past his front door.

When your compelling business plan, combined with your slick, professional presentation of it, results in your successfully raising the funds needed, by all means celebrate. After all, you have acquired the means to make your dream a reality and you will feel like you've won the lottery. Enjoy the moment; you've worked hard for this.

But when those celebrations are over, don't be fooled by all that money in the bank. You've actually achieved only the first stage. Money doesn't guarantee success; only the effective execution of your business plan can deliver that. And that task lies with you and the rest of the management team, which is why we will look at this aspect next.

5

DELIVERING AND LOOKING AFTER YOUR BABY

"Early to bed, early to rise, work like hell, and advertise." **Ted Turner**

So much has been written about the art of running a business that a search for the word "management" in the books section of Amazon returns around 80,000 results to choose from. There's no end of advice out there, everything from *"Managing a dental practice - the Genghis Khan way"* to *"Bodybuilders in Tutus - and 35 other obscure business-boosting observations"*. There's even one entitled *"Leadership Secrets of Attila the Hun"*, and another called *"Whale Done!"*, which explains why your co-workers have a lot in common with killer whales (but you probably knew that already).

All of them, I'm sure, have their merits and may well contain important and useful advice. But, frankly, there is generally so much nonsense written about management that the underlying fundamental task becomes lost. Quite simply, management is the organisation and coordination of the activities of a business in order to achieve its defined objectives.

The person at the top of the business, the chief executive, clearly sets out how the goals and plans will be achieved, with each department in the company given its respective responsibilities and tasks. The managers of those departments have the role of steering their bit of the business in the right direction so as to achieve their short- and long-term targets, and each is answerable for them. It doesn't require you to take on the persona of a Genghis Khan or metaphorically (let alone actually) don a tutu; it does require an ability to be organised, focused and clear.

It's not rocket science. During the 20-year tenure of Jack Welch, the legendary former boss of the American multinational General Electric whose tenure ended in 2001, the company's value rose 4,000 per cent. When he retired, he collected a payment of $417 million, the largest severance package paid to any American CEO in the previous decade. Welch once summed up his method of running a business: "Focus on a few key objectives... I only have three things to do. I have to choose the right people, allocate the right number of dollars, and transmit ideas from one division to another with the speed of light. So I'm really in the business of being the gatekeeper and the transmitter of ideas." He doesn't mention here that he used to fire the bottom 10 per cent of his managers annually, regardless of their absolute performance. It earned him the nickname "Neutron Jack" (in reference to the nuclear weapon) for his ability to eliminate people while leaving buildings intact.

A TV station's management in the developing world is often a family affair, or one that is usually managed by the original founder. But, as in all businesses, things are moving towards a more professional approach. TV stations are not like a factory where the manufactured product, made by the same process and with the same materials every day, is then sold through prearranged logistics in an organised distribution system. In our business, by its very nature, the content of our product changes on a daily or hourly basis. It can take time and patience to make the product, to see your content being aired on the screen, and you need in most cases to wait at least six months before ratings have settled down enough to assess what advertising pricing structure to put into place or, rather, to judge what the market sees as a fair price for advertising on your channel.

For these reasons and more, I strongly believe that it is best for the founder of the channel to adopt a professional and pragmatic approach when it comes to deciding who should be chief executive of the business (and, indeed, the other key management appointments). It's a time for ego, ambition and familial connections to be put to one side. Just because you founded the company, just because you were brilliant in coming up with the idea and raising the investment needed, doesn't *necessarily* mean you're the right person to manage the business day to day.

Only you, any other co-owners, and your investors can decide this. You need to be hard-headed and ask yourself some tough questions. Do you want to be CEO because you know you'll be good at it and have the right qualities, or because you like the idea of the title and the power that comes with the job? What will give the business the best chance of success - bringing in a professional CEO with a good track record in the industry, or giving the role to someone who has little or no such experience (that would probably be you)? It's really a very delicate, difficult, personal judgement matter in which the issues as to who will manage the business can only be answered in a self-critical mode.

If you choose the route of appointing a professional CEO, you can always sit on the board of directors as chairman, giving input into the macro decisions affecting the business and effectively being the CEO's boss. You will also remain, of course, a major shareholder. Always keep in mind that the TV business, like any other venture, requires a team effort.

I need to make a confession here. I have written the above advice with the benefit of hindsight and accumulated wisdom. When I initially established my businesses, I was a control freak. My fear was that if I was not in charge, the business would collapse or someone else would take it over and force me out entirely. I only began to learn how to relinquish day-to-day oversight when I moved to Dubai in 2000 to set up Middle East Business News, which later morphed into CNBC Arabiya in 2003. That channel needed my full commitment for at least five years, so it was at that stage that I appointed a CEO for the Pakistani production company, and later for CNBC Pakistan in 2005 and Samaa TV in 2007. Whether my timing was right or wrong, I don't know, but it's a personal decision driven by a multitude of factors such as time commitments, size of the businesses etc.

CNBC Africa, launched in 2007, has always been looked after by my co-founder and he has done an excellent job managing it. I attend board meetings and act as a sounding board for important decisions or in a crisis situation. There was no particular catalyst that made me realise that the businesses would do well if I was not there; however, after all these years, this evolution from a control freak to taking a backseat and looking only at the bigger picture has freed me up to do many other useful things. Such as spending time on the strategic direction of the businesses, looking at new investment opportunities, particularly in the technology sector, and going into the education sector by bringing international universities such as UK's Lancaster University to Africa and Australia's Curtin University to the Middle East.

My passion and love still lies in TV and, frankly, the news channels. The CEOs manage day-to-day affairs but consult me on major matters. And, believe me, being chairman of a news channel means you are confronted with serious issues on a regular basis, some of which are very challenging.

It was, for me, the best decision I have ever made. If you

initially decide to be the CEO of your business, the timing of a move from actively managing it to a more strategic role will vary, depending on the circumstances of the business and yourself. Your inner self will tell you when it's time to appoint someone. My own move gave me time to think about what really mattered in the long term and to leave the day to day to the professional managers. Don't be like me: if you have a choice of appointing versus managing, do the former. At what stage of the business cycle should you consider this? That's up to you; it's a judgement call. All I can say in the matter is that it has worked brilliantly for me. After all, it's even given me time to write a book!

How should the management of the company be structured? Broadly, there should be an executive committee in which all heads of department are members. This will normally meet once a week, chaired by the CEO, to review the performance of the business and take decisions to resolve any problems or to increase investment in areas that are performing well. Once a month or perhaps every quarter, the board of directors should meet to review business performance and to consider strategic issues, with the Chairman overseeing this meeting.

Broadly, the following represent the various facets of the management process, though not in any particular order:

Marketing
Research
Sales
Finance
Human Resources
News/Programming
Operations

We'll go through the marketing and research in the rest of this chapter, along with aspects pertaining to launching your channel. Then, in subsequent chapters, we'll look at sales and finance; HR; the newsroom; and, finally, operations. All these departments are equally important when it comes to building and looking after your creation - I'm just breaking them down into bite-size chunks.

Rather than trying to give a comprehensive step-by-step guide to all of these areas, I intend to provide you with an overview, along with some observations I've made over the years.

MARKETING

Again, a lot of dead trees have been sacrificed in the pursuit of the perfect marketing process. Type the word into Amazon's search engine, and almost as many books as for management appear - 70,000.

It's a bit like child-rearing manuals (except that there are only 50,000 of those on Amazon), in the sense that if it were simple and the answers were obvious then there would be no need for tens of thousands of different experts all claiming that theirs was the right solution, and charging US$16.99 a time for their wisdom. Everyone would have perfect children, and the perfect marketing strategy. If only.

Put at its most basic, marketing is the process of influencing consumers or advertisers to choose your product over those of your competitors. The key is finding the right marketing method and message to educate and guide your consumers or advertisers, and delivering that message to them at a time and a place when they are receptive to it.

Sounds simple, yes? I wish. Getting those variables right - the method, the message, the placement and timing - is not so much a science, as a difficult and inexact art. And measuring the effectiveness of any campaign is problematic, too, whatever some of today's digital advertising gurus will tell you.

The adage coined by John Wanamaker, the successful 19th-century American merchant, remains as true now as it was back in his day: "Half the money I spend on advertising is wasted; the trouble is I don't know which half." There have been times in my career when I have thought that Mr Wanamaker may actually have underestimated just how much is thrown away.

You'll hear all sorts of spin as to why, in today's digital age, Wanamaker's dictum is out of date, and why he would now be able to "accurately and precisely" measure the return on investment of every single dollar he spent on marketing. As one particular advocate of online advertising claims, marketing today has become "a combination of precise, measurable science, deep strategy, leading-edge technology, advanced psychology, education and, of course, execution through beautiful, engaging and creative art form. Successful marketing today is where science and art intersect to deliver superior results."

Oh, really? Why is it then that the Interactive Advertising Bureau (IAB), the online advertising industry's trade association, estimates that ad fraud, in which advertisers are fooled into paying for fake inventory, cost the publishing industry more than $US16 billion in 2017 alone? Was that click on your banner ad, or that view of your video ad, done by a human or a robot? A robot which, after all, is unlikely to buy your product - at least as things stand today.

Bo Sacks, an American magazine industry veteran who campaigns against ad fraud, estimates that just one "bot" - and there are tens of thousands out there - can produce one billion fraudulent ad impressions every minute. "We are so filled with so much fraud that it's hard to tell the good players from the bad players," he warns. "It's just everywhere."

In 2016, Facebook admitted it had "inadvertently" inflated the video viewership metrics it had given advertisers and brands by between 60 and 80 per cent. Late in 2018, a group of advertisers in America launched a potential class-action lawsuit against the tech giant, accusing it of unfair business conduct and fraud, and claiming that the video metrics had actually been inflated by between 150 and 900 per cent. Facebook, which said it would contest the action, strongly denied any wrongdoing beyond its earlier admission.

It's a minefield. So, when you come to embark on the journey of committing your hard-earned cash to promoting your new venture, beware. You need to be super smart, ruthlessly focused and have your BS detector set to maximum power, because you will be about to hear some fantastical stories about characters such as reach, branding, awareness, measurability and effectiveness.

Is the marketing of a TV station comparable to other forms of businesses? The answer is "yes" in the sense that a channel is a business that has a product (content/news) which needs to be sold through media managers to advertisers, or sold as subscriptions directly to consumers.

Marketeers the world over like to talk about the "4 Ps" - which are product, price, promotion and placement. These, too, apply to the TV business.

The product is your channel and its content, or programmes. The price is what you charge companies to advertise on it, or what you charge consumers for a subscription. Promotion is how you tell people about your brilliant programmes to entice them to buy a subscription, or, for advertisers, it's about the large numbers and attractive demographics of the viewers your programmes attract. And placement, as far as TV is concerned, is really about distribution - the ways in which your channel is able to be viewed, the platforms it is available on.

I am not going to talk much here about the product, the content, because that is your vision, and we've gone over the qualities I believe are required for success, but we will look at the three other Ps in turn.

We spoke in earlier chapters about the need to be extremely clear about who your target market is, what they currently watch and do, and how you will reach them to tell them about your exciting new offering. I also said it was important that you try to create a sustainable competitive advantage over your rivals, and keep abreast of what they are doing. How different is their content from yours? What is their pricing strategy compared to your business? What particular promotional strategies were successful for them, especially in their launch phase?

The early work you've done on understanding these two aspects of your business - your target market and your competitors - will help you put together your 4 Ps, and will be crucial if you are not to waste (too much of) your precious marketing budget.

You and your marketing director will need to draw up a plan that will cover two distinct phases: the launch of the station, and probably the first 12 months or so after that - though the latter will be subject to change as the lessons of the first few weeks and months of going live are learned. In drawing up your plan, you will probably want to enlist the assistance of some outside experts, perhaps a marketing or advertising agency that you or your marketing director have used before and trust.

You may be tempted here to try to go it alone, on the basis that you believe you know your product and your target audience best. Unless you are an experienced marketing executive by background, I recommend putting that temptation aside. If you can afford it, consult the best experts and professionals in this field. Don't try to be a jack of all trades. You may be brilliant at certain things, but everyone has strengths and weaknesses when it comes to dealing with the launch of a TV station.

Your marketing plan will not just set out the 4 Ps, but also address in a subtle way your proposed positioning of the brand or station, where it sits in the market - is it upmarket, mass market or somewhere in between? What are its values, the things it stands for, with which, in time, its name will hopefully become synonymous? This will inform your marketing message, and help give consumers, advertisers and media buyers an idea of what your channel is, and to understand why they are being asked to pay the price they are to subscribe to it or run their commercials on it. It's psychological in nature, but it needs to be addressed.

Pricing

As we discussed in the business plan chapter, trying to set the appropriate pricing for subscriptions and for advertisers can be tricky.

If you haven't already done so at the business plan stage, it might be useful at this juncture to set up focus groups, both of consumers and media buyers, to help you reach decisions on this aspect. It's amazing what these can produce by way of sound advice if structured well. If the pricing strategies weren't fixed at launch, these focus groups can help determine where you settle. Should your strategy place the product offering at a high, medium or low value? What will consumers pay for a subscription, especially now that they can be shown some of the programming that they'll receive? Don't be too hung up on the advertising pricing, as the market is a great determiner of what's right. That will come about six months into launch, when your audience numbers are real, rather than projected.

Promotion

As with the business plan, it is critical that you don't allow your marketing messages - particularly at launch - to raise expectations to such a degree that people are disappointed when they watch your content. There's no point promising to, say, be the only news source that people need, if you're only covering certain topics or covering issues from a particular political angle. Or if you are saying that yours is the most technologically advanced news channel in the world, available 24/7 on any device known to mankind, you'd better make sure that is true, and that your operations/IT teams don't drop the ball. Some of my worst moments - as you will read about later - have come when my business was let down by last-minute technological snafus. What *can* go wrong in this area, probably *will* go wrong. Only promise people what you are 100 per cent sure you will deliver to them.

It would be pointless to get into a discussion here about exactly what sort of marketing message you might employ, or the merits of the myriad methods of advertising and promoting your business that you might use. Only you and your marketing director - and any expert advisers - can decide on these matters.

Is it better to promote some of the big-name presenters that have joined your station or to focus on some of the unique content that you'll be providing? Do outdoor billboards trump ads in specialist print magazines, or is it better to go with spots on terrestrial television or targeted campaigns on Facebook? Should you start your own channel on YouTube and drip-feed videos promoting your content in the days and weeks before launch? What about online microsites for your most popular programmes? What's your Twitter strategy? How can you use social media influencers to endorse your channel to their millions of followers? What celebrities might you persuade to back you? How can you encourage engagement with your brand online and on screen, by garnering and highlighting comments, or through phone-ins, polls or quizzes?

How do you, in the parlance beloved of marketeers, create a buzz about your arrival on the scene? Can you make a video or a gif that goes viral? It doesn't necessarily have to be something that garners tens of millions of views worldwide, though that would be marvellous. It might just be something that makes people in the TV industry in your region talk about your immi-nent launch. Many of these people will be extremely curious as to what the station's look and feel will be, or what your new programmes will consist of, or what new technology you may be introducing. Or you might aim something at people working in the advertising sector. These communities are like small islands when looked at separately, but if you seed each one with something tempting, they can grow into a substantial number overall. If you can create a buzz, an excitement, either among the general public or around the industry, you will have achieved something important.

Each business will take a different marketing approach, based on its needs and the knowledge it has about its target market. When we launched Samaa in Pakistan, we did a branding awareness exercise (known as "ambient marketing") at three major airports in the country (Karachi, Lahore and Islamabad), using departure and arrivals billboards and branding luggage carts with our logo, for general brand identification/positioning and for promoting particular programmes as well. It proved useful. Our breakfast show and current affairs shows were the ones we pushed, and ratings for all of them increased; in one particular case, our 8pm prime time anchor was promoted and this resulted in an immediate spike in his ratings and viewership.

It should go without saying that you need to ensure that any influencer, celebrity or other "product advocate" you use needs to command respect and credibility. There's no point getting an endorsement from, say, a disgraced former sportsman who used performance-enhancing drugs to cheat. Unless a) that's the sort of image you want for your station; or b) it perhaps takes the form of an amusing, counter-intuitive advert. Such approaches are often fraught with danger, however. They are favoured by advertising agency "creatives", who enjoy doing something different that will earn them industry awards and the envy of their colleagues. (Indeed, I sometimes feel that some of them are often more interested in being fêted themselves than they are about the fate of the actual product concerned. After all, while you're careering on towards bankruptcy, they're just moving on with their careers and their next ad campaign.)

Yes, creativity is the key to devising a good marketing strategy and campaign, but it needs to be kept in check. Ad agency creatives can be like architects who build you a fantastic, futuristic-looking house that wins awards and critical praise; it's only when you move in that you discover that the award-winning flat roof leaks and the award-winning wall-to-ceiling windows give you no privacy or shelter from the burning sun. To these architects, it's the aesthetic that matters; they don't have to live in the damn thing. And neither do the ad agency creatives really have skin in the game; if it was their money, their business and their livelihood on the line, would they take the same decisions or such risks? I doubt it.

If you are seeking to be controversial, fine, but otherwise I'd avoid any temptation to try to be humorous. What can appear funny or amusing in an ad agency boardroom filled with like-minded people, can often have the opposite effect on the general public. Take a look online at Burger King's 2009 advert for its jalapeño-topped Texican Whopper. It showed a tall American cowboy moving in together with a short wrestler who was cloaked in what appeared to be the Mexican flag. The tagline? "The taste of Texas with a little spicy Mexican." The ad was pulled after Mexican officials complained that it was disrespectful to its nation and its flag.

A similar result befell a 2012 American TV advert for the snacks brand Popchips, which featured the white American actor Ashton Kutcher as an Indian man "looking for love" in a dating ad-style spoof. Kutcher's use of brown facial make-up and a stereotypical Indian accent was deemed racially insensitive and offensive, and sparked an online backlash, particularly from members of the Indian-American community. The video was pulled and Popchips had to apologise, claiming that the dating parody was "created to provoke a few laughs and was never intended to stereotype or offend anyone".

So it's not about creating any buzz. It's not akin to the old mantra of "no news is bad news". The buzz about your brand needs to have a positive impact, and just in case you do a Burger King or a Popchips, it's worth having a disaster recovery plan in place, to quickly counter anything that might impact your station's reception, both during launch and post going live.

Do not overlook publicity of a different kind. Public relations, or PR, which involves placing interesting stories about your venture in other media, is a very useful tool to raise the profile of the station and you personally. You can go on chat shows to talk about how you founded your business, and why your station's going to be brilliant. You can put yourself up as an expert speaker at relevant industry conferences or seminars, or offer to write a regular column in a specialist magazine. Or some of your star hires can give interviews as to why they've chosen to jump ship to you. Your station might elect to champion a relevant cause - a charity, a hospital, a sick child - that fits with the company's commitment to the local community. Any positive publicity is better than none. And better than that, it costs you nothing but your time.

You could also look into partnering with established brands in the launch or as an ongoing marketing strategy. The brands that you consider for this should be those that fit your value system, and offer synergies, or mutual interests, for the both of you. If you're appealing to a youthful demographic that's into video gaming, then might marketing executives at Microsoft Xbox or Sony PS4 see you as a great fit? Or if your target audience is the business community, might a bank or an insurance provider want to be part of that? As I write, we are in the process of launching a major new TV channel in Pakistan in collaboration with an internationally well known brand name. Because of the confidential nature of the project, I cannot reveal more at this stage, and we are still awaiting regulatory approval. It has been an interesting journey that has thrown up many questions for us. Is it the right time to launch given that the economy is in transition, or should we wait? We have lined up a slew of good brand names who will be partnering with us, which has made the decision to proceed easier.

Placement (Distribution)

Distribution is key and deserves your attention from the get-go. It should be addressed as one of the critical factors for your station's success. There's no point producing brilliant programmes presented by superstar anchors, if no one can watch them because you've failed to secure broadcasting space on a satellite, or haven't put agreements in place with cable distribution operators, or haven't enough bandwidth to stream your station over the internet. Sorting out these vital technology issues is not easy, but it has to be a number-one priority. I mean, what sort of numbskull would allow some technical hitch to mar the launch of his fantastic new station? (That's Mr Numbskull to you, please.)

Just when you think you have everything under control in terms of a perfect line-up of programming, an array of talented presenters and producers, and a slick marketing campaign, someone will ask, right before launch, "By the way, which number on so-and-so cable operator is the channel going to be?" Oops. How on earth did we forget to secure a place on so-and-so operator?

As I mentioned earlier, how the launch of your new TV station goes is key to its short- and long-term success. It involves every aspect of the business pulling together in the same direction, and no department making a hash of its responsibilities, but marketing, programming and operations/distribution are the three most crucial areas to get right.

The launch of a TV station is the most important event, the culmination of what will have been probably a year and a half of hard work. You only have one go at it. Get it wrong at launch and it will take you many years to recover, if you do at all. There are isolated examples of TV stations having a disastrous launch and emerging stronger for it in the end, but that will have taken a long time and a lot of money; hence the caution to try to get everything right at the start.

This is the moment when the CEO earns his or her stripes, and must be completely across the detail of each department's progress against its milestones leading to the big day. Every facet of the operation needs to align, in tandem and on time. It's no use having an amazing marketing campaign primed and ready to go if the operations department has forgotten some fundamental aspect that means a whole swathe of potential viewers on a particular platform or in a geographical location will not be able to watch the channel. The start date for most marketing campaigns has to be set weeks in advance, so once it's committed to, that's it. There's no reset button.

What will help make your launch - and your life - easier will be hiring a good project manager to oversee all aspects of taking the station from a concept on a piece of paper to a fully fledged live channel. After weeks of consultation and planning with key executives, the project manager will devise a timeline, a project plan and a budget to launch - on a date that will be set using their experience of how long it will take to recruit, train, design, produce, build, install, rehearse and get on air.

Once the launch date is set, all plans work backwards from that. It is a complex military exercise in reverse engineering. Real-time pilot programmes should run for at least four weeks before "go live". Rehearsals (for "blocking" shots, testing sets and technical production) should be a further four to six weeks before that. Training on the various kit will precede that, depending on the staff's experience. Things will inevitably go wrong. Technology will fail, production of brand sequences will be late as editors disagree with this colour or that typeface, and, as things slip, plans have to be adapted to meet the launch deadline. A good project manager will run a risk register outlining known concerns and plans of how to mitigate them.

There should be weekly production meetings attended by the top people from every part of the organisation - not too big a group, but not too small either. Engineering, production, creative, editorial, HR and finance should all be represented. Hold ups, hiccups and advances should all be reported, and it's here that you will be able to monitor your baby's slow progression to its birth.

As I have mentioned before, I carry scars from each of the four channels I've been involved in launching. For an illustration of how not to do it, take CNBC Pakistan. It was an encrypted channel and, therefore, every cable operator in Pakistan had to be provided with a set top box, which, by the time of the launch ceremony in Islamabad in 2005, I was assured had been done. We had President Pervez Musharraf as our first guest on the station, appearing live from the presidential palace in front of a select audience, alongside live links to some special guests around the world. These included Sir Martin Sorrell, the founder of WPP, the world's largest advertising and PR group, in Cannes; an expat Pakistani businessman in London; and a senior economist from a leading think-tank in Washington. Two things went wrong: we lost the link to London for 15 seconds during the show, and not all the encrypted boxes had been delivered to the cable operators. These hiccups were embarrassing for the launch of a major international channel but, thankfully, we got over it relatively quickly.

A similar mishap marred the launch of Samaa TV, where I was Chairman. Our CEO and the distribution department assumed that we had delivered boxes to all of the cable operators, whereas that was not the case. Here was a major launch of what was supposed to be a nationwide channel, but which instead had limited distribution. There was a mad scramble afterwards to try to make up the lost ground, along with a lot of wasted marketing money. It was mortifying. But, luckily, Samaa did very well after that and today, more than 10 years later, is now in the top four news channels in the country, and highly respected for its integrity and fairness in reporting.

On the way to launching CNBC Arabiya, in 2002, there were issues around acquiring capacity on a satellite, because there are so many stations in the free-to-air environment of the Middle East. There were just no transponders available. Various friends and connections of mine tried to gain space, but to no avail. There we were, well on our way to a launch in six months' time, with no ability to transmit our signals. We were in danger of broadcasting to absolutely no one, unless we invited a few dozen people to the studio to watch us live.

Somewhat in desperation, I went to see the managing director of Abu Dhabi TV to ask whether he could spare any capacity. He had none, but said that Yemen TV had a spare transponder, and they might well be persuaded to sub-lease it to us for a premium of 150 per cent. When I arrived back from Abu Dhabi, I called a management committee meeting. I explained the dilemma, and asked the technology experts to look at the digital transponder landscape, which was then in its infancy and somewhat unreliable, but was improving at the time. They came back saying that such space was available, but the risks of a failure going down that route were enormous. The price difference was substantial, however: a saving of US$2 million per annum using digital versus traditional. After much debate, we agreed to risk the digital transponder approach, and thankfully the call was the correct one. Within a year, most channels had followed our lead. CNBC Arabiya was the first international brand to commence broadcasting in Arabic in the region, and that generated great interest. Fast forward to 2019, and most of the major international news channels are in the region, broadcasting in Arabic. What a difference 16 years makes.

There are varying technical issues to be addressed in different countries, of course. In Pakistan, there are hundreds of cable operators, plus sub-operators, so it can be fairly crowded and chaotic. Frequent power failures don't help either. The Government has begun the process of DTH (Direct to Home) digital and, hopefully, all the channels will transition on to that in due course. It's going to take a few years, however.

In South Africa, a virtual monopoly exists in the form of DSTV, a direct broadcast satellite service owned by MultiChoice and which operates across sub-Saharan Africa. When we were preparing to launch CNBC Africa, in 2006, we approached DSTV but were turned down. It was already carrying CNBC Europe, which was quite popular with viewers. We had taken something of a gamble, believing that DSTV would have to put a local channel such as CNBC Africa on its service, particularly because our agreement with CNBC Europe entailed it going off air in Africa to be replaced by us. But DSTV didn't want to budge. In the end, it took CNBC Europe to intervene, telling DSTV it would no longer be allowed to carry its channel anyhow, before the South Africans realised they had no choice. It was not until a few months before our launch that DSTV relented. Their main concern was that viewers who watched CNBC Europe would not be interested in the African markets. We overcame this by explaining that we would be airing the most important programs of CNBC Europe and CNBC America on CNBC Africa since all three channels were in English. Thankfully, the relationship between CNBC Africa and DSTV is now good and continues to improve.

Once you've launched, and are a living, breathing broadcaster, you'll soon gather a slew of real information about which people, and how many, are watching you at any given minute of the day, alongside detailed data on their demographics. You will quickly have a fairly good idea of who your viewership is. There's no longer any need to rely on projections about audiences or their size.

The more you know about your audience, the better for your business, and the better for your advertisers. Your research department will compile the ratings data, and create a wealth of information. Each minute can now be scrutinised. Who was watching? For how long? What are their demographics, their gender, age, income, locations? Which programme, headline or story attracted the biggest audience? What's a viewer's average daily/weekly engagement with your station and how does that change over time?

This sort of data - the amount you know about your customers - is extremely important today and will be absolutely critical in years to come. The digital world allows TV channels to start amassing the same sort of insights and knowledge that the big tech giants like Facebook and Google have on their users - and which allows them to hoover up advertisers' money by the bucketload. If you are charging a subscription for people to watch your channel, then you will clearly have much more sophisticated knowledge of your customers than an ad-supported channel will.

One way of improving your data is to carry out customer research surveys, which can form an integral part of your evolving marketing strategy and enable you to know your viewership better. This research is normally carried out by professional firms who have relevant experience in the field, and understand the processes involved with collecting, collating and interpreting the data.

The broad objectives are to understand such things as:

1. Your viewers' habits and their favourite programmes;
2. Why they choose the programmes they watch;
3. Where you stack up *vis-à-vis* your competition;

4. What your viewers want to see that is not yet being shown;
5. What they dislike in your and your competitors' programming;
6. Which presenters and reporters they like or dislike.

This process can be enlightening. Sometimes, you unearth insights that can form the basis of a new programme that your team may not have thought about. Other times, the findings reinforce your hunches about what's working and what's not.

But a few words of caution: you can encounter some strange results from your marketing research. It often throws up conflicting data, the analysis of which is an art not a science. At best, it should assist in directing your programmes and promotions to increase viewership and help you gain some competitive advantages over rivals. It is very easy, though, for such research and associated focus groups to become carried away with a "fairytale idea" for a new programme or a promotional campaign, which could prove expensive in terms of resources, money and time. There must be checks and balances in place to prevent this from happening.

Should you always be on the lookout for doing something new in relation to both programming or marketing? Yes, all the time, since only by looking at things differently and doing something new can one keep pace with the changing needs and wants of your consumers. There's a reason that Number 3 on Jack Welch's Top 10 Rules for Success is: "Search for a better idea every day." Nothing stays the same, and as your viewers evolve, so must your programming and approach. Every product, every show has a life cycle; before it becomes stale or obsolete, it needs to be reinvented or discarded in favour of something new. Research is used continuously to assess what you're doing well and what you're not, and alerting you to which once-popular programmes have a waning audience.

Having armed yourself with the results of your surveys, you may wish to tweak current programming, start new programmes, change your graphics, your music or your station ID. A great deal of thought and ideas will emerge from this process.

By the way, you can pick up useful feedback from just about any quarter - perhaps from your bankers, lawyers, accountants or even the Uber driver taking you to the studio. It's always good to talk. And, more importantly, listen.

6

ALL HAIL THE RAINMAKER

"You are the product. You feel something.
That's what sells." **Don Draper,** *Mad Men*

There is a saying in advertising, "Consider yourself lucky if you get a rainmaker in your sales team." That's not the one doing a funny dance in the corner of the office and looking at the skies in anticipation, but the person (supported by his or her team) who seemingly effortlessly lands the biggest commercial deals for your station, week in, week out, year in, year out. If you are fortunate to have one of these maestros, cherish them, reward them well, and pray that they stay with you as long as they live.

At the end of the day, after the hard labours of the programming, news, operations and marketing divisions, it is the sales team that will bring in the bulk of your revenues. Its members work tirelessly to convince the various advertisers, media buyers and agencies to buy your product. The product, in this case, is your inventory: the number of advertising minutes that the station has to sell in a day. If your policy allows for 12 minutes of commercials per hour, then you have 288 minutes a day available to sell, though it's a little more complicated than that. Keep in mind that some of the night-time programming is written off as "dead time" for commercial purposes. Generally, the day is divided into morning (6am to 10am), 10am to noon (sometimes referred patronisingly as "women's hours" in some countries); an afternoon that runs from midday up to 6pm (or earlier, in some countries), and then it's prime time from 6pm to 11pm. Prime-time advertising is invariably the most expensive, overnight the least. A TV commercial generally lasts from 10 seconds to one minute; in some territories, such as in Pakistan or in Africa, this might stretch to two minutes, but that is rare.

To whom do you sell, and how? Your first ports of call are media buying houses, which act as agents for large numbers of potential advertisers. They will be the biggest purchasers of inventory, and will seek to negotiate substantial discounts for buying in bulk. They have very sophisticated methods of analytics and of dissecting data and ratings, and are most times spot on in this. Building good relationships with these agencies is paramount.

Direct sales to companies are also important and will contribute a percentage of your revenues (although probably not as substantial as that from the agencies). But there are companies that do not use media buying houses and wish to negotiate directly, and who have their own advertising agencies to provide the commercial.

Sponsorship and branding of programmes is another important area, and some long-term deals can be struck here. Ideas for this can be initiated by your sales team, or often the media buying houses will come up with innovative suggestions.

The leadership, skill-set and ethos of your sales team is crucial for the long-term success of your venture. The sales team must reflect the wider values of your brand, and demonstrate those virtues in all of its dealings.

. The head of sales is a key appointment. One must be sure that his or her personality is a good fit with the station, and that he or she shares similar views to yours and believes passionately in the product. He or she must be an evangelist for the channel, able to lead by example in the sales process, and identify, train, nurture and motivate junior sales executives, and to mould them into the company's way of doing things.

Always remember that truth and integrity pays in the long run: never seek to take a shortcut when selling. Sales people have tough targets to meet and their bonuses are often tied to achieving certain revenue levels, so there's always a temptation to cut corners or to promise the client something that's impossible to deliver, in order to get the deal signed. Over the years, I've heard of sales teams promising ridiculous things: that a star presenter will personally endorse the client's commercial just before it's aired, for example, or that a review of the client's product (in this particular case, a new movie) would be guaranteed to give five stars out of five (it received - and deserved - three).

Such over-selling, over-promising - actually, let's just call it what it is: lying - never works in the long-term. You'll gain a reputation for being unreliable, untrustworthy and unscrupulous, of being prepared to say or do anything in order to seal a deal. Be honest and never shortchange anyone in the sales process. You - and your company - will be admired in the long term for that. The media industry in every country is close-knit and matters of insincerity or greed on anyone's part take a toll not only on the salesperson's own standing, but on that of the whole sales team and that of the brand. Never fall to temptation to make a quick buck, as a quick buck today will inevitably mean fewer (or no) bucks tomorrow. Success will always come through hard work and passion for the brand you work for. Repeat business inevitably comes from clients/media buyers when they know they are dealing with upright sales personnel. Of course, you will also need a bit of luck sometimes.

At CNBC Arabiya, we made a seriously large presentation to a premier commercial bank in Kuwait for a three-year annual advertising partnership worth US$3 million. My sales team had spent months developing this relationship. I flew in from Dubai to attend what was the crucial presentation to the bank's CEO, the decision maker, because the team felt that my presence was important. As I watched the faces in the room while the presentation was being made, everything appeared to be going well. Then, at the end, the CEO said, "Wait a minute, you have one of our rivals advertising with you as well - I want an exclusive deal." Now, this was an impossible thing for us, and we tried to convince him of that, but to no avail. We were just about to pack our bags and leave, when the chairman of the bank unexpectedly walked in to the room. This was highly unusual, as he rarely interfered in the bank's day-to-day management. He had apparently received a call from the Emir of Kuwait's office asking him to come over urgently to the royal court, and he wanted the CEO's take on a certain matter which he felt might be under discussion there. He apologised for interrupting, asked the CEO some questions in private, and was about to go when, as an afterthought, he asked what the presentation was about. When told it was CNBC Arabiya, he said, "Yes, good brand, we should associate ourselves with them." Luck was on our side that day. We got the deal.

It's essential that each member of the sales team is familiar with the station's programming; they all need to know what they are selling when talking to clients and media buyers. Better still, they should have some emotional connection with the station; if they believe in the power of the product/content, then that belief will flow through their presentations and make them more effective. Data, such as ratings, rankings, reach, viewership, demographics etc, should be at their fingertips. The mindset of the sales people must be one that reflects their happiness with their job, that shows they have a passion for the product they are selling, and that they have a positive frame of mind.

Remember that details matter when negotiating a deal. Sometimes the sales team is so eager to make a deal that members overlook small, essential details, such as whether a proposed commercial campaign might not comply with a country's regulatory requirements. If it is a large deal, always consult your compliance officers or legal department. Never rush things just to get it done.

A good sales team will always look after the interests of its clients, but not, as in the examples above, to the detriment of the station. Sales people must possess good listening skills and pick up signs of uncertainty or hesitancy from potential advertisers. What aspects do they need reassurance on? What incentives or inducements might get them over the line? It might be a minor or a major matter. It is important to spot the signs and know when the time is right to find the sticking point and answer their needs to clinch the deal. Recognise and interpret the signals they are sending out.

Keeping in close communication with clients and buyers is crucial, as is never forgetting a face. Sometimes you may have a buyer who's bought just one commercial to air for a limited period of time. Not knowing whether he or she is likely ever resort to television advertising again does not mean that you should allow yourself to forget about them. Always keep in touch. You never know. Obviously, the sales team will be in daily contact with media buyers, advertising agencies and other big clients, but the smaller ones also need attention. So reach out. There's no harm in doing so. It just takes an email or, better still, a call to say "Hello".

An alternative to having your own sales team is to appoint a buying agent to represent you. In this case, the agency takes over your entire inventory under an arrangement whereby minimum sales guarantees are given and the revenues are shared between the agent and the station. I am not a proponent of this sort of pact because you are putting what is almost certainly your biggest revenue earner into the hands of someone else. In some cases, it has been a great success; in others, not so much. So I guess it depends on your attitude, strategy and how you rate the potential sales agent.

There are some types of advertising that should be avoided. This may seem rudimentary and taken for granted but it deserves a mention. You might get someone wishing to promote a product that has a dubious reputation. Or a company that is involved in a murky business. Or one that seeks to malign a competitor. Or a political party or movement that wishes to denigrate a rival. It might not always be obvious either: there are many instances when such a campaign may come in very subtle forms, so be cautious and careful to evaluate them, and do not be swayed by how lucrative the offer may seem.

There are times when the economy is going through a tough phase and the sales team feels demotivated as its pipeline is in a trough. Economies have ups and downs, and advertising is often the first casualty, as businesses cut their marketing costs. Anticipate the cycles, and make plans to counter the depression. Come up with special promotional themes. Your team may need to focus on more innovative solutions, perhaps bespoke or customised campaigns, tailored to a client's needs.

It's during such times that you will see the value of having engendered solid relationships with your clients and agencies, and of having built a reputation for being reliable, honest and looking after the interests of the clients. Use these moments to also review your costs, as you will be surprised how these go up on non-essential things during the good times. If times are tough and you have to make substantial cuts, then the first port of call will be those areas that do not impact content. Cutting your stars or editorial personnel who produce the content should be considered only if things are really bad and the downturn is expected to be of a long duration - as a benchmark, more than three years.

I have one final piece of advice on sales, which is: "God gave us two ears and one mouth." There has always been a purpose to this. Listen attentively, pay attention to detail, watch body language and don't talk too much. Never boast that your TV station is the best, or the only solution for potential clients. They will always know where the station stands by way of branding and ratings. Just listen, be focused, and offer solutions to their problems. In essence, they want to sell more of their product or raise awareness for their brand. What is it that you can do to help them achieve these goals in a cost-effective way?

The sales team will always need the support of other departments, not just by way of excellent content, good marketing and as big a viewership as possible. You might want to stage a glitzy annual conference for media buyers and selected clients towards the end of each year, at which the station's biggest stars, such as presenters and specialist reporters, give their forecasts for the following year, in politics, economics, business or sport. This can be followed by an after-party, where clients can mingle with the presenters; even people who work in the media industry get enthused by meeting the star faces they see on their screens.

Finance

It's all very well making sales, but what then? Who's ensuring that the revenue actually reaches the station, that there's enough money coming in to cover the monthly salaries and other expenses, and that the business is running on a financially stable footing?

The finance department of a TV station does not have too many dissimilarities to that in other businesses, though it is often smaller than one would find at a factory or a large corporation. However, the day-to-day working on management of cash flows and estimates of current and future liabilities to ensure stability are generally the same.

The structure is normally comprised of a head of finance who reports to the CEO. Under the head, there are various financial accountants looking after functions such as dealing with suppliers, credit policy and payment cycles.

On revenue inflow, there will be a team responsible for collection, which is always under pressure. In some countries, procuring the money that's owed can be extremely difficult, with bad debts a big issue. The sales team should be trained to be aware of players with significant credit risks. Historically, sales and collection were done by the same people. This all changed in the 1920s when, in the US insurance industry, some bright person decided to split the role between collection and sales to improve capabilities. This altered the entire structure of the sales industry for the better: sales people were left to sell, and it was others - namely in the finance department - who got the job of chasing clients to pay up. These techniques have been refined since then, however, the issue of bad debts is a pressing problem in most countries and it is important that the sales team be taken through risk-averse procedures and processes.

One of the key objectives of the finance department is to prepare weekly and monthly management reports for the executive teams and the directors, setting out the company's financial performance and profitability. These should be clear and easily understood by non-accountants because they will inform you and other executives about the financial health of the company, its cash-flow position, and whether you are heading towards a profit or a loss, allowing you to make changes to how the business is operating as and when necessary. On an annual basis, finance will prepare detailed accounts, including a Balance Sheet, Income Statement and Cash Flow Statement.

Cash flow - the amount of money coming in to a business versus the money going out - is extremely important to the health of a company. It's a great moment of celebration when the money coming in every month starts to exceed regularly what's going out (i.e., having a positive cash flow). You can then start to acquire an even more enviable position, known in financial terms as a high liquidity base.

Here's an example. Let's suppose your annual operating costs are US$10 million (salaries of staff, office space, marketing etc) which generates US$11 million in revenue from digital and advertising sales. Your company would have a positive cash flow of $1 million. If there were no loans or other debts that needed servicing, then the company would have $1 million that it could keep as liquidity, or cash in the bank.

Over time, you can hopefully improve your positive cash flow and build up this cash pile (or liquidity position, in accounting parlance), which can be used for buying new equipment, investing in better programming or hiring new stars, expanding in other ways, or buying other companies. Or the directors may choose to pay part of it out as a dividend to shareholders. Having a cushion of liquidity is a very positive sign of a thriving company.

The basic function of the finance department is to ensure good cash liquidity, looking continuously to deliver smooth operations by managing the inflows/outflows of money, and maintaining a tight control on funds, whether they be for day-to-day or for long-term capital expenditure.

Before experiencing positive cash flow (at least in the short- to medium-term; remember there is likely to be a lengthy gestation period before you become profitable), it is probable that you may need to raise more capital to keep the business running until that happy day arrives.

This will be a similar exercise, involving the same sort of potential sources to the one undertaken in your raising of funds to get the project off the ground, except that there will now be real financial results to look at, not solely projections. Potential investors will want to examine closely your cash flow and your liquidity, both the current position, the trends and likely projections. If a positive cash flow based on an acceptable return and timetable to the investor is shown as a result of the evaluation, they will probably go ahead with the investment. On the other hand, if the projections do not look good, they probably won't.

However, even if the results of the cash-flow analysis are negative, I have seen investors proceeding with the financial injection. Why? It comes back to what we spoke about earlier in the book: controlling a media outlet can give owners a direct entry into the corridors of power. This can help protect and grow their other, perhaps larger, business interests. This sort of trade-off is more prevalent in Africa and South Asia in my experience, but I dare say it exists elsewhere as well. To some wealthy people, media investments are vanity projects to be kept as trophy assets.

Your finance department will need to prepare a detailed business plan to show to the various potential investors. Assuming that you remain a private company at this stage, these would include:

- Existing shareholders willing to raise their holdings;
- Personal funds from friends or relatives;
- Bank borrowing at commercial rates;
- Angel investors who like to come in at second-stage financing rounds;
- Private equity or venture capitalists.

Once your finance department has prepared the initial business plan, it's a good idea to bring in a specialist consultant to refine the numbers. Investors will use one of a variety of complex methods to evaluate the proposal, and to decide whether it is a good idea. In essence, they will want as much reassurance as they can get that the rate of return on the money they put in will be higher than anything else they could do with it. They know that investing in a business is risky, so the potential rewards need to be attractive and justify the gamble. If, for example, people can put their money into a bank deposit account and earn 5 per cent interest a year, they would probably be indifferent to an opportunity to put that money into a business venture that offers the same rate of return over the same period. But if the investment could potentially bring in a positive return of 20 per cent, they might be tempted.

The process of sourcing investors can be long and relentless. Much will depend on how the station is getting on, obviously from a commercial point of view, but also how it is perceived: is it receiving good reviews, is it growing in popularity, does it have a good vibe about it?

When it comes to raising finance, success breeds success. While I've told you about some of the difficulties I have had in raising money for my first CNBC franchise, Arabiya, establishing backing for CNBC Pakistan was much easier. In fact, I was asked by the Finance Minister at that time to look at whether I could bring CNBC into the country. Because of my track record with CNBC Arabiya (it was in 39 countries by then), I had no issues with persuading institutional investors to back me. Although the channel proved to be a disaster in financial terms (its audiences were so small that officially its ratings were zero), it was a good experience to get an international network into Pakistan. The lesson I learnt was never take a niche channel into a country where ratings are considered primary and where the buying power of those watching the station is not considered to have any value. The other lesson from the experience was how to transition a badly rated financial disaster into recovering some money for the shareholders. All it took was to change the licence from business to news, retain the staff to produce news without spending extra and then market it as a news station. Sounds easy, but believe me it was a nightmare to transition; however, the experience itself was a good one.

It was a similar story with CNBC Africa, at least in terms of investors. I had never been to the African continent in my life when a colleague working for me in Dubai insisted that I visit South Africa. This was in 2005. I did so and was amazed at the country's infrastructure. Because of my relationship with CNBC, South Africa's institutional investor, the Industrial Development Corporation, saw no issues with partnering with me. We had the fortune of being overwhelmed with offers and had to turn down some good investors. The channel proved popular from the start, and although it had distribution and subscription challenges to begin with, all that is now a thing of the past.

7

PEOPLE: CAN'T LIVE WITHOUT THEM...

"Great vision without great people is irrelevant." **Jim Collins**

Let me be clear: the success or failure of your venture will depend entirely on the quality of the people you hire. You can come up with a brilliant idea and devise a foolproof strategy as to how to make it work, but you cannot do it alone: you need other people.

You need to surround yourself with the best and brightest people you can find, from the start. Talented people who are smarter than you, who know more than you, who will challenge you, pick holes in your plans, and sometimes annoy the heck out of you. But these are the sorts of people who will eventually make you look good. And make you rich. Steve Jobs, the legendary boss of Apple, said: "The secret of my success is that we have gone to exceptional lengths to hire the best people in the world."

This is even more critical for a new business like yours. As Jobs succinctly explained: "When you're in a startup, the first 10 people will determine whether the company succeeds or not. Each is 10 per cent of the company. So why wouldn't you take as much time as necessary to find all the A-players? If three [are] not so great, why would you want a company where 30 per cent of your people are not so great? A small company depends on great people much more than a big company does."

This is not just about hiring brilliant presenters, bursting with charisma, personality and on-screen presence. It is about hiring impressive people in every department - in operations, in marketing, in sales, in finance, and, perhaps particularly, in human resources, the department that will act as the conductor of the company's people strategy, from identifying and recruiting the right candidates, to training and equipping them with the skills they need to succeed, to rewarding, motivating and nurturing them properly so that they are happy, loyal and productive.

To begin with, the hiring of your first few employees is likely to come down to your judgement, perhaps alongside that of any co-founders. Hiring people - judging if they're an A-player or just a C+, or a B+ with a capacity to be better - is not easy; again, it's an inexact science, which is one of the reasons that there are also tens of thousands of books on this subject, doling out advice how best it should be done. Is a rigorous selection process involving several rounds of interviews, written exams, 360-degree assessments and psychometric tests better than making a decision based on a hunch, a feeling about the person? What references and background checks, such as on their social media profiles, ought to be undertaken? Do you need to like someone to give them a job, or should you take the view that what matters is only how well they can do the role?

During my time in the industry, I have personally hired dozens of people for jobs across the spectrum. So I must be able to give you the low-down on how to identify the right people, to sort the wheat from the chaff, to select the deliverers and the doers from the duffers and the dreamers?

Sorry.

My track record on hiring is mixed, at best. While, of course, I look carefully at a candidate's experience and background, and take a view on their character as they come across in the interview, I have often hired on a gut feeling, an instinct that the person seems a good fit for the role and for our company. The result? When it's worked out, it's been great; when it hasn't, it's been a disaster.

While hiring for CNBC Africa in 2005, I made a quick decision to hire a chap called Alex Leidner as an assistant producer after he came in for an interview. My head of HR in Dubai was with me in Johannesburg, where we were doing the initial interviewing for the new channel. Alex's CV was a gem and unlike any CV I had seen before. It says nothing about his education and little about his experience, and struck me as being sort of upside down. In the end, it basically just said, "Hire me". I found this intriguing! I ended up hiring him immediately. More than 11 years later, he still works for us in Johannesburg, and whenever I see him I am reminded of his CV. He has proved to be very, very good for CNBC Africa.

With CNBC Pakistan in 2005, I thought I had found the perfect anchor for one of our prime-time shows. He had a business degree, and had worked for a hedge fund and then for a leading brokerage firm in Pakistan. For a station such as CNBC, he was a great find: he was well groomed, looked good on screen, and came across impressively on the mocks we did. He was 38, full of energy and charisma, and wanted to become the guru-to-go-to on anything regarding stocks or financial matters in Pakistan. We hired him at great expense and spent a lot of resources in promoting the show. The programme proved to be a disaster as he started to freeze when on live TV. We tried various trainers to help him, but that seemed just to make him more worked up and, if anything, he got worse and worse whenever he was in front of a live camera. This was something entirely unanticipated by any of us. Three weeks after launch, I had to take the decision to pull the show and let him go. I knew that it takes time for any programme to settle down, especially when it has a new face, but the station received so many complaints from viewers that it became obvious it wasn't working and was unlikely to ever. The most common complaints were that "he does not even speak for minutes" and "just keeps shuffling around". Even my friends, who were normally reluctant to tell me their real feelings about a show, told me I had made a big mistake. And so I had.

So patchy is my record in hiring on an instinct that nowadays I am not allowed to interview candidates by myself, let alone offer jobs on the spot. One of my HR professionals always accompanies me, with strict instructions to keep me in check and to make sure I don't do anything rash.

These HR professionals would not approve of what I am about to say: despite my hits-and-misses, I still believe that if you spot someone you believe has the right stuff, you should offer them a job immediately, and work out the details later. Yes, there are many talented people out there, but they are in great demand in the TV industry, and you often need to be bold and strike fast to capture them. Not that they all always appreciate such efforts.

I remember, during the hiring process for CNBC Africa, someone coming in for an interview for head of sales. As we went through the details of his life, he seemed to me to have a good voice, and was someone I thought would do well in front of the camera. So after the salary he had wanted was agreed, I said to him, "How would you like to become a star?", and went on to explain that I thought he would do well as an anchor. He asked for some time to think about it and said he would come back to HR the next day. On the way out, he told the head of HR: "You know, if I am to take the presenter position, I think I would need a 25 per cent raise on the salary I wanted." On the way back to his house, he rang HR and told them "perhaps 35 per cent more, and not 25 per cent". HR simply said: "You have until tomorrow, think about it and come back to us." The next day, after speaking to his wife, he rang to say he would be delighted to accept the position, but needed a hike of 50 per cent on the initial salary. The HR head said thank you and goodbye, and that was that. The man continued to phone back for several weeks, but his calls were never taken. I suppose the moral is to "never look a gift horse in the mouth"; if it's a good thing that's being offered, seize the opportunity.

Talent and teamwork play a critical role in TV. The HR department needs to be on the same page as the management of the station to ensure that it comprehends the overall strategy and the inner workings of the business. HR must understand the key drivers, so as to be in sync with the entire executive team. That's not only good business practice: as and when you are contemplating raising capital, potential investors will be looking at HR to see whether it is strategically aligned with top leadership in terms of goals.

Each department, whether it be management, sales, distribution, operations, news or administration, will work at different paces and directions, and have varying needs, especially when it comes to hiring and retaining people. Some will want to move fast to fill gaps, and others may be more circumspect. HR's job is to be the blender that brings it all together to make certain that overall objectives are being achieved.

So what are the principal functions of an HR Department?

- Preparing an overall staffing plan in conjunction with all heads of departments, to ensure that the right people are put in the right place;
- Setting out the company's employment policies and procedures that need to be followed by managers and employees;
- Mapping out the marketplace to assess industry

norms, identifying talented individuals to hire now
and in the future, and constructing remuneration
packages that are attractive enough to draw and retain
employees;

- Devising training programmes for staff designed to
improve their skills and flexibility so as to meet the
needs of the business now and in the future; and

- Ensuring that integrity and ethical standards are
strictly maintained in line with overall company
policy and values, and in line with regulatory
requirements.

Its overriding function, and its biggest challenge, is the
ability to attract and retain talented people. That's what the
department - indeed, the overall business - will be judged on.

This factor will help determine your success, or your failure.

Of course, remuneration - the salary and the benefits you
offer - is key in this. You're unlikely to persuade people to leave
their good jobs with other TV stations unless you're paying them
better or offering more attractive benefits, such as higher pension
contributions, private medical insurance, longer holidays,
company cars or more flexible working hours. It may seem - and
is - an expensive option, but it will pay dividends. As Robert
Bosch, the founder of the German engineering company, once
said; "I don't pay good wages because I have a lot of money. I
have a lot of money because I pay good wages."

A promise of continuous professional development - through
internal training and/or external courses - can also be a lure for
potential employees to join and a good motivation to stay. In all
four of my stations, we always used professional trainers, and I
found that it is a major attraction for staff. Most are eager to
learn and to improve themselves. When CNBC Arabiya started
in Dubai, it was not only difficult to get well-trained staff, we
had to create a new mindset because this was the first time an

international brand name had launched in the Middle East and there were extremely big expectations. Our policy of bringing in professional trainers was enormously successful, and much appreciated by employees.

Once you are fully functioning amid the incessant ups and downs of the news cycle, the chasing of revenues and the general demands of the day-to-day business, it is easy to forget about the morale of your staff or to simply think, "They're ok, I haven't heard any complaints." It's important to set aside some time every week to these matters, however. Human beings have an inherent need to feel wanted and valued by the institutions for which they work. Take time to make staff members feel they are important and appreciated. The last thing you want is a work-force that gets up in the morning feeling, "Oh, another day." If that is the prevailing emotion, then you are headed for trouble. It's HR that needs to help put forward the right incentives and motivational aspects that help people feel excited about their work.

Some sort of employee recognition programme can be vital in making staff feel part of a team, as can regular staff satisfaction surveys to gauge sentiment towards their working conditions, the workplace and their bosses. Use rewards to publicly praise those who have done particularly well, perhaps giving them financial bonuses or holidays or other gifts. Nothing is more demotivating or likely to make someone look for another job than their hard work and extra effort going unrecognised.

While standards and zero tolerance on misbehaviour are important, one must always respect the dignity of all staff. The results obtained by showing kindness and complimenting people when they have done well can be amazing. The team spirit that often results because of this can be inspirational for everyone. A by-product of such schemes is that it allows staff to better understand and appreciate the company's business strategy and philosophy.

Of course, you will occasionally lose staff to new jobs with other employers. The lure of higher salaries and promotions are constants that drain your employee base and put pressure on your costs. I have always maintained that if people wish to leave for a higher salary, you should generally let them go. There is a loyalty factor that comes into play, and sometimes trying to dissuade them from leaving can be disruptive to other team members. There may be a case for keeping some of them occasionally, but it should be rare.

As I have said before, always try to hire people who are more intelligent than you. They may cost a bit more than your average, but the payback can be wonderful in terms of your business goals. If you hire the right people, then let them get on with their jobs: don't micro-manage. As Lee Iacocca, the former boss of America's Chrysler car company, put it: "I hire people brighter than me and then get out of their way." Of course, you and the HR department need to set overall standards of behaviour, such as having red lines on matters you consider of critical importance to your company, but within those parameters, let your managers manage.

Effective and honest two-way communication between managers and staff is crucial. This is about more than putting a box marked "suggestions" on the office floor. I know this because, as chairman of Samaa TV in Pakistan, I had the bright idea of having just such a box, and sent round a memo asking all employees to put in their ideas about ways to improve the station or the business. I expected to get a lot of complaints, along with one or two useful ideas. The result? I did not get a single message. At first, I thought it was because it was located on the floor near my office, and that people were reluctant to be seen putting something in it. I had it moved to another floor. It was the same result. Depressingly, but not surprisingly, many staff start with an in-built suspicion about their employers.

To help overcome this, managers need to have a regular,

genuine dialogue with their staff. A weekly team forum where any topic is allowed to be raised is a good thing, as are regular one-on-one meetings. Managers need to be able to listen to their staff, and to accept constructive criticism, even if it puts them in a bad light. Open discussion usually produces good results. One must always encourage staff to speak frankly and give their opinions, whether it be about a particular business decision they disagree with, a personal problem, or a moan about your behaviour. This may be tough to take for some, but I believe it creates a better understanding of each other and the respective points of view. Diversity of thought is always a good thing. Everyone must have the patience to listen, and the courage to change one's mind. No one - but no one - has a monopoly on calling things right 100 per cent of the time.

I believe that fair performance appraisal systems, done correctly and professionally, are good for individuals and the business, allowing both to prosper and grow. Each employee - from the CEO down - should be given an annual set of performance targets. These will include tangible goals, such as hitting a revenue target, obtaining a set number of new customers, or achieving a certain audience rating, to some intangible ones, such as improving one's presentational style or giving better feedback. The more relevant, specific, measurable and attainable these can be, the better, though inevitably there will be an element of subjectivity. Staff should also be encouraged to have a say in what the targets are. Done properly, both manager and worker should be able to assess how they are performing in meeting the challenges and responsibilities of the job.

When someone falls down in their objectives, it's important that they get a chance to put things right. Of course, those that fail time and time again, even after all assistance, training and encouragement has been directed their way, certainly need to be fired for the sake of the business. But I am no believer in Jack Welch's philosophy of kicking out the bottom-performing 10 per cent of the workforce every year just to encourage the others to work even harder. It strikes me as slightly inhumane and counter-productive. We are all human beings, and we all make mistakes. Most of us learn from them and move on. People should not be penalised for honest mistakes, or one year's drop-off in perfor-mance. What if it were due to their partner or child having had a long-term illness, or having to care for a dying parent? As employers, I believe we have a duty of care towards the people who help build and run our businesses.

When a particular post needs to be filled, should the recruit-ment be done internally or should you look outside? It depends. Giving it to someone already with you may be sensible because they are a known entity, it takes less time for them to get up to speed, and is generally not as expensive as hiring an outsider. They will be familiar with the culture and values of the organisa-tion. They will also be grateful for the promotion and the pay rise, and it sends a positive message to others in the company that they, too, can progress and prosper with hard work. Hiring from outside also has it merits. It brings you a fresh face and new thinking, and allows you to select from a multitude of people available in the market.

It's important to discuss disciplinary procedures. These should be formalised and staff made aware of the procedures. These include an initial notification or what is called a "show cause notice". This is then followed by a second warning and then a last-chance warning. If matters are not resolved with the potential employee and an event or a failure occurs again, then a termination notice is sent.

Finally, a word on when things go wrong in a serious way. We all know that economies and business cycles go up and down. When things are going well, everyone is generally happy, cash flows in and pay rises and bonuses are given out. But you should not assume that this is how it is going to be forever more; bad times should be anticipated. Every year, businesses close down or are forced to reduce staff. If you are prepared for a downturn, by building up cash reserves, you may be able to avoid the rough patches and ride it through.

In case you can't, you may be forced into terminations at some scale. In such a scenario, it's important that you are as honest with your staff as possible, that you keep them well informed as to why it is necessary, that you have a transparent selection process, and that you treat those chosen for redundancy with dignity and give them as decent a financial settlement as you are able. It may not necessarily appease those that you lay off, but the employees who remain will see that you have treated their former colleagues decently, and they will be more likely to stay with you as a result. Once it is over, focus on the future.

Here's how not to carry out a redundancy exercise. In 2005, the Middle East was hit by a recession. Advertising was down. The management team of CNBC Arabiya met at our Dubai head-quarters in Dubai Media City. Our financial projections indicated that unless we cut costs we could soon go into a spiral from which there would be no return. We had no choice but to conduct a belt-tightening exercise and reduce costs. I asked the heads of each of the major departments to draw up a list of people they felt we could let go without impacting our operations in any significant way. We had a number of news bureaus across quite a few countries, but I decided not to touch those as a first step. A list was prepared and discussed with HR, which then started the process. It went horribly wrong as the heads of the department did not sit down with their staff and explain why it was neces-sary, what the process of selection would be, and to allow staff to ask questions.

Instead, HR simply called in those selected for redundancy one after the other, and told them they were no longer required. I blame myself as the CEO. I should have gone through the process minutely to ensure that the principles outlined above were followed. Within hours, we had a demonstration of disgruntled former employees outside our offices, loudly complaining that they had been the victims of wrongful dismissals. In fact, I knew that this was not the case: although we had dealt with it in a crass and insensitive way, we had been within the law and our contractual obligations. We could have taken the demonstrators to court for defamation, but that would have made things even worse and been awful for the brand. We decided to invite them in, and I addressed them, gave them assurances of their financial settlements, and offered a little bit more money. They had appointed someone to represent them all and he must have been a vicious union leader in some previous life. He was very threatening and even went on to say, "You will not get away with this! We will all chase you until we get what we are due." I explained to him, very politely, that the staff were being given what was due to them, but it was to no avail. They were angry and this man, the leader, was inciting them. Even though we had severe cash flow problems at that stage, I decided to give them a bit more than they were due, and the matter was eventually resolved.

It was a salutary lesson for me, our HR team and all of our managers; had we handled the matter well in the first place, the outcome would have been markedly different. It was an important reminder about the need to always treat one's employees as you yourself would want to be treated. Or as Stephen Covey, the businessman who wrote *The 7 Habits of Highly Effective People*, summed it up: "Always treat your employees exactly as you want them to treat your best customers."

8

THE CREATIVE HEART - THE NEWSROOM

"A great journalist wants to make the world watch and care, even when it would rather look away." **Orla Guerin**

At the heart of any news organisation is its editorial team, the journalists who will find, report and put together the important, compelling, vividly told stories and programmes that will define your channel, and ultimately decide whether it will be a success or not. Good journalism helps people make sense of the world and provides them with the information they want or need to live their lives.

The newsroom is where all this happens. It can be an exciting - and sometimes scary - place, especially in a 24-hour news channel when a big story is breaking. A newsroom in full flow becomes an adrenaline-fuelled, hyperactive scene where everyone seems to be working in fast-forward mode: reporters and camera crews being scrambled to the scene, presenters trying to ad-lib over live footage, editors and producers viewing multiple incoming picture feeds and having to make instant decisions whether to transmit them live, save them for later, or ignore them, and yet others chasing guests or witnesses to interview. It's at times like these that the heart beats faster, collectively and individually, and your editorial teams prove their mettle and demonstrate their professionalism. Or not.

As a startup, you have the enviable opportunity of designing and building your newsroom from the ground up, to ensure that it fulfils the creation of the content that you need for your channel. The importance of getting its structure, relationships, design, workflow and staffing right cannot be underestimated. No two newsrooms are exactly alike, though most share a lot of similarities. Clearly, its design will be defined by what you are seeking to achieve and the audiences you are seeking to serve - a newsroom for a 24-hour international news operation will be markedly different to one existing to cover one specialist subject in one country.

While this chapter deals primarily with "television news" - that is, telling stories through moving pictures and sound - we exist in a converged media world, and you need to think about all the platforms you want your content to be on and what is required for them. Just as a newspaper can no longer solely churn out text stories and still pictures, a TV news channel can no longer simply produce bulletins consisting of two- or three-minute videos - written stories will be needed, along with galleries of still pictures, explanatory charts, podcasts, tweets etc etc. And what's going on Snapchat?

Trust me, it is difficult, if not impossible, to bolt on additional platforms to existing newsrooms. There needs to be intricate planning and organisation so that your newsroom has the capabilities to produce text, video, audio and social media content, and doesn't fall into the trap of mimicking traditional workflows and practices. Mark Thompson, the President and CEO of *The New York Times* and a former head of the BBC, made that point very clearly at the Oxford Media Convention in

March 2019. He said: "It's incredibly difficult and disruptive to turn around a news organization - and really painful." He estimated that *The New York Times* had replaced 85 per cent of its sales staff and 40 per cent of its journalists over the previous five years to ensure that it had the digital skills and approach needed. News is now multimedia. Traditional newspaper and publishing groups are broadcasters and vice-versa. And it is a global media landscape - even the smallest news organisation in a one-horse town in Idaho has the means to serve an international audience. So what we will be looking at here is how to create a multimedia newsroom, one capable of delivering the various ways that people consume news and information, and one flexible enough to be able to adapt to whatever new platforms emerge in the future.

This last point is critical. One thing that I have learnt over the years is that adaptability is essential to a news operation. If you are setting up a newsroom, make sure above all that it is designed to be agile and can change to take advantage of the evolving media world. The experience of some digital news providers illustrates this beautifully. Don't become too reliant on certain platforms and business models (see, for example, what happened to Mic.com in Chapter 13). Have processes in place that allow you to manoeuvre, or pivot, to the next thing, and quickly.

The 2018 Digital News Report from the Reuters Institute for the Study of Journalism underlined how quickly change is happening. Facebook's dominance of the online news world has stalled in many countries as users look for more private spaces to communicate and source their news - for example, around half of online users in Malaysia and Brazil surveyed by Reuters are using WhatsApp. And Reuters found big differences around the world in the performance of traditional media - in some places, such as Brazil and Hong Kong, the top TV news brand was also the predominant online news brand. But, in others, like Malaysia and Taiwan, the premier TV brand was a long way behind the leading online news brand.

The metaphor of the oil tanker turning slowly is a good example here. Traditional news organisations may be powerful heading in one direction - however, when they are forced to change course, problems can arise.

The simple fact is that news organisations continue to have an important role in society, and that is to provide the audience with information. The job of the journalist remains the same: to find an interesting story, make sure it is true and tell people about it in the most engaging manner possible. What's changed is how that story reaches people. The flexibility of the newsroom and the ways in which it can adapt to different circumstances will prove invaluable.

This chapter sets out the most important components of a multimedia newsroom, using my experiences of what works and what doesn't. It is also based on how a general news broadcaster operates today - naturally, the design, scale and organisation of your newsroom will differ depending on the content that you want to produce.

In the following chapter, we will then look at the basics of storytelling itself: what makes an exceptional journalist, what makes a good story, how to film and create it, how to conduct interviews, and some of the sort of kit that's needed.

Newsroom Organisation - the basics

In its very best form, the multimedia newsroom should be a conduit for quality journalism, not a factory that pumps out news. The model employed across the world by almost all multi-media, multi-platform news operations is a coordinated system where the newsroom is divided into two separate teams: "Input" (or "Intake" or "Newsgathering"), and "Output". Simply, the first team gets the stories, the second one packages them together for transmission or publication on any given platform.

The newsgathering team is responsible for commissioning and controlling all the stories/content coming into the news operation, whether it be from reporters in the newsroom, correspondents out in the field, freelance contributors, news agencies, social media alerts - in fact, anything and everything that can lead to news stories.

The output editors and producers then take this material and re-version it for their platforms or programmes, dependent on their remit and their audience. Editorial responsibility for what is broadcast out on air lies with the output editors.

All the information and content is coordinated through a central computer system shared between the two teams.

The newsgathering team is managed by a "Newsgathering Editor", or news editor. Alternative titles could be "News Organiser", "Intake Producer", "News Coordinator" or "Head of Newsgathering". The title for this role is often different in news organisations around the world, to reflect naming conventions and cultural considerations. This person will be in charge of the entire newsgathering operation, and they will need to have a specific set of skills to make this role work. This is set out in the job descriptions later in the chapter.

The success of the operation will rely largely on this person. They will be the vital link between the newsgatherers - the reporters, journalists and correspondents - and the output teams. Most importantly, they will be across all of the stories coming into the newsroom and can make calls on what would suit the different platforms.

The benefits of multimedia working are profound. They enable the teams to function in a more productive and efficient way. Everyone in the newsroom should be able to operate in a multimedia way - to be able to do all aspects of the editorial job, to film, to write scripts and text stories, to do voice-overs, conduct interviews, and edit and create packages.

Every newsroom should be built in a bespoke way, to meet the needs of the business. Its design and layout is vital in encouraging coordination between departments. In some, the technical teams, directors, producers and presenters for the TV channels all sit at the same desk. In others, newspaper, video and digital editors sit side by side. There is no one-size-fits-all answer to the newsroom design, and great teamwork doesn't just flow from simply putting people in the same room. What you need to do is decide what output it is that you want, what workflow is required for producing it, and then assign the resources needed to achieve that.

I have a lot of admiration for the BBC, its skills and training programmes. I got to know it in a small way when I produced a programme called *Question Time Pakistan* for BBC International. The BBC went through a lot of trial and error when it tried to devise its first multimedia newsroom at its London HQ in the year 2000. The radio and TV news teams were put together in one room in an attempt to create synergies between them - however, they could not have remained more separate. They may have co-located, but they didn't cooperate. The editors running the TV bulletins remained steadfastly aloof from the radio news team, and vice-versa, while the online team was the unwanted stepchild, banished to an eyrie several floors away. There are many anecdotal stories of BBC online running contentious news stories, unaware that there was a problem with them, simply because the radio and TV news teams had failed to notify them of the issues. Editors of flagship TV news programmes were so fiercely protective of their stories that they would submit false running orders ahead of editorial meetings, to put their colleagues off the scent of a scoop or major exclusive.

Two decades on, thankfully, things have improved somewhat, partly because of time and partly because of the BBC's adoption in 2013 of a "hub and spoke" operation at its vast new newsroom in central London. This puts the newsgathering team at the heart of the operation, and allows for very clear lines of communication between the newsgathering and the output teams.

The central newsgathering team, along with the regional and the social media news teams, sits in the "hub" in the middle of the newsroom. Its members work with correspondents and field producers to bring the news and information into the building. They form the control centre that feeds the output teams.

Each of the "spokes" coming off the hub represents an output team, such as online, radio news, BBC world, or a programme like the corporation's flagship 10pm news bulletin. Each of these output teams has differing needs and demands, which the newsgathering team has to seek to accommodate. This is a big beast to feed and it requires intricate planning and coordination.

In the past, the BBC has been guilty of hideously overmanning a story. Dozens of reporters, producers, camera crews and satellite trucks would descend on a story, each competing for the best material and shots. Rather than working together, they were notorious for battling against each other, instead of against rival news organisations.

In a well-organised and defined system, all the newsgatherers know exactly what they are doing, for whom and when. The reason for this is elementary: it's a much more efficient way of working. One person can coordinate all the different components of the story and feed in what is needed.

Life may have been so much simpler in the olden days, when a journalist had only to produce an article for a newspaper, or one filmed package for TV, or one audio report for radio. Today, he or she has to be ready to do all three and more, often in short order.

The benefits of multimedia working are many. Journalists working across all platforms can produce stories that have much more impact when delivered in text, video and audio; these stories will reach a far bigger audience than they would have when done for just one medium. It's why newspaper journalists are now broadcasting live on Facebook and producing videos and podcasts for their masthead's website and social media sites.

There are, however, some pitfalls to this way of working. There needs to be an acceptance of what is possible and what is not. Just because someone *can* produce all of the material, doesn't mean they *should* all of the time. Creating video is no longer about producing one film for a TV news channel and clipping it into different durations and aspect ratios to suit different other platforms - YouTube, Facebook, Twitter, Instagram, WhatsApp, Snapchat, etc. Ideally, each platform requires a different way of telling the story. How can any one person find the time to do all that? Even the best and most multi-skilled journalists can be so distracted by the time and effort it takes to do multiple versions of a story that they can neglect the most important aspect of their job: obtaining the story in the first place, exercising news judgement and crafting a beautiful, compelling account of it. Sometimes, surely, it's better to do one perfect version, than five or six mediocre ones?

David Hayward, an experienced former BBC reporter and editor, helped create some of the first multimedia and multi-skilled newsrooms at the corporation and now runs a business that does the same for news organisations around the world, including broadcasters and non-governmental organisations in the UK, Nigeria, Pakistan, Kosovo, Moldova and Russia. He says: "You need to be realistic about what can be achieved. You need to play to the strengths of the team. Recognise that everyone has different skills and take advantage of that."

The first time Hayward appreciated the value of multi-skilled working was in 2006, when he helped run a pilot for the BBC to create six local TV stations, broadcasting online and on digital satellite. "We did not have the conventional news reporters, camera crews and picture editors. We had a team of video journalists, who were expected to shoot, script and edit their own material.

"We got reports of a shooting at a Kanye West concert at the National Exhibition Centre just outside Birmingham. Sending three video journalists to the scene meant they were able to produce three packages rather than the one that the conventional team produced.

"Each journalist had a brief and they worked as a team, filming for each other, sharing the shots, gathering the material and interviewing contributors. Because they were multiskilled, they were able to work far more efficiently and adapt to the surroundings far better.

"This was before social media, live social broadcasting and the widespread use of podcasting, which would today have to be factored in, but it very clearly demonstrated to me the importance of the multi-skilled, multimedia reporter."

Hayward adds a note of caution, however, that not every story can be covered by one person. "The pressure this can put on them is immense," he says. "There also needs to be a recognition that the skills that people have need to complement the team.

"Not everyone is going to be a first-class journalist, filmmaker, picture editor, writer and social media expert, all rolled into one perfect human being. In designing and recruiting for a multimedia newsroom, you need to make sure you have a combination of all these skills.

"The reason the team worked so well on the Kanye West story was that there was a mix of skills there. One of the team was a great digger and journalist. She got the best interviews and inside information, which she shared with the team. There was a second person who had a background as an excellent camera operator. He got the key shots and added the visual creativity to the pieces. The third journalist was excellent at writing scripts.

"So recognising the importance of the diversity of skills and making sure people work together are the keys. All three of the journalists working on that story interviewed people, filmed material and edited the video. But they played to their strengths and worked as a multi-skilled team."

Hayward advises his clients that while "everyone should be able to do everything" in a multimedia newsroom, they need to hire journalists who have an all-round mix of skills and one or two specialisms: some who are experts in filming; others who are clever writers or excellent editors. He also recommends that each story then needs to be assessed as to which mix of people is right to cover it.

News - how to find it, how to cover it

How do you define what news is? How do you decide what stories you cover, and the ones that you pass over? And how do you make sure you don't miss anything important?

At its most basic, news is anything that is interesting, or new, or out of the ordinary, or which helps people to make sense of their world and assist them to make better decisions or improve their lives. Or a combination of those things. It encompasses the whole gamut of human activity: from a fatal traffic accident that's closed the road you normally take to get to work to a senior politician being arrested over a bribery scandal; from a full-blown war between two countries to a panda giving birth to twins. It might be something that's predictable, such as a court case, an election or a sports event, or it might be something unpredictable, like a fire or a terrorist attack. As Charles Anderson Dana, the 19th-century American journalist, said: "When a dog bites a man that is not news, but when a man bites a dog that is news."

The journalist's job is to make sense of these events for viewers, to report them truthfully and without distortion, and to give people the facts. Joseph Pulitzer, the publisher whose name lives on in the annual awards given to those journalists involved in the most esteemed stories in America, explained it this way: "Put it before them briefly so they will read it, clearly so they will appreciate it, picturesquely so they will remember it and, above all, accurately so they will be guided by its light."

So how do you go about doing all that? Putting the unpredictable, breaking news to one side for the moment, in TV news channels most stories begin with the planning desk. Its importance to the smooth and successful running of the operation cannot be underestimated. The planning desk maintains a meticulous and detailed diary that gives an overview of all the potential news events that are known to be coming up on a daily, weekly, monthly and even annual basis. Such as court cases, important votes in parliament, the release of annual crime statistics, the anniversary of a terrible tragedy, a presidential visit, or a company's launch of an exciting new product.

The planning team discusses story angles with the producers of the programmes in the days before a scheduled event, allocates crews and reporters to cover them, and briefs them on the expectations of the programmes, who they are going to file to and when.

On the day of the story, the newsgathering teams take ownership, liaising with the reporters and producers out in the field who are gathering the material, and communicating closely with the output teams, ensuring that what was promised and what is wanted is delivered.

The editorial angle of the story is decided by the output teams, with feedback either directly or through the newsgathering teams to the reporters in the field. This process can often be a source of conflict, as the reporter in the field believes that the story should be told in one way, while the producer back in the studio wants it done in a different way. The newsgathering editor will also have a view. The balance of power here can prove difficult. While the reporter is on the ground and (usually) most knowledgeable about the story, the producer is looking at how this fits into his or her programme or bulletin as a whole. It is important to state that this has to be a two-way conversation, and that excellent communication, at all levels, is vital.

Aside from talking on the phone or in person, this can be done through a variety of mechanisms:

A shared **electronic diary** of all the stories being covered by the newsroom that day, so that everyone has access to the very latest information on each individual story - the content that can be expected, i.e. video, images or text, the reporter working on it and when it will be delivered. This will be the central planning hub for all future stories and will be available to all output editors and producers. It allows everyone to be aware of the stories being covered, how and by whom, and creates greater collaboration and coordination.

A shared **newsgathering operational grid** to keep all editorial staff informed about operational information and of the progress and status of stories on the day, such as when the reporter is due to file, who is being interviewed and what content the different platforms can expect. For instance, if the story is from parliament, the grid will record what is being discussed, when, who is likely to be interviewed, what content is expected: video, text, or pictures. With this information available to all at the same time, the editors can make judgements on how they will frame and version their stories.

A **central server** to host all content that can be shared and accessed by all editorial teams.

The use of **messaging app** groups for the immediate sharing of information and material on all of the breaking news stories being covered by the newsgathering teams. The messaging groups act as an additional means of communication between the intake and the output teams. All the latest story developments should be uploaded to the messaging app groups, allowing all of the output editors to be across the stories as they evolve. The decision about which messaging app to use should be carefully assessed and agreed upon. The groups will depend upon the stories being covered, but they should include all senior editorial staff - output editors, digital editors, the newsgathering team, the reporters working on the stories and the central management team.

A **daily morning editorial meeting** will inform the editorial teams about the stories being covered and set the agenda for the day - for example, what are the three big stories we want to "own" today and which require resources? - and provide an opportunity for requests to be made for a particular angle or story from the different output areas. In a 24/7 newsroom, these meetings ordinarily take place at 08.45 (or a more suitable time if agreed upon by the senior team). Attendees will include the newsgathering editor (who normally chairs it) and all the output editors, or their deputies, and, in big organisations, will probably need to be carried out as a multi-location virtual meeting.

The newsgathering editor will lead the meeting by outlining: the stories being covered on the day; who is covering them; what content can be expected, i.e., text, video, audio or pictures; when the content is due; who are the contributors to the story - who is likely to be interviewed?

The editors will tell the newsgathering editor the stories that he or she is likely to be interested in. They can also suggest or request different lines of approach from different contributors. For instance, this might be the case in stories that have different angles depending on their audience. There may be a story of interest to all output - but some may need a different angle or contributor.

Weekly planning meetings are an essential element of the process. They take a similar format as the morning editorial meeting - however, they look at future prospects and inform the output editors of the stories and content that the newsroom is working on long term. This meeting will consist of the same people as the morning meeting; the output editors and newsgathering editor. Again, this is also an opportunity to request bespoke material for each platform.

Sharing material and content. With the demand for more multimedia content, a fast and effective mechanism to share the content will be required. This will need to be discussed and the best application decided by the digital and the senior team of the news organisation. There are a number of tools for this, such as Google Drive, Dropbox, WhatsApp, Telegram, Viber and WeTransfer.

Key Job Descriptions

As mentioned a number of times earlier in the chapter, the roles of journalists and editors within the multimedia newsroom need to be defined and clearly adhered to. What is eventually viewed on the screen is the end result of the work of many people.

It's important that certain roles are described to give an overall view of the complex and wide-ranging skills that are required, and also provide an overview of what's involved. The job descriptions below give the central demands for each of the key roles in the typical newsroom of a 24-hour TV news channel. You can pick and choose the ones that are suitable for your venture, or create new ones as you see fit.

INPUT

Head of Newsgathering

The head of newsgathering is a strategic leadership role. It is designed to implement and creatively lead the entire newsgathering operation. He or she will need to be an inspiring and forward-thinking leader, with an excellent pedigree in journalism. They must be fully conversant with the multimedia platforms that the newsroom will be operating. This will require a strong and in-depth knowledge of TV, radio, digital and social media.

They need a proven track record in leading change in the news environment and should have the ability to spot and react to changes in the news media landscape, to see what's coming down the track. This is a very senior role and requires diplomacy. There will often be conflicts in the priorities of the daily news output. The head of newsgathering should have a first-class knowledge of the priorities for the newsroom.

While they must be a strong team leader, they have to be able to delegate. This is not a day-to-day operational role, but a strategic one. There needs to be a level of separation from the daily news team.

News Organisers

The news organisers are in charge of the day-to-day coordination of the newsgathering operation. They report to, and work closely with, the head of newsgathering, to agree the strategy and goals of the newsgathering operation. They will need to have an intrinsic understanding of the demands of TV, radio, digital and social media.

On breaking news stories, they will prioritise the greatest needs and demands, and meet the appropriate deadlines across radio, TV, digital and social media. They will manage the day-to-day team on the newsgathering hub and coordinate with any regional offices and the central output teams. They will have a first-class journalism background and be conversant with the needs of different platforms. They will have a good understanding and appreciation of the evolving and developing media landscape on a global, regional and local level.

They need excellent coordination skills and be able to react to fast-moving news stories. This will require diplomatic skills and the ability to make clear and well-thought-through decisions under great pressure. The news organisers will be the day-to-day facilitators of the elegant and cohesive working between the correspondent, planning teams and the output teams.

They will monitor the output of the news organisation and be across all other relevant forms of media from social media to competitors to the international news wires and agencies.

Production Coordinators

The role of the production coordinators is to support the news organisers in the day-to-day news gathering operation. They will assist in the logistics of deployment for the newsgathering teams, including camera crews, live broadcasting equipment and maintaining contact with newsgathering teams on the road.

They will need to have an intrinsic understanding of the demands of multimedia working and the demands of different platforms. It will be their role to make sure all the output teams are serviced with their needs and requirements from the newsgathering operation.

They will be the contact point between the newsroom and the correspondents, crews, producers and journalists in the field. They will, in turn, ensure that the in-the-field teams provide the material for each programme and output area.

Regional Coordinator

The regional coordinator role is to provide an on-the-day link between the central newsgathering operation and the regional offices they are communicating with. This is a particularly important role in large news organisations. For example, CNBC Arabiya has operated out of 20 countries, CNBC Africa covers the English-speaking nations on the continent, and Samaa TV is in all provinces of Pakistan.

The co-ordinator will feed all the relevant information both ways on stories being covered and convey the demands of the output teams. This is a two-way conversation - helping both the national and regional teams get the best out of the news operations. This is a very important job; it should cut down on duplication and allow a more harmonious and effective way of working.

UGC/Social Coordinators

This is a vital role for the success of the newsroom. The UGC (User Generated Content) and social coordinators, monitor social media and networks to ensure that the newsroom is aware of all social media trending events as soon as possible.

It is their role to verify the content and to pass it on to the relevant teams for production. They need to work closely with the digital and newsgathering teams to follow up on breaking news stories and trending events, but also to be across the content and scheduling of the social media teams at the newsroom hub. This is a research, monitoring and fact-checking role, providing the newsroom with fast and verified social media content.

Head of Planning

The head of planning works closely with the head of newsgathering to oversee all long-term and future prospective news stories, ensuring the newsroom has the most creative and comprehensive coverage of all forthcoming events. They need to allow all outputs to be serviced in a fair and balanced way. The role requires a great deal of diplomatic skill and inspirational leadership. They will help design and define the newsgathering strategy and oversee the running of a robust, effective planning diary.

OUTPUT

TV Editor

The TV editor leads, inspires and manages the news team to produce informative and engaging TV and digital content. He or she is primarily the day-to-day editor of the news programmes and bulletins. They need the ability to turn complex information into compelling, easy-to-understand broadcast material, and have a nose for original, creative journalism and broadcast innovation. The role oversees and manages all aspects of production and journalism, and controls the commissioning and production budgets. It is essential that they have a clear understanding of a collaborative multimedia, multi-platform working environment.

TV Producers

The TV producers are responsible for producing the daily bulletins and the daily news programmes. Their role demands a deep understanding of TV production and the grammar of film-making. They will write scripts, introductions, headlines and the building blocks of the news programme, create running orders and oversee the structure of the output. They will also carry out editing of material and re-version content for other platforms, including radio, digital and social media.

Radio/Audio Producer

How big a radio team you need will depend very much on what scale of radio operation you are running. Some television news operations - such as Sky and CNBC - offer news bulletins and coverage to commercial radio stations around the world. Others, like the BBC, NHK in Japan, Al Jazeera in the Gulf and the German broadcaster Deutsche Welle, run their own 24-hour radio news channels. The radio producer primarily focuses on producing the live bulletins, programmes and podcasts. They write and produce the content and, in some cases, present the broadcast. They will also work to the wider radio/audio/pod-casting output and contribute to it as a whole or in individual segments as well as producing, reporting, planning and the overall running of the programme. They will work alone or alongside other journalists, conduct interviews and chair discus-sions, live or pre-recorded.

Social Media Editor

The social media editor works directly to the head of newsgath-ering. They will develop strong links with all other editors and executives in the newsroom. They are responsible for defining best practice on all social media accounts, as well as assessing what developments or new platforms are coming next. They need to be an expert in this field and have great connections both inside the newsroom and the wider social media community and industry. They will be a champion for "digital" within the multi-platform newsroom, leading the thinking on how to engage with audiences generally.

They will identify and analyse appropriate performance data around core social media activities, draw up insight from them in relation to key objectives, and give feedback to individuals and teams across the newsrooms. They will also identify new trends in social and digital media to maintain existing audiences and engage new ones.

Social Media Producers

These are the lead producers and managers of the social media accounts for the newsroom. They will be responsible for setting the social media agenda and providing editorial guidance on relevant stories, tone and community management across the social media platforms.

They work in collaboration with relevant colleagues across the newsroom, ensuring that all those contributing to the accounts understand what's required of them and oversee comment moderation. Working closely with the social media editor, they will track and monitor performance of the social platforms in tandem with the objective of reaching and engaging all audiences.

They need to have a passion for producing social media content that is engaging, compelling and will drive audiences to the newsroom platforms.

Web/Digital Editor

This editor will help create and implement a digital first video and content strategy for the newsroom website and its social platforms. They will run a team that will deliver smart, original videos, visual stories and related content, for the website and social platforms. This editor is a manager and leader but also a talented and visionary creative, who knows how to make content that will delight digital audiences every day.

They are digitally literate, social media savvy, and have the ability to source ideas and execute high-quality stories. The role requires day-to-day liaison with other multimedia producers, journalists and editors.

Live Feed Editor

The live feed editor and producers are responsible for the live feed on the news organisation's website, including social media feeds and SMS alerts. The key role of the live feed editor is to produce breaking news stories and keep across the developments of the story as they evolve throughout the day.

This will involve monitoring the wires, other news organisations and social media, and liaising with reporters in the field and the central newsgathering hub. This is a crucial role within the multimedia newsroom and will provide the first port of call for breaking news stories. They will need to be expert writers, be able to judge what media fits the news story, and edit and re-version material gathered by the TV, radio and digital teams.

They will also be expert in the verification of a news story. Their role is crucial: Al Jazeera's coverage of the Gaza conflict, the Arab Spring and the wars in Iraq and Syria pioneered the use of citizen journalism and social media in areas where conventional coverage was limited and where verification to avoid "fake news" was essential. Euronews, the pan-European news channel, in which NBC now has a stake, has put its social media desk - The Cube - in the heart of its newsroom, both verifying and debunking stories on social media in real time.

Web Producer

The digital web producers will be responsible for creating distinctive content on a variety of platforms. Their primary focus will be establishing and maintaining the online platforms for the newsroom. They will work effectively with other departments across the newsroom, ensuring it maintains excellent relationships throughout. They will be first-class digital journalists with a clear understanding of how digital fits into the overall strategy and dynamic.

Editor in Chief

Overseeing and managing the whole editorial operation is the Editor in Chief. The title changes from station to station and continent to continent - sometimes Head of News, Editorial Director, even News President or Vice President - but the role and responsibility are always the same. In editorial terms, the buck stops here. This is the senior editorial figure in the company - usually reporting directly to the chief executive and sitting on the executive board of the company. The Editor in Chief has to set and monitor the editorial output, standards and agenda for the service - but his or her role is strategic rather than hands-on. The daily teams described above have to be trusted to make the detailed decisions - but they need to know what is expected. Is the journalism honest, accurate, objective, fair? The daily teams are inevitably very close to what they are doing, and even the best of us make mistakes occasionally. The Editor in Chief has to stand back and judge the output by the standards that he or she has set.

That also means establishing clear guidelines and policies for the service - how do its journalists cover politics, or terrorism or stories involving young children? The Editor in Chief has to ensure that every journalist employed knows and applies those standards in their work. All broadcast news is subject to the laws of the lands in which its programmes are viewed. The laws of privacy, defamation and confidentiality apply to journalists as well as other citizens, though in some countries journalists can claim special treatment under freedom of expression laws. In many countries, television journalism is also subject to regulation, sometimes by public bodies, sometimes by government departments, requiring, for example, the news to be accurate and impartial.

In the fast-moving world of 24-hour digital news there is only too much truth in the warning that "the technology means you can now make your mistakes at the speed of light". Employing lots of young, keen and comparatively inexperienced people (as is the case with many news channels) just accentuates the risk. The Editor in Chief can't check everything or even watch more than a fraction of the output. So everyone has to know the rules - which means compliance with the station's guidelines and legal and regulatory requirements. The Editor in Chief is ultimately responsible for compliance - but most large news channels will have a compliance manager or managers, including in-house lawyers, to give legal and regulatory advice when there is a tricky policy issue and to help the editorial team members when they have a query. The most effective way of ensuring compliance is through training - making certain that as well as journalistic and technical skills, everyone on the team knows and understands the channel's ethos, its guidelines and policies.

And finally, the Editor in Chief has the really important responsibility for the safety of everyone working for the channel. Journalists are often targets these days - research by organisations like the International News Safety Institute (INSI) shows that it is not only teams in the field covering conflicts who are at risk - many journalists around the world are killed or injured while investigating crime and corruption. Many of the world's leading broadcast news organisations such as NBC, CNN, Globo in Brazil and NHK in Japan, together with news agencies such as Reuters and AP, have adopted the INSI Safety Code which sets out clear safety policies and guidelines such as providing the right training and safety equipment. A large organisation will probably have a safety manager and even employ safety advisers to work with crews on very dangerous assignments. A smaller channel will probably delegate that responsibility to the news desk. But however you do it, safety has to be the first priority. There is no such thing as risk-free journalism, but there is no excuse for not doing everything you can to keep that risk as low as possible.

Congratulations to those of who you noticed that there are two newsroom roles missing from this list of job descriptions. I deliberately omitted those for journalists and presenters, not because their roles are not key, but rather the opposite: they are so important that they and their work deserves a chapter or two all of their own. So they're coming up next.

9

LET ME SHOW YOU A STORY...

"The only qualities essential for real success in journalism are ratlike cunning, a plausible manner and a little literary ability." **Nicholas Tomalin**

The TV journalist is a complex beast, often thin-skinned and egocentric, frequently a gossip, occasionally a whiner (about resources, money, lack of time, bosses, the weather, you name it). But they are commonly driven by an abiding passion to report the news, a dedication to break stories and are insatiably curious. And they are generally worth their weight in gold (though don't tell them I said that or I'll have a queue of them outside my office demanding pay rises).

Their story-getting and telling abilities, aided and abetted by their camera crews and other support staff, are the stuff of legends. The BBC's John Simpson donning a burka to enter Taliban-controlled Afghanistan before the US-led attack in 2001. Bob McKeown, a correspondent for America's CBS, being the first Western journalist to broadcast live from liberated Kuwait city in 1991. The same year as CNN's Peter Arnett reported live from under a desk at the Al-Rasheed Hotel in Baghdad as air raid sirens blared and US bombs exploded around him.

Often the most compelling stories combine great reporting with pictures which do far more than illustrate the story. Ted Turner, the founder of CNN, once said "the news is the star" and the history of television news is one of compelling images which have moved the audience and sometimes changed the course of events.

On October 23, 1984, the BBC's Michael Buerk reported on the appalling famine in Ethiopia which had been largely hidden from the world. Buerk's reporting was powerful and compassionate - and I give an extract of that later as a good example of writing of the highest quality - but the global impact of the story owed as much to the great skill of his cameraman - Mohammed Amin, the brilliant Kenyan photojournalist - in portraying horror with humanity. The pictures led to an international response to the disaster.

On August 7, 1992, when ITN's Penny Marshall and Ian Williams revealed the dreadful conditions in the Serb-run concentration camps of Omarska and Trnopolje in Bosnia, their reporting, together with that of their newspaper colleague Ed Vulliamy of *The Guardian*, was a model of how to report evil and inhumanity - but it was the images of Fikret Alic and other terrified, emaciated Bosnian prisoners in the camps taken by cameramen Jeremy Irvin and James Nicholas which provoked outrage around the world.

With the digital revolution making cameras much lighter and less cumbersome, the growth of video journalism - courageous individuals often working unobtrusively on their own or with minimal backup - has become more and more the route to the exclusive stories that capture the headlines. Miguel Gil Moreno de Mora, a Spanish corporate lawyer who became a war correspondent, was one the greatest of this select and courageous band. In 1999, at the height of the crisis in Kosovo, he filmed ethnic Albanian Kosovans being herded by the Serb government into overcrowded trains as part of the "ethnic cleansing" policy of deporting them. As with the 1992 ITN pictures of the Bosnian prisoner Fikret Alic behind barbed wire at Trnopolje camp, these images of inhumanity were close enough to those of the horrors of the Nazi era, with Europe's Jews and others being sent to concentration camps in railway box cars, to cause international outrage - and shortly afterwards, NATO decided to intervene against the Serb regime.

Another good example is the work of "Max Stahl" - the professional name used by Christopher Wenner, a former British TV presenter turned investigative video journalist. In 1991, he found himself one of the only outside journalists reporting on the independence movement in East Timor. The country had been occupied by the Indonesians in 1975. During incursions ahead of that invasion, the Indonesian army murdered five journalists working for Australian television and then killed another Australian journalist sent to investigate what had happened to them. East Timor had become a very dangerous place for independent reporting. On November 12, 1991, Stahl was the only cameraman in Santa Cruz cemetery, Dili, when the Indonesian army opened fire on unarmed independence protesters, killing 250 of them. His pictures, smuggled out, drew worldwide attention for the first time to the plight of the Timorese, who eventually gained their independence in 1999.

In Africa, one man's courage transformed the world's knowledge about the civil war in Sierra Leone. When Revolutionary United Front (RUF) rebels captured the capital, Freetown, in January 1999, they celebrated with murder, rape and looting on an appalling scale. Sorious Samura, a Sierra Leone journalist and cameraman, took the incredibly brave decision to go out on to the streets alone with his camera to record what was happening - persuading the RUF fighters that he was on their side. His pictures, smuggled out, helped bring about the international intervention that brought the civil war to an end.

More recently, some of the most compelling journalism of the conflicts in Iraq and Syria has been by citizen journalists and local cameramen and women. The UK Royal Television Society, for example, gave its 2006 judges' award for television journalism to Iraqi Camera Operators, a 100-strong camera crew working in Baghdad, often in situations too perilous for the international media.

However, there is still plenty of scope for great, enterprising reporting by a star correspondent. Sometimes it is also a feat of technical wizardry - such as when Alex Crawford, one of the top reporters at Sky News, entered Tripoli on August 21, 2011 at the fall of Gaddafi, reporting live from a rebel truck - thanks to the ingenuity of her team members who used a mini-satellite dish powered from the vehicle's cigarette lighter to allow her to describe the scene as the rebels drove into the city.

And as television news has become truly global - with news channels in every part of the world - a new generation of reporters from Africa, Asia and the Middle East is taking an increasingly important role in international coverage. Nima Elbagir, the Sudanese-born senior international correspondent for CNN, has won countless awards for her investigations into human rights abuses, slavery and people smuggling, often at great personal risk, as you will see from the example of her work later in this chapter. The same can be said of the Syrian video journalist Waad Al-Kateab, whose coverage of the horrors of the siege of Aleppo won international recognition - again, there is a brilliant example of her work in my choice of great stories later in this chapter. And as well as excellent reporting and video journalism, there is also an important role for the well-informed, persistent interview. One of the best practitioners of that art is Mary Ann Jolley of Al Jazeera English - her spectacular confrontation in 2018 with the former prime minister of

Malaysia, Najib Razak, is well worth watching and is also in my list of great pieces of journalism.

Of course, most reporting is more mundane than these examples and being a news correspondent is not as glamorous as it looks. You need to be able to churn out finely crafted, imaginative reports, often to tight deadlines, while maintaining the highest editorial standards, perhaps four, five or more of them in a day. There are sometimes countless hours spent waiting around for something to happen, or wasted on fruitless attempts to crack a story, or days when the story you've been covering gets pushed out of the schedules by a bigger, more interesting development. On a 24-hour news channel, you'll be expected to work at all hours of the day and night, weekends included. When something major breaks, be ready for the call that will get you out of bed in the middle of the night. Every day in news is relentless and like a clean sheet; you'll rarely know what you are going to be doing, because your fate is in the hands of the news gods. Some people find that exciting, others terrifying.

So what exactly does it take to be a good broadcast journalist? Vin Ray, a former BBC foreign editor, puts it this way in his informative 2003 book, *The Television News Handbook*: "It takes excellent craft skills such as writing, storytelling. Traits like curiosity, passion and courage; and certain physical attributes such as a good voice and an ability to speak naturally into a microphone."

We'll look at some of those requisite skills in this chapter, alongside how best to film stories, interview people and edit. We'll also talk about what it takes to be an accomplished TV news presenter.

The best TV news reporters think visually. They are, after all, storytellers who tell their stories primarily in pictures (though their accompanying words are very important, too, of course). The strongest, most memorable, television news stories are about the power of the image - strong images that remain long in the memory. So when reporters are on their way to cover a story, they need to think about what sort of footage they want, and to talk about it with their cameraman or woman, if they have one with them and aren't shooting the material themselves. It's not so much how do I tell this story, it's how do I *show* it? What would best illustrate the event and bring it to life for the viewer, such as a child's teddy bear lying abandoned at the scene of a dreadful plane crash, or the last breaths of a whale stranded on a beach.

How to shoot a story

Many a seasoned journalist or camera operator will tell you one of the golden rules of filming for TV news: shoot what you *need* first, before shooting what you *want*. Get the critical shots and sounds in the can, then do any fancy, nice-to-have stuff later, if there is time. The adage - "shoot it quick, before it goes" - is a good one: always capture the action first ahead of doing the interviews.

The basics of filming a story are that news tends to work best with static shots, not fast-moving ones. It's not just a question of pointing the lens at the subject; the shots need to be composed well and framed properly, be in focus, zoomed in and out as necessary, and to be as steady as possible (always use a tripod when you can). Try to film a selection of angles and sequences. There are three types of shot that form the basis of most news stories: long or wide shots to establish the location; medium shots (generally where a person is filmed from about the waist up); and close-ups of people's faces to see their reactions and capture their voices. You'll also need to get some over-the-shoulder shots with the reporter talking to interviewees for cutaways.

The sound of a story adds much to a viewer's understanding of it, and helps give them a sense of being there. So record relevant background noise that will add atmosphere and context.

Police sirens wailing as they approach the scene, people shouting, someone crying, laughing, or sighing. The rain beating down, waves crashing on a sea shore. You almost always need more sound than you thought you would, so let it roll.

You or the camera operator should always carry a lighting kit. Using it can greatly improve the quality of your pictures; allow time to set it up. Even the most interesting interview, piece to camera, or footage of a news event will be ruined and quite possibly unusable if it looks like it's been shot in the dark.

Writing and Editing

Great writing for television news is a rare skill. The best at it let the pictures breathe. They don't make the mistake of talking over pictures that tell their own story. Or by trying to explain pedantically what's going on in the pictures, when that is obvious to anyone who is watching. There's a reason why we all know the expression "a picture's worth a thousand words". Don't talk too much, full stop. Less is more when it comes to TV reports. Simple, clear and succinct beats wordy every day of the week. As one correspondent puts it, "Understatement is an art, overwriting is a crime."

Complex issues need to be distilled, explained and put into context with clarity (don't conflate this with simplification). Explain why this story matters, why it's important. You are the eyes and ears of your audience; give them an opportunity to be there as a witness to the event. Tell the story in the compelling and clear way you would tell it to a friend over a cup of tea, using a strong, chronological narrative and memorable phrases. Most stories have an arc - a beginning, a middle, and an end. Use your words to add to what the pictures show. Don't let your words distract viewers as they watch something interesting, or you'll lose them. Get rid of any unnecessary detail.

Structure your story before you start, and work out what will go where. What are the opening and closing shots? What clips from your interviews do you want to use, and where?

Watch and learn from the masters of the craft. Such as the veteran BBC reporter Martin Bell's opening line as a trainload of smiling, waving Soviet soldiers left Czechoslovakia for the last time in 1991: "They overstayed a welcome they never had." Or his opening line over a panning shot of the war-ravaged ruins of Vukovar in the same year: "To the victor, the prize and the prize is a heap of rubble."

Or that from another BBC reporter, Kate Adie, starting a piece on the funeral procession of 28 victims of a terrorist car bomb in Omagh, Northern Ireland, in 1998: "Through country green and quiet, through towns grey and sad, the coffins moved today. Carrying young and old, Catholic and Protestant, nationalist and unionist, a baby and a grandmother. Coming together in mourning, the like of which has never been seen on one day in the Troubles." She used the tolling of church bells to punctuate each of her sentences.

The editing of the shots and sounds usually happens simultaneously with the scriptwriting. The words need to be matched to the most relevant pictures, the best clips of interviews selected, and the less impactful footage discarded. The editing process is often nowadays done by the multi-skilled journalist himself, or in some cases a specialist editor.

In both the writing of the script and especially in the delivery of it, be authoritative and interested. Don't just intone a script - tell someone a story. Television exposes insincerity and boredom with great ease, and there's nothing more likely to turn off viewers than a correspondent who's coming across as if he's deeply uninterested in the whole subject and looks and sounds as if he or she would rather be down the pub. Why should the viewer continue to watch, if that's the case?

When you have finished recording your script, watch it, then listen to it again, with your eyes shut. If you've got a camera operator with you, get him or her to listen to it and pass judgement. Ask yourself the question: what is it about this report that's going to stop the viewer from wandering off to put the kettle on, never to return?

Live TV

Live reporting on TV can be a fraught, hazardous business for a correspondent out in the field. Lines can be stumbled over or forgotten, equipment can fail, people can wander into shot, a pigeon can drop something nasty on your head. Or, as in the case of a reporter for a Russian broadcaster, you can get run over by a car live on national television (he wasn't badly hurt, thank goodness).

As with the writing of scripts, watch and learn how the greatest storytellers put their packages together. Try to gain an understanding of what works for different platforms - what is good for traditional TV might not work or be best for your website, let alone Facebook or Snapchat.

With the help of some acquaintances and colleagues who are television news journalists, I've compiled a list of memorable reports from around the world. Some were produced for TV, while others were made with online platforms in mind and probably would not work on a conventional channel. David Hayward, the former BBC editor, was of particular help with the latter. He believes that many legacy news organisations have failed to understand the medium of online video and simply continue to ape the traditional TV news conventions, which often don't work in the digital landscape.

You can find most of them on the internet. The thing that unites them is that they all tell powerful stories, in a watchable, compelling way. The universal truth still remains - it's about the content. Look at them, study them, learn from them, and be inspired by them. And do what artists do: steal from them.

1. The Ethiopian famine

Michael Buerk's original report of the Ethiopian crisis in 1984 for the BBC provided a chilling picture of the ravages of famine on the land and its people, and forced the world to act. His opening words were as powerful as the distressing pictures that accompanied them: "Dawn - and as the sun breaks through the piercing chill of night on the plain outside Korem, it lights up a biblical famine, now, in the 20th century."

2. The Slum

This is an epic and moving documentary of how the poor exist in Manila. Produced in six parts by Al Jazeera, it shows the stark reality of what it means to live in a world of abject poverty, rising crime, and little hope.

3. The Fallen of World War II

This is a wonderful interactive documentary that examines the human cost of World War II and the decline in deaths in battle in the years since. It combines cinematic storytelling techniques and animation to provide viewers with a fresh perspective of the conflict. It follows a linear narration, but allows viewers to pause to interact with charts to dig deeper. It was made by Neil Halloran, an American data visualisation expert and documentary filmmaker. It is nearly 20 minutes long, but the use of data, the scripting and the production values make it compelling viewing. "There is no way it would have been shown on TV," says Hayward, "[but] it works so well in the far more intimate world of digital."

4. The Children of Gaza

This video from Britain's Channel 4 has more to do with the ethics of impartiality and objectivity on TV news, than the production techniques and style of video. Jon Snow gives his views on the children of Gaza, based on his experience. In it, he is more akin to a newspaper columnist than a TV reporter or presenter. "It is a passionate and polemic account," believes Hayward. "It works very well in the context of digital media. It would not have been allowed on a TV broadcast [due to British regulatory requirements around impartiality]."

5. The 126-day sit-in or 'Dharna' by PTI in the heart of Islamabad, 2014

This was the moment that TV coverage of big political gatherings went airborne for the first time. Drone cameras used by Samaa hovered high in the sky showing visuals that otherwise weren't possible. Since then, drones have become a compulsory gadget for a news channel, giving all the benefits of helicopter coverage, for a fraction of the cost. Drones are transforming media coverage, and it can be safely assumed that their use will only increase moving forward.

6. The European refugee crisis

This was an interesting experiment by the BBC's John Sweeney to report on the 2015 European refugee crisis for a younger audience, through Snapchat. It was the first time that BBC News had published a mobile-only digital short documentary in portrait format. The techniques here have become commonplace - but this was a really revolutionary step.

"It took an established BBC brand and personality and told a story in an entirely different way," says Hayward. "It was filmed in portrait [vertical] to suit the social platform and the mobile devices most people watched it on.

"There continues to be a debate raging about vertical video vs horizontal video. This film illustrates that there is room for both, as long as the content is produced and versioned to suit the platform. It's clear this would not work on TV, not only for the aspect ratio but the nature of the content."

7. Tim Peake's rocket launch

When the British astronaut Tim Peake set off for the International Space Station in 2015, the BBC made a 360 video. The producer simply placed the camera between the crowd and the launch area. The reaction of the crowd and the sound of the rocket taking off combine to allow you to fully see what's happening. It is best viewed on a mobile device, but it can work on a desktop or very smart TV. "This is the moment I finally understood 360 video," comments Hayward.

8. Drowned Syrian Boy Symbolised the Refugee Crisis

Hayward describes this film by AJ+, an online news and current events channel run by Al Jazeera, as one of the first and still one of the very best examples of combining powerful imagery, text and social media. There is very little audio - just a few lines, which are also subtitled. It plays to the strengths of social media platforms and especially Facebook, where people are often watching without sound - an important consideration.

9. Cry Freetown, by Sorious Samura

This brilliant and hard to watch documentary, with terrible violence from the first few seconds, tells the astonishing story of Sorious Samura, a Sierra Leonean journalist who chronicled the atrocities of the civil war in Sierra Leone at great personal risk when the RUF rebels captured the capital Freetown in January 1999. By pretending to sympathise with the rebels, he was able to film their atrocities. In the documentary, he also reflects on the risks he took and the decisions he made.

10. A Message from Aleppo, by Waad Al-Kateab

In recent years, Waad Al-Kateab, a Syrian citizen journalist, has won multiple international awards for her courageous and unflinching portrayal of life under siege in the city of Aleppo, focusing on the human cost in the last functioning hospital, where her husband was a doctor. Few pieces of recent modern television news have reflected the impact of war on civilians with such humanity and honesty.

11. Najib Speaks, 101 East

Sometimes a great interview makes the news. This exclusive is the reward of dogged persistence and meticulous research. In October 2018, Al Jazeera English's Mary Ann Jolley challenged former Malaysian prime minister Najib Razak over corruption allegations, provoking a spectacular walk out of the interview. It shows that just two people sitting down to talk can make compelling viewing and create a major news story.

12. Smuggled by Nigeria's 'Pushermen', by Nima Elbagir

This is a chilling and very dangerous undercover investigation for CNN by the Sudanese-born journalist Nima Elbagir into the Nigerian gangs which offer to smuggle people into Europe via Libya. In one sequence, the smugglers press her to take condoms for the trip and advise her that on the journey she may be raped - in which case she should not resist - and/or be forced to trade sex for help. The viewer is relieved to see her get off the bus heading north, but it is an unforgettable piece of evidence of the incredible risks people are prepared to take to try to reach Europe.

These are just a few examples of countless great television news stories over the years. You may well have your own favourites. If so, I'd love to hear about them and why you found them so moving: please visit my website, TVNews3-0.com, to leave your comments.

Anchors

The stars of TV news are, undoubtedly, the men and women who present it. In America, where the cult of the anchor began in the 1950s, the powerful network news presenters became known as the "voices of God". Men like Walter Cronkite and Ed Murrow became celebrities, revered for their presentation skills, gravitas, authority and their nightly sign-offs - Murrow's was "Good night and good luck", while Cronkite's was "That's the way it is".

Cronkite defined broadcast journalism for decades, and polls named him the most trusted man in America. It was an era of no cable news, no streaming internet, and when a single broadcaster's voice could change history. In 1968, Cronkite came back from a trip to the Vietnam War and declared it unwinnable. President Lyndon B. Johnson reportedly watched the broadcast, and declared, "If I've lost Cronkite, I've lost middle America."

While there are now hundreds of news channels - and presenters - to choose from, the cult of the celebrity news anchor remains as strong as ever. Channels pay small fortunes for the best of them, in the knowledge that their on-screen charisma and charm will boost ratings. Their salaries can be enormous: a co-anchor of NBC's *Today Show* in America was reported in 2018 to be earning US$23 million a year. Which, I hasten to add, is not the norm in other countries. The most highly paid news presenter at Britain's BBC in 2018 earned just over £500,000, while the range for the presenters on my channels is markedly lower.

So what makes a good news anchor? Typically, they will have backgrounds as extremely good reporters and have reputations based on their knowledge, experience and integrity. As with all journalists, they need to be steeped in news events and be on top of what's going on. They also generally require on-screen presence, charm and charisma, a "special something" that viewers find attractive. They need to deliver the news with gravitas and authority, but be warm and relaxed, to be able to interview people well, and to cope without scripts when big breaking news events happen. They need to look good on screen, dress smartly and have a voice that carries authority (some stations audition candidates only by listening to them, not looking at them).

The best sometimes do unexpected and powerful things - like Cronkite's uncharacteristic personal outburst about Vietnam or his shedding of a tear as he announced the assassination of President John F. Kennedy in 1963. In early 2018 in Pakistan, the gruesome rape and murder of Zainab Ansari, a six-year old child, shook the country to its core. One of Samaa's anchors, Kiran Naz, decided to host the opening part of her show with her young daughter on her lap to starkly highlight the appalling crime. She told viewers: "Today, I am not Kiran Naz, rather I am a mother today and that is why I am sitting with my daughter." Referring to Zainab, she said "the smallest coffins are the heaviest, and the entire society is burdened by the weight of her coffin... this day marks the funeral of humanity." The emotional segment earned widespread praise from viewers and sparked international attention, with channels such as the BBC, NDTV and Huffington Post interviewing Kiran Naz and praising the way Samaa took this issue forward.

Presenting is a high-pressure job, and it's not for everyone. Unlike the reporter who will occasionally do a real-time broadcast, the presenter is on live almost all the time. Being live on camera can do funny things to people: they can panic, lose self-control, find themselves unable to speak, they can sweat under the studio spotlights, look nervous or burst out laughing even in the midst of a serious news item. To prevent such "corpsing", as it is known in the business, some presenters will dig their nails into their hands or squash the toes of one foot with the heel of the other. Better to stay cool and calm in the first place, but that's sometimes easier said than done when things go wrong in live TV, and they frequently do - the autocue goes down or jumps to the wrong place, the presenter is given the wrong name for an interviewee, studio lights explode, outraged guests walk out, a planned package fails to play. Throughout it all, the presenter needs to stay unruffled and somehow find the right words to explain what's going on to viewers or to ad lib coherently until the problem is fixed.

Now that we've dealt with the editorial front line, we'll look at all the other operational functions a news station needs, without which it would fail utterly to get on air.

10

ARE YOUR ARTERIES OPERATING?

"Some people want it to happen, some wish it would happen, others make it happen." **Michael Jordan**

If the newsroom is the heart of a TV news channel, then its arteries and other major organs are without doubt all the non-editorial roles - technicians, engineers, camera operators, editors, graphic designers and the production control room and studio teams. Without them, you simply won't have a channel on air. Journalists need them to help tell and broadcast their stories. A good presenter is nothing without his or her studio director, make-up artist or floor manager; a good reporter nothing without his or her camera operator or editor.

The term "Operations" is a catch-all for all non-editorial functions in TV News. In the management chain, a good Head of Operations may also oversee the finance side of the newsroom and be the main liaison with the engineering and production departments which span the Operations roles.

This chapter is not intended solely for engineering students or technicians but for anyone interested in launching and running a TV news channel. It is not an engineering manual that explains how each piece of kit works in great detail, but an overview of operational roles and a spectrum of the type of equipment needed to run a channel. Every journalist should understand how their written word, interview or packaged edit gets to air; this chapter will help to unravel the mystery for them and prospective Operations staff.

When I started my first TV production company, Telebiz, I did not have a clue what went on behind a TV camera; the technical equipment required to produce programmes was a mystery to me. I hired good people with the expertise and I learnt. It was a journey of discovery, so let's go on ours.

To begin with, let us divide the Operations roles into "out-of-house" and "in-house". Quite simply, the tasks fulfilled by Operations staff are either newsgathering on the road, or in the newsroom or studio. If they work in-house, they are output staff, just as reporters and camera crew are newsgatherers or input staff. Slightly confusing, perhaps, but there you have it.

Traditionally, this broad range of roles has been defined by specialist craft skills (by which I mean the ability to not only perform certain manual techniques, but also having the knowledge of how and why tools or appliances work and the capability to fix technical problems with them, and to deal with constantly changing circumstances) and staff rarely moved between roles. However, in the 1990s in television production there was a move towards multiskilling for the purposes of cost reduction. This wasn't a bad idea, but there were pitfalls. Where craft skills were eroded, quality tended to suffer. When people moved companies or were sick, finding freelancers with those same combinations of skills was difficult and sometimes impossible. This meant hiring two freelancers sometimes to cover one role, negating the cost saving. That is the negative side of multiskilling. However, lessons have been learnt and, in general, most news companies today combine multi-skilled staff with single-craft-skilled staff, and depending on the output, time of day or segment of the channel, make use of those staff appropriately.

Let me give you some examples. If a news channel has a very small audience at midnight with a single presenter and simple links into VTs (videotapes), then filling the control room with staff with single skills - a director, vision mixer, sound mixer, production assistant, lighting director - is not cost effective or necessary. Having the technology to enable a single multi-skilled operator to use a pre-set lighting rig for the presenter, fade up a single mic and roll VTs, especially on an automated system, is the right choice. However, if 10pm is peak time for this channel and there are two presenters, live interviews requiring someone to set up comms (communication links) to outside sources, and hit ad breaks at specific times, then you would fill up your control room with more staff to maintain the quality of output. This ability to flex up and down and use craft skills and multiskillers at different times for different parts of the output is generally optimal, if the business model can afford it.

Another example is editing. There was a time when the vogue was for every journalist doing their own edits. Why employ craft editors in edit suites? They are expensive, as is the high-end edit kit and the soundproof rooms they need. Why not have all the journalists cut their own pictures on their desktop PCs? Ten years ago, many channels decided it was an all-or-nothing decision: the reporters would do it themselves. The more sensible ones deemed there was a place for both. As with the example of crewing a control room according to the time of day and type of output, editing can be done both by the journalist and/or the craft editor. It's not a case of either/or, but both/and. A TV news programme or channel has headlines, underlays (VT where the presenter talks over the picture live rather than having the sound laid down on the picture as in a reporter package) and shorter packages down-bulletin (i.e., not the lead stories). Why not have a presenter or producer cut these less important items on their desktop in the newsroom? Why waste a craft editor's time and skills on these? Let the craft editor cut the main stories that are leading the bulletins, or to re-cut the piece coming in from the field that needs fast work to get it on air quickly.

Similarly, moving to the field or outside the newsroom where reporters work with camera operators to "gather" their stories, get their interviews and shoot the pictures that tell the story, do we really need camera operators with their large cameras? Why can't the reporters shoot on their smartphones and send the files back to base via email or an application like Dropbox or WeTransfer? Should all the reporters be made into video journalists (VJs) with small broad-cast quality video cameras in a backpack and do it all themselves? Well, of course they can. But I refer back to the "horses for courses" argument. In a war zone or disaster area, would it be sensible for a reporter to be on their own shooting pictures with no one to watch their back? If a reporter is interviewing two politicians, could he or she continue to ask pertinent questions and listen to the answers, while also properly filming the interviewees? If a reporter is "door-stepping" someone being challenged to account for their actions as they exit a building, could they do this safely and effectively while holding their own camera and walking backwards? The answer, of course, is "No". At least not safely, or with any certainty of recording a piece good enough to go to air. But if a reporter is covering a local, "safe" story that is going to be pre-filmed for an edit, for example, of course they can shoot it themselves. If a reporter is doing a piece to camera where they can set their own small camera up on a tripod and film it themselves, then they don't need a camera operator. A newsroom that operates both models is a flexible newsroom and makes the most of its kit and staff.

We haven't yet touched on the digital output of any news channel. Presenters, reporters and producers should not only be presenting and reporting news in all the traditional ways but also in new ways that are appropriate for non-traditional platforms (as our chapters on the newsroom set out), such as Facebook, YouTube, Instagram etc. Most channels will favour a particular social media outlet, but without doubt if a journalist is not tweeting then they should consider taking up another career. With clever software, the tweets from journalists or indeed the viewing public can be displayed by a character generator (CG) on screen (by which I mean the "TV channel" output) - if appropriate for the content and style. Mostly, though, reporters' tweets are there on Twitter to complement and promote the TV output, to break stories and to give their followers a more personal view to a story ahead of it appearing on TV. The journalist doing this does not require any Operations staff (unless it is a clever software designer who has written the interface to get the tweet on air or a talented graphic designer who has created the template to make sure it looks good on air).

Of course, behind all those bright Operations people is a whole raft of technology. Usually, engineering or technology departments will advise on what kit to buy, but the best newsrooms will take their journalists and production staff with them to technology conferences and involve them in the decisions. If there is a choice of desktop-editing technology, for example, why let an engineer make the decision on their own based on the technical specifications of the kit and its cost? Have a producer test it and only then will you find out what the editorial functionality, speed and ease-of-use is in order to make the right decision. The same goes for ENG (Electronic News Gathering) cameras for the camera operator, or a vision mixer for the vision mixer (the only example, I believe, of the role and the kit being one and the same name).

With a brand new installation for a start-up TV news operation, or an upgrade for an old newsroom, having a team of engineers, journalists and production staff to test and make the purchase decisions on the kit is the key to a successful operation. This buy-in from the people who will use and operate the kit is crucial. I have seen many times when the engineers have chosen the kit and the operators struggle with its functionality because of a lack of initial involvement with the end-user.

Before we drill down further into the specific Operations roles and some of the technology required for running a channel, what attracts people to become a camera operator in the field or a studio or being responsible for the timings of a live news output as a production assistant? It's the same for the operations staffer and the journalist alike. Live telly is fun, terrifying, never boring and, most of all, never lonely. If ever there was an industry that requires teamwork, it is television news. When things go wrong - and they do, despite all one's best efforts - it's up to the members of the team to put it right. Some of the technical things that can go awry need back-up or quick thinking, or both. For such eventualities, it is sensible to have pre-recorded "buffers" of graphics that reflect the channel with its branding to be able to roll quickly in the event of any major technical hiccup or gap to fill leading up to an ad break or "top of the hour".

In live interviews with reporters or interviewees in the field, communications can break down (paradoxically, this seems to happen more with an interview down the road from the studio you are transmitting from, rather than from across the world in a war zone). If a presenter loses comms, the control room staff have to move on to something else or try to stick with the interview if they believe the problem will be resolved quickly. This decision has to be made in seconds so as not to be appear messy to the viewer. Clear direction from the control room (via the director or technical director) is paramount. The director will make the decision with the help of the sound engineer or master control engineer (MCR is the master control room in which all signals - picture and sound - get routed in and out of the building); they are the staff best placed to advise whether the fault can be rectified or whether it's best to cut out of it quickly. The presenter is the person who carries the can as the drama is unfolding, and has to appear calm and carry on regardless while one of the Operations staff makes the decision to bail or not to bail.

Of course, not all failures are technical issues. Sometimes the presenters themselves can do that all on their own. I remember when a hostage was being flown back from Lebanon to RAF Lyneham in Britain in the 1990s and the great Sir Trevor McDonald, the celebrated ITN presenter, said that the plane carrying the hostage was being flown in by the RAC. For those readers outside Britain, this meant that a car breakdown service - the Royal Automobile Club - not the esteemed Royal Air Force, was behind the rescue! Much mirth is to be had in a control room when such gaffes happen, but it is quiet mirth, so as not to add to the presenter's woes.

Let's examine Operations roles in more detail, starting with those who work outside the newsroom "in the field", such as the news camera operator. It is not a coincidence that most - not all - ENG camera operators are men. It is a physical job with heavy equipment to carry, from the camera to the mics and lighting rig. (This is absolutely not to say that women can't be camera operators and they do operate in many newsrooms.) Often, they will carry a backpack satellite kit, too, such as a LiveU or AVIWEST. Sometimes news organisations will also send an engineer with this kit, not so much because the camera operator could not set it up and use it but that the bulk of all the kit does tip over the optimum carrying weight. It is also not a coincidence that many camera operators end up suffering from shoulder, back or hip problems.

It is fairly obvious what the ENG camera operator does. Many would have begun their careers as sound recordists/technicians historically, but as this role has been largely phased out in news, bar for specialist recordings or live broadcasts. Camera operators who work in news have to be physically strong and mentally resilient, too. From the extremes of a war zone to standing on the same spot for a reporter's piece to camera, they must concern themselves with the pictures and sound and, of course, their own safety and that of those around them. They will be the eyes and ears of the reporter.

In my first production company, I engaged an ex-BBC chap. He was from Scotland and very rigid in the ways he trained his staff. This was a time when there were no static camera positions in the studio in place ready for interviews. He was training the local cameramen to set up camera and lights for a quick interview. His method was simple. He asked two cameramen at a time to take their camera and lights, run across the production facility to the farthest room and set up the camera and lights, while he timed the exercise on a stopwatch. He would then instruct them to come back and do it all over again, until he was satisfied that the crew was routinely completing the task in an acceptable time. Any grumbles would be met with a withering stare and stern rebuke: "Practice makes perfect, laddie." Visitors to the studio were amazed by this spectacle, and asked, "Why are these guys running around like madmen from one end of the building to the other?" They were told that the staff were "being punished for being late". Not true, of course, but it was amusing, and typical of the humour that runs through a TV news operation.

Camera operators are often responsible for some of the funniest incidents in TV news, and are particularly fond of capturing the bloopers and out-takes that bedevil the business. One of the most infamous such pieces was the sign-off (the end of a reporter's piece to camera) recorded in the pouring rain in London as follows:

"Colin Baker for Thames News, Westminster... [PAUSE]... soaked, with cold feet and an aching heart, married, several children, p****d off, really dreadfully p****d off."

The camera operator kept rolling, recording it for posterity, and it has become one of the funniest and enduring out-take sign-offs. It can still be found on YouTube - look it up!

The other peril to beware of is the live microphone. There's a saying in TV: "Never start to talk about anything other than what is scripted when the mic is turned on." With good reason. The list of politicians who have been caught saying things that they later felt embarrassed about is long and not so distinguished. Who can forget how US President Ronald Reagan, at the height of the Cold War in 1984, while doing a sound check shortly before his weekly radio address, announced: "My fellow Americans, I'm pleased to tell you today that I have signed legislation that will outlaw Russia forever. We begin bombing in five minutes."

In 2010, the then British Prime Minister Gordon Brown's election campaign was marred when he forgot that his mic was still on after stopping to chat with an elderly voter, who complained about the amount of immigration into the country. Safely, he thought, back inside his car, Brown complained to advisers: "That was a disaster. They should never have put me with that ridiculous, bigoted woman." Cue headlines, cue humiliating apology, cue lost election.

The then French President Jacques Chirac was caught on tape in 2005, attacking Britain, as both countries sought to win the right to host the 2012 Olympics. "The only thing that they have ever done for European agriculture is mad cow disease," he told Russian President Vladimir Putin and the then-German Chancellor Gerhard Schroeder. "You cannot trust people who have such bad cuisine." Despite its supposedly dodgy food, London won the bid.

Sadly, we must return to the camera operator's main functions. If shooting for a recorded package, they have to be mindful of storing up a good selection of shots to tell the story that the reporter will later voice and package. A powerful selection of wide shots, which include pans (the camera moves from one side to another), and zooms or pull outs (the camera is being used in the Z-axis to move in or out), is not necessarily enough for a two- to three-minute package (an average length news piece). The good camera operator should include static close-ups and wide shots; the pull outs or zooms should have good depth of focus so that the viewer can be drawn out or into the object(s) of focus to complement the words. If the piece has a human angle (which one would say most good news packages should have), then human faces in close-up always tell a powerful story. The best camera operators do not need direction, only guidance from the reporter since it is they who know the story they want to tell.

Why do so few ENG camera operators move in to the studio and vice-versa? Framing a shot is a skill both jobs require, though clearly the studio camera operator will mainly be framing presenters and guests, i.e., people, rather than a mixture of people and scenes. Both will know that an eyeline should be horizontally a third down a screen whether in a close up, an MCU (medium close up) or a wide shot. Both will know to allow for some headroom (above the person's head) and some "looking room" if they are not straight to camera (i.e., some space to one side of their head rather than framing them dead centre of screen if they are being interviewed). Both will know not to "cross the line", i.e., to film from one side of a shot then the other as this cannot be edited together, or to cut from one shot to the other due to the effect it will have on the viewer.

Having said all of this, it is probably more down to temperament and lifestyle choices than different skills as to why the ENG and studio camera operators rarely switch over. Studio camera operators always have the director in their ear; the operators in the field rarely have such guidance - they work unaided, steered only by the reporter.

Often accompanying the camera operator in the field is an

engineer. At the end of the day, a trained engineer will always understand the mechanics between setting up a good picture (and sound) and how to transmit it back to base via satellite truck, links vehicle or a studio. The engineer may set up a portable satellite dish to send the camera operator's pictures back to base, or they may "link" the signal to a truck that, in turn, gets either radio-linked or more probably satellite-linked (from a dish on the truck's roof) back to the studio or MCR.

A few decades ago, there were only large and unwieldy satellite dishes that had to be rigged by a team of engineers to send signals up to space and down again. They were very rarely used live. Now - as has been described - these dishes are much smaller, and can be carried in a backpack and operated by one person if needed. One thing is for sure, though, if the kit breaks or fails to work, it is invariably only the engineer who can fix it.

Out in the field, then, who accompanies these roles from the editorial side? If the story is not complicated, it is likely to be only a reporter. If more complex, then a producer will also accompany the shoot. He or she can liaise with the newsdesk back at base, help with the logistics, trace interviewees, and also carry kit.

Most news organisations have garages or warehouses where vehicles or trucks they own or lease are stored. Often, there is a small team of logistics people who help keep those vehicles safe and roadworthy. They make sure that there is always a vehicle available for a shoot. They can also look after the cameras, lighting and sound kits and portable satellite dishes to make sure they are serviced or fixed and available for the next shoot. This part of Operations is extremely important but often overlooked. Sometimes the same logistics team looks after the PPE (personal protection equipment, the protective clothing used by staff working in war or riot zones). Usually, these logistics staff work back at base, but can often go out on the road if they need to transport kit or a vehicle to a particular location. As such, they, too, are classed as newsgathering staff.

As we move in-house, we'll stick with the more technical and engineering roles that support the newsroom. There are support engineers who not only fix things, but also cover major events. In news, there are often set-piece events - political or royal, for example, which need OB (outside broadcast) facilities, such as temporary studios or platforms for presenters or reporters with iconic backdrops or positions along a route. These need linking to make sure that signals get back to the main MCR and onward to the studio. Engineers make sure that this happens by using satellite, radio or fibre links (more often than not fibre nowadays).

Then there are support engineers who fix kit, whether it's a newsroom PC, editing kit, vision mixer, camera etc. Traditionally, broadcast engineers were different to the IT engineers who fixed the computing side of the technology. Now so much technology relies on chips and IT that the roles are merging into one with a new type of engineer combining both broadcast and IT skills.

The engineers in MCR are technicians who may also perform as engineers on the road in a links vehicle, for example. They understand the mechanics behind routing signals (video and audio) in and out of the building, often around the world and via the studio and/or editing server. MCR can be the most exciting room of any news organisation. It will have more monitors, more "hubbub" and excitement when news is breaking than any other part of the operation.

MCR engineers must be good communicators because they are talking to reporters, camera operators and engineers in the field as well as the studio director and sound mixer in-house to meet the demands of the running order, as the programme editor or producer requires.

If the news channel is being distributed via another broadcaster, MCR has to connect to that broadcaster's transmission control (which may be next door or many miles away); if the channel transmits its own output as a broadcaster in its own right, then it is likely that the output will be put through a presentation suite which will be allied to the MCR. The presentation or transmission suite will have operators who control the running of the ads and any promos or buffers played throughout the main news channel output.

That just about covers working in the field in the key areas outside the newsroom from an Operations perspective. We shall now move indoors to the newsroom or around the newsroom to the in-house or "output" Operations staff.

We have talked about the editing of pictures to a certain degree. Pictures come into the building from a variety of sources. Most news organisations will subscribe to agencies such as Reuters or Associated Press (AP) and as such will get raw (unedited) pictures of worldwide events. Then there will be the newsroom's own pictures from its camera operators and journalists. Nowadays, a central server (or large computer) will store all the video and there will be some kind of media manager function. This may be in the MCR or a Traffic department where a media manager will look after the content: label it (so journalists and editors can find it), delete what is not needed (as there will be finite space even in the biggest server), and often decide where packages are edited and how edit suites and edit desks are assigned and used. The media manager will often come from an editing or engineering background.

The craft editor in news is a skilled Operations professional. They will understand picture selection from the volume of pictures or "rushes" (unedited material) shot by the camera operator. They will understand how shots should go together to make the best piece or package. They will know how to interlace close-ups with wide shots, how not to place a pan next to a zoom and how to create the most impact with picture and sound for any news piece. They will sit with a reporter as they write their words so they can bring the words and the pictures together in harmony. A good editor and reporter will not have a wall-to-wall script, but leave some natural sound (known as "Natsof" - coming from the original phrase "natural sound on film"). This will create more impact than just the reporter's voice. They will be able to manipulate the picture if necessary and add graphics into the package. The best craft editors are calm, quiet professionals who work with picture with a seamless, natural flow, cutting and re-editing as the words demand.

Now we come to the graphics department. Every channel is packaged with graphics that reflect the broadcaster's brand. A brand will have a set of colours, typefaces (fonts) and rules which the designers should follow for consistency's sake. The titles, stings, promos, break bumpers (the "stings" before and after an ad break) will reflect this identity and would have been designed and produced often by a branding company outside the news organisation, which the design department then has to follow in terms of style.

Graphic design is another craft skill mostly learnt at art college. Graphic designers who work with moving images and in news are a very small percentage of the field as a whole. Understanding and executing typography and images that work on television and can be read and understood with immediacy alongside a reporter's or producer's script is a skill often taken for granted. A graphic designer will create everything from the two-line "supers" (the text at the bottom of frame that may show someone's name and designation, "superimposed" or "keyed" over an interviewee) to the most complicated 3D-animated graphics explaining complex news stories. The "crawlers" at the bottom of the screen, summing up a breaking story, will have been generated by a designer before being made into a template.

Many graphics, including the supers, crawlers and text-heavy graphics that fill the frame, can be turned into templates in a character-generator (as the name suggests this is a graphics output machine that concentrates on text, which are "keyed" or "super'ed" over people or live backgrounds). Once the designs have been templated, journalists can type the required text into their newsroom PCs (there will be a pre-set character maximum) and this can be used live on air or in a recording, without the direct involvement of a graphic designer on each occasion.

As in the case of editing, the craft designer can then be used for more complicated work. The most common example of this is a reporter "explainer" package, perhaps on a business story for which moving pictures cannot explain a complicated issue or concept. The reporter or producer will brief a designer as to what they are trying to get across. It is a mistake to be prescriptive at this stage since the best designer will help mould how the animations explain the story and the reporter's words can then be adapted to move the graphic along. Also, with animations or "reveals", the script must synchronise with these so that the viewer can follow the explanation exactly.

The most graphic-heavy content is perhaps election programming for which moving picture is minimal (apart from shots of people voting or candidates winning or losing). Election results are often the most demanding subject matter for graphic designers. Keeping a viewer engaged, especially when there are several channels competing for eyeballs, is challenging. Talented presenters and interesting guests are crucial, as is a good set, but it is the graphics that can capture the imagination and keep the viewer interested for longer.

This plethora of analytical graphics data needs to be informative as well as innovative and how long the viewer stays engaged as well as the ratings as a whole are the yardsticks by which channels judge their election programme success. Election programmes are undoubtedly one of the biggest events for any news channel and certainly for the graphics department. Hence, why we have a chapter dedicated to such "specials" coming up.

For speed, the best newsrooms will automate the results with stylish, 3D graphics; journalists are able to enter them in real time and they appear simultaneously on air. The best graphics department will include software designers who can write this automation and produce the most innovative 3D designs.

News graphics designers are often called "information designers" because their graphics inform the viewer with easily understandable text and pictures. Some newsrooms give a proportion of their producers the title of "graphics producer". These are often the most creative of producers who are able to collaborate with designers to create the best graphic explainers.

Before we move into the studio, what other roles outside editorial help support the newsroom? Most newsrooms will have a library of material either from their own copyright material (shot by them) or from affiliates or agencies. There may be a library of stills (once, these would have been physical photographs or transparencies) or even newspaper cuttings, though these are likely to be digital now and sourced through a third-party agency. The people who are responsible for retrieving, labelling and managing all this material are called library researchers or loggers. In the past, there would have been a whole library department but journalists can now access such material via their PCs. Nowadays, there usually remain only a few researchers who help manage the material and copyright, or to do more detailed research when needed. The most valuable researcher can recall material and events from time long past and often appears to have a near-photographic memory

Now we move into the studio and control room. This is where everything produced in the field, the newsroom, design department and edit suite come together to complete the full package: the studio presentation and all the other sources become a channel. The studio floor can vary from a few square metres for a simple one-presenter output to many thousand square metres of space that can take multi-presenter and guest formats.

Surprisingly, there may be very few staff even on the biggest studio floor. These Operations staff can flex up and down according to the output and time of day. Apart from the presenter, it may be that there is nobody on the studio floor at off-peak times. The cameras can be "locked-off" (framed on the presenter with fixed shots), the lighting rig fixed for a single presenter, the autocue or teleprompter rolled by the presenter with a foot pedal or hand control, and all cues done from the director in the control room without the need for a floor manager. That's one extreme of the studio floor manning - almost no humans at all.

If we take the other extreme - a large studio floor might have four pedestal cameras and one jib camera, two presenters (including one standing up) and several guests - then this output could not be produced without some seriously skilled Operations staff. The cameras will be "manned", to allow moving shots and re-framing according to direction. The studio camera operator will always follow direction but be able to "offer" alternative shots while "off-camera" (not on air), so that the director may preview these and take them to air if he or she wishes.

There will be a floor manager, who like all other floor staff will wear a headset to hear direction. Their main purpose in a multi-camera studio will be to stand next to the camera on air (or about to be cut to) and count down with their fingers to the next live cue for the presenter. They will "mic up" the presenters and guests. The floor manager is in charge of the floor - including having responsibility for who comes on to it during rehearsals and transmission (TX). Interviewees, make-up artists and others who need to come on to set will look to the floor manager to be able to enter without appearing on camera.

It has been known for guest interviewees to take offence at a particular line of questioning, rip their mic off and storm out of the studio mid-interview. This is always difficult for a director as to what to do, but the camera operator will invariably focus on the guest, showing parts of the studio not normally "on camera", including the floor manager, other technicians and the studio door. It can be entertaining for both the viewer and the crew.

If the autocue is being rolled for a presenter, the operator will usually sit in a corner of the studio; although they could be situated remotely away from the floor, the presenter will often want them to roll a script or change the odd word, and being physically nearby aids this process. In the modern world of telly, this can be quite a junior role, as can the floor manager. Some organisations have "news assistants" who perform both roles, though not at the same time.

One Operations role that may take the staff member into both the studio and the control room is that of the lighting director. All studios will have a lighting rig which is usually pre-designed and pre-set according to the format. For special programmes, the rig may be changed to accommodate different arrangements, such as more presenters or guests. The lighting director may be up a ladder tweaking the angle or gel on a light before a transmission or during a break, but they will then sit in a control room during TX to adjust any lighting levels for the output via the monitors.

We will talk more about set - "hard" (physical furniture) and a "soft" set or virtual reality (VR) - later, but the lighting director's role will vary according to its nature. If there is chroma key or VR involved (where the background is replaced by a graphic or computer-generated set), the lighting director is responsible for ensuring that the key or matte around the presenter is smooth with no flaring or buzzing edges. A keyed background will be created by replacing the colour of the curtain or hard background wall with the computer-generated one; the colour will usually be green in news, though it may also be blue or red (red, green and blue are the three pure colours or signals of a television picture, often referred to as RGB). Channels tend not to use blue because it is worn by so many news presenters - the juxtaposition of blue clothes on a blue background causes them to disappear or, most disarmingly, seem to be just floating heads. Red pulls colour from some skin tones, which all combines to make green the go-to chroma key colour of choice.

A control room (or, to use its full name, a production control room or PCR) is the hub that pulls all the sources together before they on-pass through MCR and to air. The lead in the newsroom for any programme or channel will be the programme editor, while the lead in a control room is the director. All direction must go through them, even if the programme content belongs to the editor. The director is the captain of the ship once it's on air, even if the editor will have plotted the course beforehand.

The director may roll the VTs via buttons that control the server's playout. He or she will have a mic into the presenters' ears, and into the reporters in the field (though this will probably be "keyed" so that the reporter hears the director only when a key is pressed rather than the constant talk from the control room that might be disconcerting). Every studio floor team member will have a headset to hear the director along with the MCR operators, media managers and any other live Operations staff. The director will be looking at the multi-screens in the control room, which will show every edit output, graphics output, camera and "outside source" camera or studio location.

The director will have sat in the newsroom alongside the next on-air presenter, programme editor and producers in the lead up to their on-air slot to contribute and understand the segment that they will be in charge of. This is unlike any other Operations staff, who tend to work outside the newsroom or in the field. The director is the prime link between Editorial and Operations.

Back in the control room, the director will have a vision mixer alongside them (usually to their right), who cuts or mixes to the next source or picture, unless the director is doing it them-selves. Often the vision mixer will act as a director, or technical director, in other segments of the channel, so they understand the role intimately. When they are mixing, however, their role is largely silent and technical as they follow directions from their left. They will always put on "preview" the next "event" or source to be cut or mixed to air or transmission. You will always see a TX monitor in front of the director and next to it will be the preview monitor for the director to see what source - camera/edit/graphics/outside source - is due to be on next.

Usually sitting on the other side of the director is a production assistant (PA). Although a 24-hour news channel can be more fluid in terms of duration of each segment than a finite-length programme, there will still be junctions or events to hit at specific times. The top of every hour or half hour needs to be marked on the very second because viewers tune in for those slots. Ad breaks (on which the channel's business model relies) will also need to run within an agreed time slot or segment, for example, perhaps three an hour. Therefore, someone needs to be responsible for arriving at these junctions on time. It is often an underestimated job. The PA may use a stopwatch or the automated timing control on the newsroom system as the running order counts down. As the camera operator is more often than not male, the production assistant is more often than not female. Whether this is tradition, or if there is an underlying "female trait" that leads women to this role is not certain. Probably, in decades gone by, newsroom secretaries who typed scripts became production assistants, timing programmes as well as generating the scripts on paper and maybe it's because of this that most PAs are women.

The last role in the control room is the sound mixer. Often sitting in a separate, glassed-off, sound-proof room next to the control room, the sound mixer will be concerned with one thing - the quality of the audio output and any comms needed to be set up to allow sound to be heard by the presenter or interviewer. With more complicated segments or programming, for example where there are many live outside sources, a second sound engineer may be in the sound control room, one concentrating on live output and the other on setting up comms. The sound mixer will have many sources on their sound desk, just as the vision mixer has all the picture sources on his or her desk. Faders can be slid up and down as mics go live or off air, VTs are rolled or outside sources cut to. The good sound mixer will do this in synchronicity with the vision mixer cutting to the source. The bad sound mixer may leave presenters or reporters mouthing silently or VTs with their sound coming in too late.

That completes the studio and control room operation and roles, which, above all other parts of Operations, has to be the most tightly knit team, its members having to follow each other while concentrating on their own jobs to produce a seamless and "clean" output. Adrenaline will flow, particularly when news is breaking and the output is more fluid than with a fixed running order. When a story is unfolding, the newsdesk staff will assign reporters and crews, look at agency pictures and wires (written stories describing the event) "dropping" on to their computer screens, and the news editor will ring the control room to inform the programme editor of the details of the story as it happens. The programme editor will then tell the director where to go to next and every single person will, hopefully, be performing at their very best. It is at times like this that on-air errors may happen, but it is also at times like this that the viewer is most forgiving, aware of the fast pace of a breaking story and almost enjoying a loss of sound or picture or a presenter "fluff". It's all part of the drama of breaking news.

Inevitably, while describing the roles, we have touched on the technology but let us now delve deeper into the kit.

ENG cameras used by the skilled camera operator are not very much smaller (although lighter) than they were when ENG came in during the 1980s; back then, they needed to be big to carry the large tapes onto which they recorded. Now, with disk cameras using SD cards, the cameras can be much smaller (as cameras used by VJs - video journalists - are). It is a matter of robustness of the camera. These cameras will and should last years and need to be taken to war zones, disaster areas and carried about for many hours a day. They need to be strong. All the major Japanese camera manufacturers compete to provide kit for the news business and often leapfrog each other in engineering the best tool for the job. There was a time when news broadcasters wanted to use the same manufacturer for their cameras because tapes were often swapped in the field for non-exclusive events. With SD cards, that is no longer a requirement.

The means of getting the pictures back to base is the single, biggest technological change of the past five years. Once upon a time, it went via terrestrial radio links, large satellite dishes or a link to the studio. We have already mentioned laying fibre links if the event is big enough. However, for day-to-day news coverage, the new light-weight satellite packs are the favoured technology. In the UK and Europe, these are often LiveU or AVIWEST units. They require fewer people (i.e., not a team of engineers), and can be hand carried onto planes for coverage overseas. They rely on stable broadband for the signal, so if a hotel room is not available or the conditions poor, then SIM cards, which have to be locally compatible, and a WiFi dongle will do. 3G and 4G networks can be used but watch the cost - many accountants are shocked when whopping bills come in for streaming pictures from certain territories overseas.

The other kit that the camera operator will carry with him or her is a tripod for steady pan shots or a reporter's piece to camera. There will be some kind of simple lighting on a stand (now most often LED, which again keeps the overall weight down). Every camera will have a "top light", too, as well as a built-in microphone (or "mic") that tends to be used for natural sound (Natsof) which can be mixed on a separate soundtrack to the reporter's voice-over.

Each camera operator will carry a stick mic that they or the reporter can hold for an interviewee, for example. A reporter in the field may either have a hand-held mic perhaps with foam or fur over it to cushion wind noise (referred to as windjammers), or a radio mic, which is attached to a lapel or other piece of clothing and wired to a radio pack often clipped to the back of the wearer's trousers or skirt. Radio mics are fine for interiors or when there is no wind noise, and are the least intrusive. In a sound booth or edit suite, a lip mic will be used by the reporter. This gives the clearest sound because it is held right up to the mouth, but for live broadcasts - at least in vision - they are unsightly. Sports commentators use lip mics for the clearest sound over a match or other sporting event since they are often off camera, and the aesthetic is of no matter.

Returning to the method by which pictures are sent back to base live or for recordings: many newsrooms still deploy satellite trucks, particularly for the reliability of signal for live presentation, for example. This kind of newsgathering followed the introduction of ENG, and is known as SNG (Satellite News Gathering). You may also hear the term DSNG, which is Digital Satellite News Gathering. Inside the truck, there will be the capacity to play and record on to card or tape and, of course, send material or live camera signals to the news organisation's MCR. There should always be enough cable length to park a vehicle a good distance away from a reporter's position. An engineer will accompany the camera crew for obvious reasons - it takes two to set this up.

Unless there is a really significant event, an OB or Outside Broadcast unit will rarely be used. Most, if not all, news organisations do not own large OB vehicles, also known as "scanners", but instead hire them from specialist companies when required. A scanner is basically a mobile production control room laid out like any control room. An OB vehicle may be preferable in order for the editorial and production crew to be physically nearer the location, or there may be several OBs along a route, for example, all sending one single video and one audio signal back through an MCR to the control room at base. This brings down the number of sources that the main control room has to mix, and this is logistically easier if there are many multi-camera locations.

Moving back in-house, presuming all the signals and sources arrive seamlessly into the MCR and if it is not required live but needs recording, then a recording video "port" will be put across the signal. In days gone by, this would have been a tape; now, most newsrooms are fully digital. Many newsrooms will have one Newsroom Production System (NPS). The journalists will use this system to write the running order, scripts, view wires, insert video and do simple edits.

This system will often be supplied by one manufacturer and include the newsroom PC software, editing software, and, of course, the video server which holds all the picture, as well as the transmission server which lines up the required packages to go to air along with titles etc.

Usually both the MCR and any Traffic area will have the ability to set ports to record before on-passing to the control room or an edit suite for editing. These ports will be limited (up to eight is typical), so that's why the control of them is often limited to the MCR or the media manager area of Traffic. When something is on the server, anyone with a login to the NPS can see it. Depending on the permissions of the user, the pictures can be edited by multiple users (if needed) at the same time. For example, a package can be cut by a craft editor while a producer writes a headline from the same material.

Now a bit more detail on the editing. We described earlier the different kinds of news picture and who might do the edits according to the complexity or time constraints, so what might the different levels of editing capability be? The manufacturer of the newsroom production system will usually have three levels of picture usage: viewing only, simple edits and complicated edits (usually in a suite or standalone workspace). All editing done with modern server technology is called "non-linear"; unlike linear editing in which the editor had to lay down his or her edited picture on tape in the order he/she wanted it, non-linear editing allows the editing of a piece non-sequentially. An example might be when the editor has the library picture and the end sequence, but not the picture of the day; he or she can still start the edit. It makes for greater speed and efficiency.

As mentioned, the graphics department is obviously a creative hub in any newsroom. It will work closely with producers, directors, editors and technical staff. What kit do the graphics designers tend to use? In the 1980s, companies such as Quantel started to dominate news graphics with the ability to create graphic images using real news footage that could be manipulated to produce realistic images to illustrate the stories. This was dedicated hardware that replaced cardboard graphics. In the subsequent decades, the software used by designers in print started to be used for television news. Adobe still dominates - Photoshop for still graphics and After Effects for animation. Designers always have a preference for the Mac as opposed to the PC; whether this is design snobbery or because the Mac operating system and interface genuinely aids design and is a better platform is often debated.

There are other systems that sit alongside the Adobe suite. Character generators (which produce text, both static and animated) can be standalone or integrated into other packages that can produce 3D animations for full-frame graphics or virtual-reality sets, such as Vizrt, a Norwegian company. If Vizrt is unaffordable as an integrated real-time graphics machine for 3D graphics, software packages such as Cinema 4D can be used on a Mac or PC. The advantage of having a system such as Vizrt, is that a virtual set can be produced with text or graphs or histograms laid over it for an election or business graphics, for example - all from one box. Vizrt has acquired other companies now and has moved into transmission automation as well as graphics. More on that later.

Moving into the studio, we can now elaborate on the hard set versus the virtual-reality set and how the latter works. Chroma key (when a blue or green screen is replaced with a flat picture or graphic behind a presenter or interviewee) has been around for many, many decades, with film companies "blue screening" special effects for a long time. However, virtual reality brings with it another dimension - really - with the ability to replace the green or blue backdrop and floor with a 3D model allowing the cameras to move in real time and the environment or set with them.

Virtual reality for live programming came in during the 1990s when companies like Orad developed what they were doing for movies for other genres. Curtain or hard backdrops have criss-cross pointers or targets printed on them and the camera looks at the backdrop, registers the targets and replaces them with a computer-generated scene. Later, specialist graphics companies like Vizrt developed true 3D virtual reality with the ability for a camera to "look up" to sensors built into the studio ceiling rig to generate a set.

The technology for 3D virtual sets today is quite brilliant, but it is only as good as the set that is going to replace the green screen and floor. Why use a virtual set when hard, real sets can be less expensive? For one thing, many 3D sets need multiple monitors around them to replicate a real newsroom, which can be expensive.

The main advantage of a virtual set, though, is the flexibility. Different "sets" can be designed for different parts of the day, or for special productions and events. The only limit is the creativity of the designer. With hard sets, changing them takes time, with the need for people to move the furniture; if the channel is on air constantly, how is this done without having a second studio?

One of the limitations of a virtual set is the floor and the shadows (or lack of) that presenters and their feet make, bringing an "unreality" to the viewer. The best news sets are a combination of hard and soft. Real desks, for example with real rostra where the presenter sits or stands, combined with virtual sets. It is often a mix of traditional set designer, graphic designer and 3D designer that brings the best results.

In the control room, it can take time to get used to viewing presenters and guests with a green screen, only seeing the set come together with the presenter on preview (the next "event" the vision mixer will cut to) or the transmission (TX) monitor. Guests must be warned not to wear green clothing (which is why spare ties and jackets are often kept in dressing rooms). When Her Majesty, Queen Elizabeth II visited the ITN studios in the UK on May 8, 1991, she turned up wearing a bright green outfit, and matching gloves and hat. The vision mixer demonstrated to her how all but her face and legs disappeared from view on the set. Fortunately, she was only there for a visit, and wasn't appearing live on air.

A studio floor will typically have three to five cameras, depending on its size and numbers of presenters and guests. The pedestal cameras can be robotic (moved and operated remotely from the control room) or manned. Sometimes a jib camera (a camera with an "arm") is used to take wide sweeping shots of the whole set. The jib camera (unless locked off) has to be manned to achieve impressive results. In the control room, a transmission controller or multi-skilled lighting director will balance the colour and intensity of all the shots taken from each camera to ensure that one does not look different in colour temperature from another. This will be done by eye as well as using waveform monitors to check and adjust the signals. If keying the background, this technician will also smooth the edges so that there is no buzzing around the presenters. If the cameras are not manned, the remote-control levers or knobs will be used by the same technicians to frame and zoom in to different shots.

Every studio floor has a teleprompter or autocue scrolling through the words that the presenter will read. Without these, presenters would have to read from paper scripts or ad lib. This isn't ideal, as I can testify. Our production company was all set to roll out our first programme back in the 1990s. The only snag was that the presenter was having to read the links from paper or having to memorise it, and was struggling. We had a problem. I remember taking a plane to London, going to an autocue company and saying I wanted to buy one of their units. It seemed a strange request to them because they normally took sales orders over the phone or the computer, and delivered their products directly to the TV companies or to the large production houses based in London. Yet here was this guy coming into the reception and wanting to buy an autocue over the counter. Weird. Anyway, they finally arranged for one to be available late in the afternoon. I had to pay them in cash since I didn't have a UK credit card. I then jumped into a black cab to Heathrow airport to catch a flight back to Karachi, where I had the teleprompter installed in our studio. This was the first teleprompter in the private sector; the only other one was with the state TV company. It made our presenter exceedingly happy, and our programme much more professional.

The vision mixing and sound mixing of complicated live news broadcasts requires great skill, cool temperaments and nerves of steel. To compete with the best, these specialists also need the latest technology. Traditional, larger vision mixers can have many "banks", meaning they can composite different sources upstream (for example, text over graphics or live images, virtual sets behind cameras) and then concentrate on previewing, cutting and mixing the correct output (which may be a composite made on another bank) to the signal going to air. These banks can also have programmed timelines or sequences of events that mirror set parts of the running order.

Digital Video Effects (DVEs) used to be done via separate hardware boxes cabled to a vision mixer (and still can be), but nowadays they are usually an integral part of a mixer. DVEs can manipulate a source, bend it, zoom it, fly it around the screen and combine an image with other sources or pictures. More often than not in news, a DVE will be used to shrink an image to a half or quarter of the screen, known as "boxes". The combining of sources through a DVE is meat and bread to a news channel.

A sound mixer, too, can have many tracks, 10, 16 or 24, which means that, as with the vision mixer, it can combine multiple sources from mic inputs, to music tracks, to the different tracks of a VT package, to a live interview source or anything else with sound. Multitrack sound mixers will have as many faders with individual tracks available and it is the skill of the sound engineer to align the mixing of the inputs with the vision mixer's mixing of the vision. In addition, there will be panels to set up comms with outside sources when a reporter might be live in the field and coming into the programme. These panels may appear to be the least technological with plug-in cables patching up the remote source into the control room - not unlike an old-fashioned telephone operator.

The larger mixers - vision and sound - need skilled operators. Sometimes, if the channel is small or it is transmitting at a non-peak time of day, either the same kit can be used but in a much simpler way, or technology is now available so that a single operator can get a channel to air. These "studios in a box" can run a simple studio floor and manage all the sources needed for a relatively simple output. This area of automating as much of the running order as possible is the way that live channels are moving. It inevitably brings down the number of staff needed in a control room and, with that, the cost.

In recent years, many news organisations have adopted these

"gallery automation" systems, which attempt to reduce the complexity involved in running a more traditional control room. Typically, this is a template-based software system that controls some or all of the live production equipment, from the vision mixing desk to robotic cameras on the studio floor. Rather than the running order providing the sequence that a crew is reading and following, an automation system functions through a series of technical instructions comprising individual templates edited and saved in the newsroom production computer before going live. A single template might cue up and roll a clip, cut to it on the vision mixer, fade up the correct channel on the sound mixer and animate in name supers, while another template might set up the DVE and graphics systems for a down-the-line boxes sequence ("down the line" means an interview from a remote source and "boxes" is the DVE reducing the camera outputs of presenter and interviewee together in one screen).

These systems allow the entire technical operation to be run from a single desktop PC position, enabling a one- or two-member technical team to run a programme or channel by playing through the template list in the control room, making any last-minute changes as they go. In some cases, channels have done away with technical staff altogether and have news producers directly in control of running the output. This is an extreme, with no Operations staff in the control room, but it may well be the standard in the future.

Early automation systems tended to have limited ability to cope with complex, fast-changing output but better tools are being developed all the time to allow the on-air staff to operate dynamically. It is still fair to say that automation comes into its own on well-planned, more structured channels, though, and working this way puts greater emphasis on carefully managing the running order beforehand, with editorial staff needing a deeper understanding of and involvement in technical operations and the output. Both the BBC and Sky News channels in the UK have opted for this route, using automation technology called Mosart, which Vizrt acquired recently, and Ross automation, respectively. Euronews in Lyon is one of the first channels to run the latest version of Vizrt's Mosart. Coupled with Vizrt's different engines for generating virtual-reality sets, graphics and text, it is a very powerful piece of kit.

While a control room automation system will typically still sit "on top" of more traditional equipment, controlling stand-alone kit such as the vision mixers, video servers and character generators, there are also a number of "studio-in-a-box" solutions on the market that can replace all of that equipment with a single system. Products like Newtek's TriCaster or Livestream Studio are PC-based systems that can mix sound and vision, generate graphics, play clips, link live to contributors and interviewees, record and stream live online, all from one box.

These systems are developing all the time, but at this point still involve some compromises operationally in each area when compared with stand-alone traditional tools. It is perhaps no surprise, when an entire "studio in a box" can be 95 per cent cheaper than a traditional vision mixing desk, that some channels are opting for these solutions. These systems offer greater access to tools that may previously have been beyond the budgets or skill level of potential content producers. This lowering of barriers to entry has already made such systems perfect for video podcast producers, educational institutions and radio stations seeking to produce video, and is now increasingly appealing to more traditional broadcast producers desiring to add extra channels of output online in addition to the main broadcast channel. For younger entrants to the world of news channels working to tight budgets, this is definitely the go-to solution.

At the top end of the market, television news requires skilled technical people as well as a bunch of smart technology that those engineers will need to operate and fix. Operations staff are the glue that keeps the output going. Without Editorial, you can't have news content; without Operations, you can't have a news channel. From the person just out of media training to the most experienced director, a news channel needs all of them. A junior floor manager can save a presenter from fluffing their lines by being there to point out the right camera, or running in a paper script if the teleprompter fails. A make-up artist can help fix that same presenter before going on air, not just with the right application of powder on his or her face, but with the right mix of calm conversation. Operations staff are the often unappreciated, unsung heroes of the whole enterprise.

11

GOTTA LOVE YOUR SPECIALS

"There are no secrets to success. It is the result of preparation, hard work, and learning from failure." **Colin Powell**

Televised events can unite a nation. Sometimes the world. On the biggest occasions - the Olympics, the World Cup, the Super Bowl, India versus Pakistan in the Cricket World Cup Final - they bring hundreds of millions of people together for a shared experience. And what is true for sport is also true for news: television is still the pre-eminent cultural unifier. I believe live TV coverage of consequential news events can capture and reflect a global moment with greater impact than any other form of mass communication. These are the instances when a news channel builds its reputation, much more so than when it's reporting the day-to-day news. A news channel has the potential to devote air-time and resources that sporadic bulletins on multi-genre channels simply cannot match. We call it "owning" a story: viewers know that every twist and turn, every picture and personality associated with the story will appear on our channel. It's the power of a mass audience event.

When the team at Sky News, the British 24-hour-news channel, throws its entire operational resources at one momentous story, there is a term for it: "monstering". The normal schedule is abandoned. Instead, Sky offers little else but single-story coverage, relocating the whole presentation team from the studio to the heart of the action, making sure that the event is covered from every conceivable news and visual angle. Its hope is that its broadcast and digital rivals simply won't be able to compete with the Sky News "monster". This defines the channel's brand.

Often it's breaking news that offers the opportunities to "own" and "monster" stories. But equally important are set-piece events, elections and inaugurations, and ceremonial occasions such as state funerals and royal weddings. And in this era of instant globalised communication, it may not just be a national coming-together but a worldwide one as well. When America inaugurated its first African-American president in January 2009, the live video streams carried by news channels, websites and social media platforms attracted vast numbers of international viewers: the demand to see Barack Obama take the Oath of Office was so great that the surge in viewing crashed the live video stream of one of the world's biggest news organisations, the BBC. Obama became the ultimate global news celebrity whose televised persona helped to burnish America's reputation. Donald Trump is every bit Obama's equal in the television celebrity stakes, although the world sees and judges him, and the United States he oversees, very differently.

Of course, democracy has long lived in the shadow of monarchy. In 2011, when the second-in-line to the British throne, Prince William, married Kate Middleton, the wedding attracted a worldwide audience of almost two billion, roughly the same number of people had witnessed the funeral of his mother, Princess Diana, 14 years earlier.

Monarchy is only another manifestation of celebrity. Pop singer Michael Jackson's memorial service in 2009 was also seen by two billion, just as a quarter of a century earlier two billion had tuned in to watch *Live Aid*, the fundraising concert which, alongside searing news reports like Michael Buerk's, put famine in Ethiopia in the international spotlight.

And who could forget how, in 2010, the rescue of 33 Chilean miners, trapped 700 metres underground for more than two months, became a remarkable global television news event. On October 13, the day that the miners were safely winched to the surface one by one in a specially built capsule, more than a billion viewers across the world, myself included, breathed a collective sigh of relief as each man emerged blinking into the sunlight for the most part unscathed. The extraction operation lasted more than 25 hours and was transmitted by multiple domestic, regional and international news channels, many of which deployed presentation and production teams to Chile, and cleared their schedules to offer live special programming of one of the most nail-biting and ultimately joyous human-interest stories of the 21st century.

So, in spite of the relentless rise of social media and the ubiquity of digital hand-held devices, from the ancient traditions of royalty and the frenzied focus on celebrity to the compelling drama of a news story with an unknown outcome, there's still a seemingly insatiable demand for live television coverage of big news events.

Set-piece televised events can play out across a global stage or a region; they can resonate in their country of origin or be aimed at a niche or specialised audience. Whatever the market, the successful delivery of special events is an essential component of any outstanding television news channel. How you handle these historic events may well be the determining factor for viewers in their decision about whether to stay with your channel or to go somewhere else.

World-class coverage of important events calls for special skills from newsgatherers, producers, anchors, technicians, operations staff, designers and control room teams. Everyone knows that breaking news stories - a terrorist bomb, a natural disaster, an air crash - demand quick decision-making, mobility, flexibility, nimble footwork and rapid fact-checking. But the successful coverage of a major special event embraces an additional skills set: exhaustive planning, creative production, meticulous budgeting, dexterous negotiation and attention to detail, often carried out over a period of years.

It also demands innovation. As I said in an earlier chapter, people are now accustomed to having access to all the entertainment and news they could ever want, right there in the palm of their hand. It's given them the ability to shape their own viewing experience - and this interactivity and personalisation is challenging the inflexibility of linear, single-stream television broadcasts. We are already seeing this in the coverage of big sports events - multiple angles on offer, the facility to access statistics and archive while still being connected to the main action. News cannot afford to be far behind. Special set-piece news events, with their lengthier lead times and stringent planning requirements, offer the ideal opportunity to experiment with multi-stream live coverage, created in real-time so that viewers have multiple points of view and can switch between story lines and angles as their mood takes them.

Today's viewers want to get closer to the drama - this is evident with the growth of virtual reality and 360 degree content. Ultra-high definition television sets, both 4K and 8K, are expected to be in more than 600 million homes worldwide by 2023, with the largest market for sales in the Asia-Pacific region. In these areas, viewers will demand the best quality viewing experience from their news services as they already do from sports and entertainment platforms - and the coverage of big set-piece events will be at the heart of the news offering. How the media organisations orchestrate their output to meet this demand and to exploit technology to the full will, I believe, play a significant part in determining who survives in the disrupted media landscape and who thrives in the 24-hour news business.

Covering Elections

In 2010, Peter Bazalgette, now Sir Peter, the TV executive responsible for the globally popular *Big Brother*, likened television coverage of elections to the reality show formats on which he built his reputation: "A live competition with no-safety net, a winner-takes-all popularity contest, a ruthless exposure of personalities." What works for football and talent shows, he said, works for politics as well. Only it's much more serious.

Today, almost every country in the world *calls* itself a democracy, even if it is a single party state governed as a dictatorship, or a kleptocracy run for the personal benefit of a wealthy few. Only a handful of regimes refuse to hold any elections at all. Of course, many states run elections in name only, with voters offered no real choice or facing intimidation at the polls. But experts agree that roughly 70 nations can be counted as fully fledged liberal democracies, with dozens more having so-called "partial democracy", in which at least some parts of the media are free to investigate, criticise and reflect competing political opinion.

In 2018 alone, citizens went to the polls in elections in more than 90 countries from Afghanistan and Armenia to Venezuela and Zimbabwe. In all those elections, whether entirely free or not, television offered millions of voters their primary source of election news. For many journalists, those elections were among the most important stories they will ever work on. For news teams, an election campaign in your own country is the time in your career that you are likely to be subjected to the most pressure, both internal and external.

Tragically for some journalists, when elections turn violent in the cauldron of unstable democracies, reporting can be a matter of life and death. In 2014, two Canadian journalists travelling in a convoy that was delivering ballot boxes for upcoming elections in Afghanistan were shot - one died. Four years later, journalists in Afghanistan were still being murdered with appalling regularity. In one horrific attack in April 2018, with the country preparing for parliamentary elections later that year, 10 were killed in a single day. The Committee for the Protection of Journalists rightly called it "an assault on democracy". Broadcast reporters were among those targeted because election-time television carries a democratic burden; it helps to shape opinion in a process that affects everyone. It is still the primary platform for information and debate, and to some it is a threat. "Journalists are targeted because they are witnesses," noted Philippe Leruth, the president of the International Federation of Journalists, at the end of 2018 - a brutal year in which 94 people working in the media across the world were killed.

So, television news matters at election time. Why else would politicians work so hard to cultivate their on-screen image and to stage manage the visual theatrics of their campaign? Take the ubiquitous electioneering scene of a presidential candidate delivering a speech in front of an army of cap-wearing, placard-waving supporters. Familiar? As the media historian and blogger Luke McKernan points out: the supposed audience is actually staring at the back of the speaker while the true target of this constructed event is the remote one, the audience watching at home: "Reality is subverted to televisual reality."

In territories and regions with independent television news channels, elections are the journalistic, reputational and commercial battleground on which they compete most fiercely. Whatever the intellectual or political merits of the fractious fight for the US presidency, there is no doubt that the 2016 election was good business for the American cable-news channels: revenue across

CNN, Fox News and MSNBC grew by 20 per cent to more than $5 billion. CNN reported record profits; Fox News was again 21st Century Fox's most profitable channel.

Indeed, election content is invariably viewed in substantial numbers - especially in developing nations - and watched with eagle-eyed scrutiny by politicians, opinion formers and other parts of the media. Errors, whether real or not, are pounced upon by political parties and the press: allegations of bias and favouritism, whether unfounded or not, come with the territory. "Fake news" is no longer just Donald Trump's favourite abusive term for media organisations he doesn't like - it's a phrase that has international currency, unfortunately deployed both by dictators and democratic leaders alike.

In some countries, such as the United Kingdom, a regulated media environment tries to ensure that television election coverage is impartial and balanced. In South Africa, the Independent Communications Authority frequently reminds its licensees of their obligation to broadcast equitable coverage of political parties. France has among the tightest rules to ensure election fairness: there is a blanket ban on reporting opinion polls the week before election day, and candidates from even the smallest parties are legally entitled to the same airtime as the presidential frontrunners - not only how much they speak on screen, but also how often they appear in pictures and how frequently they are discussed by pundits. Of course, if your channel has a pan-regional or international remit you will inevitably report on elections from outside the territory in which you are licensed - leaving you to enforce your own standards of fairness and impartiality. While there are rules, there is no rulebook that covers every eventuality.

In many other territories - from the United States to Iraq - independently owned news channels are free to take a political line: it's up to the viewer what they choose to watch and whether to believe what they see. As I argued earlier, I believe that even in these cases it's in the interests of the broadcaster, both ethically and commercially, to cover competing viewpoints fairly, to hear all sides of an argument and treat them with respect. But whatever the regulatory landscape or business model, if you are operating in any sort of democracy, delivering compelling election coverage is vital to build a successful news channel.

Planning Election Coverage

Firing-up a news channel for coverage of an election campaign, capturing the story of citizens voting and then reporting the results quickly and accurately demands continuous and detailed preparation. It requires planning that can stretch over years. With social media now such a potent weapon, deployed by almost all political actors, it also calls for the deep integration of broadcast and online news operations. The election cycle is so important that many broadcast news organisations assign a permanent team of producers to election planning, often giving them full-time technical and operational back-up, with administrative and financial support.

The election-planning process is drawn out - but it can essentially be divided into three stages: **(1) the "long" campaign,** which begins the day *after* an election and looks forward to the next one; this is the time when lessons are learned, future election coverage is shaped, programme and coverage ideas cultivated, budgets set, teams and talent recruited and trained, and technology is purchased and trialled. The long campaign runs into **(2) the "short" campaign**, usually covering the immediate weeks before polling when the politicians lay out their manifestos and make their most active appeals to voters (of course, in countries such as America, with its extended primary election season, this "short" campaign can, in fact, amount to a two-year tussle for the presidency). Output during this period can include programming such as televised debates, current affairs specials and themed days, as well as the day-to-day campaign news coverage. Finally, there's planning for **(3) the election results programme**, when the channel will report the verdict of the people and its implications for the nation. This is a channel's showcase output in which talent and technology, television and online combine to tell the story of a country's democratic decision. Let's look at each of these in more detail:

(1) The Long Campaign. Planning for the next election begins the day after the last one. A detailed post-mortem of your own election coverage, and that of your competitors, will reveal its strengths and weaknesses. It begins, of course, with comprehensive audience research. How many were watching and who were they? When were they watching and what were they doing while they were? For example, how many were engaging with their mobile or tablet - so-called "second screens" - while at the same time watching the results on television? Were they watching your digital output or someone else's? Online or on social media? Knowledge of this kind of data is imperative to commercial success.

But there is a string of other editorial and operational questions that should be asked at the outset of this period. Many of them are qualitative as well as quantitative: was the story told engagingly and creatively? Did the set-piece ideas for programmes, debates or current affairs specials work? Were all the themes that drove voters' preferences captured - or were some missed? Was there a broad geographical and social spread of contributions, from all parts of the country and all levels of society? Or were you taken by surprise by a demographic whose political intentions and preferences you failed to spot? Was the results service accurate, comprehensive and fast? Did the technology aid storytelling or did it get in the way? Was it, as so often happens, style over substance? Was too much spent or not enough? Did the election branding and marketing have impact? How did the teams perform? Were the right people doing the right jobs? Were they adequately trained and resourced? Were television and digital services seamlessly in sync?

The answer to all these questions - and many others - will inform the planning process for your next round of election coverage. They all need to be addressed during this "long campaign" period, so let's deal with some of these themes individually.

Technology should be the servant of storytelling, not an end in itself

The rapid development of broadcast technology - lower costs and higher portability in the field; cheaper forms of delivery and distribution; the harnessing of social media as a newsgathering tool; the prospective use of immersive technologies (360 and VR); and the explosion of options for live video streaming via new devices and platforms - all have played, or have the potential to play, an influential part in delivering more vibrant election coverage. With the advent of bonded cellular transmission, using portable IP systems like LiveU, and streaming via mobile apps has come the expanded scope of live, cost-effective coverage from the multiple venues where results are tallied. In the United Kingdom, where votes are counted by hand and results announced by a local election official, this type of technology made it possible for Sky News to be recognised in the *Guinness Book of Records* for offering viewers 138 concurrent live streams from count venues on the 2015 general election night. The technology enhanced both the conventional TV coverage and the on-demand platform: television producers had a much wider selection of outside broadcasts available, giving them the editorial assurance that they could tell the story effectively; online users were able to type their postcode into a specially developed app on a dedicated web-page to view live coverage of their own local count. Not content with one world record, Sky News had increased the number of counts covered to 250 by the time of the next UK election two years later.

Increasingly sophisticated databases are driving on-air and digital graphic content, both during the campaigns and in the delivery of results, offering viewers and users the opportunity to perform deep statistical interrogations of election and opinion data, while at the same time generating content for producers.

Equally, the competitive instinct of the electoral broadcast battleground can get the better of news organisations when they become technologically self-indulgent. I well remember CNN's experiment with "holograms" during its 2008 election-night programme. "I want you to watch what we're about to do, because you've never seen anything like this on television," the anchor, Wolf Blitzer, said in gasping tones in New York, before a fuzzy live image of Jessica Yellin, CNN's reporter in Chicago, was projected a few feet in front of him. "You're a terrific hologram," Blitzer enthused, even though she wasn't a hologram at all, but a sophisticated piece of computer-generated imagery, and Blitzer himself couldn't see her anyway - she was visible only to viewers.

The "hologram" was actually a tomogram, admittedly an impressive technical feat filmed simultaneously by 35 high-definition cameras in Chicago and synchronised to the studio cameras in New York by 20 computers to give it a 3D quality. But it seemed to me significantly less momentous than the election of America's first black president, the story it was elbowing off stage. "It's like I follow the tradition of Princess Leia," Yellin ventured, unconvincingly drawing comparisons with the *Star Wars* scene when the character's image is projected out of R2D2. But the Force was not with election holograms (or tomograms): fortunately, there was no repeat performance by CNN in 2012.

Holograms notwithstanding, important decisions on technology are crucial and inevitably must be made during the long campaign period. They have enormous implications on budgets, on the content and tone of election output, and the storytelling of an election results programme. A channel could build its distinctive coverage around a highly mobile newsgathering operation to allow it to chase after candidates on the campaign trail and to establish a broad geographical spread of its storytelling. It could be poll-driven, people-driven or a combination of both. It could opt for more studio-based coverage with an emphasis on information, interviews, debates and detailed dissection of the issues. If so, will the studio be virtual or real? Will election night be primarily centred on the data or guided by the discussions with guests? Of course, it could also be a mixed offering - but if you have a clutch of bright ideas, the only restraint on ambition is technology and cost.

Budgeting: US$130 or US$20,000,000? You choose

In May 2015, an enterprising group of students in the west of England mounted a 10-hour election-night results programme. Their show featured live results from 20 counts, studio interviews, graphics and was streamed on *YouTube*. It cost a total of around £100 (about US$130), with all of that spent on four 5G mobile phone dongles for the outside broadcasts. Admittedly, the students weren't paid, and the university offered the use of its studios for nothing. And occasionally Skype links went down. But it was a quintessential high-tech, low-budget effort. The mainstream UK and international broadcasters and news channels, on the other hand, were not so frugal that night: CNN International, BBC, Sky News and ITV News, who all carried special results output, are thought to have spent around £15 million (about $20 million) between them. The BBC alone was reported to have had a team of 2,000 working on its election night programme. But even these behemoths in the market have their budget constraints. Very few enjoy the financial luxury of one former senior executive whom I know of, at a government-backed English-language news channel in the Middle East: facing a snap election, he was simply told to spend whatever it took to make the channel look like "a player on the world stage". He says: "I was the Director of Operations and not once did I have a budget meeting!"

Of course, it's almost unheard of for news channels - and certainly for commercial ones - to have such deep pockets. So, with an election's almost limitless capacity to devour cash, drawing up a realistic election budget, and sticking to it, is one of the most important planning tasks for the long campaign period. In many countries, the rhythm of the election cycle is predictable, allowing some certainty around financial planning. But matching editorial and technological ambition with available money can be a complex process of pitching ideas, making business cases, tendering and allocating funds. Some organisations set aside a defined election "pot" and then leave the allocation to the editorial hierarchy. Others, particularly in cases of big-ticket election spending, prefer to rely on their usual financial systems to make judgements on value to the business. That would be common for investment in major election-driven technology which may have a spin-off value once the election is over. Many regular budget lines - such as mobile phone bills, transmission, transport, guests' fees and overtime - will need to be boosted. New budget lines will be required for special programming such as debates, themed days of coverage, current affairs investigations, new data sources, a temporary studio build or to commission your own polling. And this list is by no means exhaustive.

One way to dampen costs is to partner with other news organisations. "Pooling" - sharing live camera shots and gathered picture - is common among many news organisations, allowing a breadth of coverage at reduced costs. It is particularly prevalent on election nights, which have an uncertain outcome and when the story is spread over multiple locations. All news organisations will be chasing the same shots of victors and vanquished, at party headquarters or election night rallies, so it makes sense to divide some of the burden and costs of coverage.

Polls are also often jointly commissioned between media outlets, including both opinion surveys of voter intention during the campaign and on-the-day exit polls. The case for commissioning your own campaign opinion polling, even jointly, is finely balanced. On the positive side, it can be a useful marketing tool to increase awareness of your brand during the campaign. And polls have editorial value: they can give a snapshot (although not always a particularly accurate one - see the UK's Brexit polls of 2016) of the state of the race, provide important context for interviews and point to issues which are "hot" with the public. But the headline figures are available to all media organisations once they are published. If you decide to use a poll commissioned by a media rival, it won't cost anything to report the headline figure. The commissioners, of course, will get some free publicity, access to a deeper dive into the figures and, thanks to early sight, some time to prepare content around it. However, the price for that can be high. Some broadcasters prefer to calculate a single, rolling poll-of-polls, averaged out of all the surveys commissioned by other organisations. It's free and usually more accurate.

The other major polling investment choice is an exit-poll, in which people are asked how they actually voted as they leave the polling stations. It's assumed to be more accurate than the voting-intention polls used during the campaign - and it can form the basis of several hours of content during the early part of an election results programme, once voting has closed but before the first official figures are announced. It will usually lead to news organisations forecasting the outcome of the election long before final tallies are known.

Although exit polls are now a common feature of election broadcasting, they have a patchy record for accuracy with potentially damaging reputational consequences. Skewed exit polling data on election night can lead to skewed coverage on the most high-profile programme of the election period. The more accurate you want your exit poll to be, the more expensive it will be: more interviews with more voters at more polling stations across the voting day takes longer and puts the costs up. As with many things, you get what you pay for: cheap polls produce poor data.

Most exit polls worldwide are commissioned by individual news organisations. But in some countries, such as the US and the UK, broadcasters and news agencies will contribute to a shared exit poll, commissioned from a reputable market-survey company in an effort to improve the accuracy - and then use their own analysts to add an extra layer of number crunching and interpretation to the incoming data. Even so, arguments about sampling methodology are commonplace with partner organisations having different editorial priorities. In 2017, Fox News and Associated Press announced that they were withdrawing from the National Election Pool (NEP), the consortium of American television networks and cable news channels, after its jointly commissioned exit poll initially pointed to a Hillary Clinton victory on election night in 2016. The Hillary-is-going-to-win narrative certainly dominated the early hours of results programming, an error which no doubt embarrassed the bosses at the Trump-backing Fox News. So, when Fox pulled-out of the NEP, the network said it would conduct its own exit polls in each of the 47 states holding Governor and Senate races in the 2018 midterm elections - an expensive editorial decision indeed.

On the other side of the balance sheet, elections bring in viewers and, therefore, on commercial channels at least, extra revenue. However, there are revenue risks associated with election content in some markets. For instance, when negotiating the terms and conditions of live election debates, candidates might insist on dropping advertising breaks. Neither American nor British television election debates carry ads. And at certain peak-viewing times, such as when results are flooding in, you may choose to forgo ad-breaks for a period of hours, to avoid diluting the power and momentum of the storytelling. It is a subtle judgement, but one that can be made only after consultation between commercial and editorial departments.

Beyond pooling and polling, there are opportunities for other, more commercially driven partnerships during an election campaign - the joint sponsorship by media organisations of special programming (where allowed by regulators). Complementary partnerships between traditional and new media organisations for events such as candidates' debates carry considerable potential for reaching new audiences, exploiting new distribution streams and creating distinctive content. In addition to cost and resource sharing, this cross-fertilisation of audiences can offer exciting opportunities for business growth. For example, in 2016 during the United Kingdom's referendum campaign on European Union membership, a counter-intuitive partnership of media organisations - the conservative and pro-Brexit Telegraph Media Group and the avowedly liberal Huffington Post - teamed up on YouTube to stage Europe's first major live political debate on that platform.

People: Identifying and Training

During the long campaign, it is imperative that election teams are identified and assembled early. People must not be uncertain of their roles as the election cycle swings, sometimes unexpectedly, from the long campaign into the short campaign - the very moment at which coverage needs to be ramped-up. Teams need to be equipped, trained and ready to go from the outset: from newsgatherers who track the candidates and file election stories, to news-desk staff who direct operations and logistics, to output producers who run programmes, and, of course, the anchors, the public faces of election coverage.

Staff need to be assigned and take ownership of their election role. If a reporter or producer has been told they will be covering a particular political party for the duration of the campaign, they should independently begin building contacts and talking to press departments. If they know their job is covering a high-profile count venue or party headquarters, then an early "recce" is essential to investigate connectivity and to establish the best live-shot positions. If someone has been selected as executive producer of a specific segment of election programming, a set-piece debate, or the results coverage, then the long campaign is not downtime, but an opportunity for exploring formats, commissioning high-value graphics, nailing-down venues and establishing how technology will realise their ambitions.

Above all, there needs to be accountability - regular sessions where progress against specific time-limited targets is monitored. I admire the simple and effective system used by the British channel Sky News. There, election planning is driven by a single list of election specific tasks with a name assigned to each task and a monthly, then weekly, then daily, then twice-daily meetings at which all those names are simultaneously held account-able - the frequency of these large gatherings increases as the clock ticks down inexorably towards polling day. It's a very open but effective way of ensuring accountability and ownership of each task in front of one's managers and peers.

The choice of anchors for election coverage is among the most important decisions to be made. It's another that should come as early as possible: election presenters need to do a tremendous amount of self-briefing to be able to handle whatever is thrown at them during a campaign. I wrote about earning the trust of the viewers at the beginning of this book, and at no time is that more important than during elections. It goes without saying that anchors should possess the usual potent cocktail of charm and intelligence, but the integrity of the election output causes other factors to come into play: a breadth and depth of political knowledge and the capacity to recall it on demand; the ability to absorb multiple sources of information and relay it smoothly to the audience; a firm and persistent interviewing style. Election night is not an autocue reading job - it's about holding it all together on a programme that's a combination of rules and chaos, a mixture of predictable events and surprises. Huw Edwards, one of the BBC's top anchors and a former political correspondent who cut his teeth on the BBC News Channel, says the trick is to appear to be a journalist who happens to be presenter: the anchor needs to be "tied into the journalistic nitty gritty", he says. Of course, a whole stable of presenters may be needed for a domestic election, in which case a team with complementary strengths should be assembled: a ringmaster to bounce between the multiple outside broadcasts from the studio, a forensic interviewer to challenge politicians and a specialist in-the-field anchor for your most high-profile outside broadcasts.

A team - think of it as a repertory theatre company - of pundits and experts also needs to be assembled well in advance, both for the campaign and for election results programming. There can be a competitive market for punditry as elections approach - you don't want to be on the back foot. You may want to offer exclusive retainers to bring down their unit cost per appearance and to prevent a particularly good pundit being swallowed into the studio of your competitors. If you plan to use "surrogates" for the parties, you will want the broad ideological spectrum covered; and you should aim for a gender, ethnic and demographic representation that matches the electorate. I make no apology for believing that both the media and, indeed, elections have long been too male-dominated. If it's a domestic election, ask yourself: does our on-air election team - presenters, reporters, pundits and experts - look like the country that is going to the polls? Make sure that the answer is "yes".

Training is another long campaign priority. Everyone needs to be aware of the legal and regulatory regime affecting broadcasters during elections in the territory in which they are working. In addition, all mature news organisations will have their own editorial and policy guidelines that supplement the official rules and regulations. These include a clear statement of the news organisation's responsibilities and complaint mechanisms which they will put into practice during the election period. If teams are being deployed on elections in unstable democracies where election-related violence is a threat, they need up-to-date certificated hostile environment training before being deployed. So overall, there is a big familiarisation and training task - and it needs to be done *before* the main business of the short campaign gets under way.

(2) The Short Campaign. This is the time when dedicated election coverage really springs into action - when the political parties and actors make their concerted appeal to the electorate, when a highly stage-managed political campaign bumps up against your own election plan. Now is the moment to introduce an election "sub-brand" across television and digital platforms. This is the look that differentiates an election offering from regular programming. Although the channel's overall tone and style will be retained from the "master" brand, a sub-brand should signpost election content from the moment the short campaign kicks-off. It will be visible in on-screen graphic furniture and backgrounds, on set-builds and promotional films, on election pages on the website and the presentation of polling data, right through to election night itself. Think Amazon as a master brand and Amazon Prime as a sub-brand. Election examples of sub-brands on 24-hour news channels include: CNN's *America's Choice,* Sky News's *Decision Time* and Fox News's *America's Election HQ.* Of course, you need to be reactive to the stories and controversies as they emerge during the campaign - that's the day-to-day business-as-usual of breaking news - but the framework for newsgathering, content and sub-brand should already be in place.

In the Studio or in the Field?

You will already have made some big decisions, with corre-
sponding resource implications. Perhaps the biggest will be how
much you plan to get away from the studio, to report the issues
and the campaign from around the country. For many years,
particularly in the Middle East and the United States, news channels have devoted hours to studio-based discussions, in which
pundits and surrogates, mainly middle-aged men, endlessly argue
about the merits of candidates, parties and policies. Of course,
animated political discussion is an essential part of any election
coverage. But it is a stale format: cheap television driven largely,
I believe, by a fear from producers about filling 24 hours of
airtime. Meanwhile, the real battle for votes is taking place away
from the studio cameras. Capturing the mood and colour of the
campaign in towns and rural areas across a country should, in my
view, be the main objective of any news channel's election
coverage. And with the increased mobility of newsgathering and
its decreasing costs, it's an entirely achievable ambition. When
the news channel of the Turkish national broadcaster TRT
launched an English-language sister-channel in March 2015, it
faced the challenge of two Turkish general elections within a
year. While the original, domestic-orientated TRT stuck reso-
lutely with the studio discussion-based formula, the new
international-facing service adopted a more expansive approach,
by reporting live from around a country whose regions had
distinctive partisan and ideological flavours. The content
presented Turkey's complex political map in a way that global
viewers had previously not witnessed.

There are multiple options on how to deliver nationwide
coverage: most of it can be planned. Identify big themes and
make issue-driven packages built around case studies and filmed
entirely with voters. Take live capability to towns and villages in
electorally significant locations to hear a real variety of the

voters' voices. Build themed days around issues - such as the economy, health, climate change, religion, immigration, rural aid, women's rights - which include both live and packaged elements. Send presenters into the field to anchor special coverage, introducing films and conducting interviews. Together, this makes the important statement that you don't only report from the city where your channel is headquartered. Indeed, build a grid that identifies on each day of the campaign the issues you will be addressing and from which locations you will be reporting. The political parties will have *their* grid that identifies which topics they plan to push on a given day, so why not have your own? That way you can rigorously ensure that you are reporting the election from the whole of the country, whatever the parties decide to do. Don't get caught out by a trend you failed to spot. Own the story.

Equally, don't ignore the parties, the candidates or the dynamics of the campaign. Live coverage of what the politicians are doing and saying is part of the election narrative, as much as reporting the latest opinion polls. What candidates say and do changes elections. But often what they say is also repetitive - the same "stump" speech delivered day-after-day from their campaign platform. A 24-hour news channel should not feel obliged to carry every speech. Editorial judgement must still play its part. Indeed, a British news executive was telling me that his channel no longer deploys large teams of reporters to follow political party leaders on their election "battle buses" which stop for stage-managed speeches in small towns around the UK. It was invariably the same speech in front of a handful of friendly supporters at which broadcasters pointed cameras simply because it was happening, while voters were hoodwinked into believing they were witnessing a major event by virtue of the TV coverage itself. Indeed, it seems that the politicians have also cottoned-on to the futility of the exercise. By the time of the 2017 British election, the number of "stump" speeches had dramatically reduced, reflecting the politicians' realisation that social media was a far more efficient way of delivering their undiluted message to their supporters. That's why the monitoring of the "buzz" on social media is now such an essential part of modern-day newsgathering.

The scaling-down of the battle-bus tour in the UK also diminished the jeopardy for politicians of embarrassing encounters with "real people" being captured by live television cameras. In 2001, British Prime Minister Tony Blair, on a televised campaign visit to a hospital, was berated by the wife of a cancer patient about the state of the National Health Service; nine years later, as already related, Blair's successor, Gordon Brown, never quite recovered from labelling a pensioner he met on a televised walkabout "a bigot" - a remark caught by a live microphone on his lapel. Brown was forced to apologise, as was Hillary Clinton when she called Trump supporters "deplorables" at a fundraising event where the cameras were rolling. If the lesson for politicians is that there is danger in mixing with unfiltered members of the public, the lesson for news organisations is that when such encounters do happen, they can generate strong election stories and be televisual gold.

Interviews and Debates

Being liberated from the tyranny of stump coverage offers a news channel the time and space to explore issues through its own journalism and creative formats. Rather than giving candidates a "free hit", it's an opportunity to hold them to account with challenging, thoroughly researched interviews, carried out by authoritative, well-briefed anchors. A half-hour set-piece exploration of issues and positions by a well-prepared interviewer will reveal more to the viewer than extensive live television coverage of campaign rallies. The examination of the leader of each party or each presidential candidate, one-on-one, scheduled across the short campaign offers viewers the opportunity to make a genuine comparison.

The only occasion in the short campaign when all the main candidates are likely to be in the same place at the same time is during a television debate - an increasingly common set-piece event in the election schedule. According to the US State Department, almost 80 countries, from Argentina to Zimbabwe, have held some sort of televised election debate. The face-to-face nature of these encounters offers viewers the opportunity to see policy differences between candidates more sharply defined: contrasting leadership styles are revealed; the extended length and unscripted formats mean that candidates are challenged to expand on the pre-rehearsed, sound-bite messaging of their usual campaign appearances. Pointed questions from the live audience, or questions sent in advance from viewers and website users, can elicit more candid answers, and pressure from a political opponent can expose a genuine clash of ideas. I was struck by something I read in *The Times of Israel*, reporting on an eight-way election debate in 2015: "Time and again, the candidates, forced into a single room to debate in front of a national television audience, saw their carefully wrought rhetorical thrusts crumble in the face of a direct challenge from their competitors."

Importantly, in some territories, television debates can help propel a range of messages into the election arena where one political voice would otherwise dominate, whether through government control of the media landscape or the accumulation of media power in a few hands. In short, they help to create a level political playing field. Even in Iran's restricted democratic system, televised election debates can throw up moments of unexpected ideological drama. I remember the fiery exchanges during the final three-hour presidential debate of Iran's 2017 campaign when Hassan Rouhani was fighting for re-election against his hard-line critics. Astonishingly, Rouhani took aim at the judiciary and the Revolutionary Guard, publicly criticising institutions that had previously been untouchable. He had gone way beyond the traditional limits of Iranian political discourse, and did so in front of millions of television viewers. Rouhani went on to win a decisive victory by almost eight million votes.

Indeed, debates have been the setting for some of the most significant moments in political history: from Richard Nixon's sweaty performance under the television lights, which is thought to have tipped the 1960 US election in favour of John F. Kennedy, to Nelson Mandela's historic debate with President F.W. de Klerk in April 1994, seen and heard live by 40 million South Africans just 12 days before black citizens went to the polls for the first time in the post-apartheid era.

Academic research into the impact of debates concludes that they help voters learn more about the choices available to them and enhance democratic engagement. And, of course, debates can be runaway ratings winners as well. When Donald Trump faced off against Hillary Clinton in the first debate of the 2016 campaign, it was seen by 84 million viewers on 13 channels in the United States - a bigger number than watched the decisive game in that year's baseball World Series and a record for the 60-year history of presidential TV debates. And that figure did not include those watching in bars, at their workplaces or at parties; nor did it count any of the millions like me, watching this gripping American political drama from abroad. In 2007, 20 million watched the French presidential run-off debate between Nicolas Sarkozy and Ségolène Royal.

In developing nations, debates have proved to have an even wider reach. In 2008 in Ghana, presidential and vice-presidential debates attracted a 70 per cent share of TV viewing. In Jamaica, the leaders' debates of 2011 were witnessed on television by two-thirds of the population. In 2013, four out of five households in Paraguay watched their country's presidential debates. These remarkable numbers are a testament to the democratic appetite satisfied by the global trend towards election debates - and the enduring power of television.

However, despite my optimistic vision for the future of televised election debates, I don't underestimate either the difficulties in making them happen or the production challenges associated with carrying them off smoothly. Even in a mature democracy like the United Kingdom, a televised head-to-head between the leaders of the three main parliamentary parties has only happened once, in 2010. Despite the three debates attracting immense engagement, especially among the young, and helping to arrest the trend towards lower election turnout, the next two election cycles saw British politicians ducking and dodging debate commitments. The result was messy, over-complex debate formats in 2015 and the refusal of the Prime Minister even to take part in 2017.

And therein lies the problem. Ultimately, successful election debates can happen only on mutually agreed terms between the political players and the broadcasters. Many risk-averse candidates can be reluctant to join in, especially incumbents who fear they have more to lose than their rivals. Very few countries have laws that compel candidates to take part in televised debates: almost always, it's a matter of delicate negotiation and persuasion, a process which can often take months. Chris Birkett, one of the Sky News executives who brokered the historic first UK debates in 2010, told me the negotiations were like "playing a game of three-dimensional chess". Not only were three British news organisations, BBC News, ITV News and Sky News, jointly taking part in months of secret talks with the political parties to reach agreement on a format, but each broadcaster was also keen to protect its own interests, whether on matters of editorial or commercial integrity. And there was always the risk that at any stage of the process one of the main political parties would simply walk away.

In response to the challenges of organisation, many different models of debate sponsorship have emerged. In some countries, it is left to an independent civic body to organise the debates and then invite the broadcasters to cover them - an example is the US Commission on Presidential Debates. In other countries, a coalition of broadcasters and interest groups comes together to arrange debates. This is how the non-partisan Nigeria Electoral Debates Group, which embraces all the country's main news organisations, and several civic and professional groups, attempted to put together vice-presidential and presidential debates in December 2018 and January 2019. The breadth of the coalition was impressive, but not enough to ensure that the two main contenders would actually show up.

Of course, any single news organisation can try to go it alone and organise its own debate - and that may well be possible lower down the political ladder, at local or regional elections. But on a national level, where maximum exposure is one of the main attractions to potential participants, it is almost inevitable that broadcasters will need to cooperate with each other to make them happen. That means editorial compromises will be necessary.

Once the organisational model has been decided upon, the real work begins. How many debates, where and when? If more than one, will different broadcasters stage each debate? Which candidates will be invited - is there a minimum threshold of support to obtain a place in the debate? What is the preferred format: podium presentations, round table or town hall? Or perhaps all these formats could work in multiple debates across the short campaign. Will the debates be themed - the economy, social issues, foreign affairs? Time limits, rebuttals, the opening and closing handshakes all need to be negotiated - the political parties will certainly have a view. How do you decide who speaks first and who gets the last word? In some countries, the language chosen for the debate can be of immense symbolic importance and thus subject to negotiation.

If there is a live audience, how will its members be selected? Candidates always fear a partisan audience whose boos and hisses could become the focus of television coverage. So, will they be silenced? That's exactly what happened in the UK's 2010 debates when the broadcasters paid more than £100,000 ($130,000) to a research company to provide demographically and electorally balanced audiences, only for the parties to insist that while the audience could applaud at the beginning and the end, they were otherwise not allowed to make any noise at all.

The editorial direction of the debate is usually shaped by the questions put to candidates. They can be formulated by the moderator or selected from those offered by audience members and viewers. Either way, a robust and transparent question-selection process will be needed, one that is capable of withstanding accusations of bias and favouritism. And how will you choose a debate moderator or moderators? What will their roles be: as referees who simply ensure participants abide by the rules and stick to time limits; or as interrogators, permitted to challenge the politicians on matters of opinion and fact?

All these issues - and dozens more - are potentially the subject of prolonged and complex negotiations with candidates, with any unresolvable issue potentially offering a reluctant candidate the excuse to walk away. Delicacy, flexibility and compromise in negotiations are more likely to lead to success than editorial or production intransigence. As Birkett explains: "You have to understand the candidates' perspective - debates end up with winners and losers, and some have a great deal to lose." When a deal is secured, try to get all those involved to sign up to a public statement confirming its terms - such a transparent commitment gives all parties less wriggle room. Public opinion and expectation exerts some pressure but, in the end, it's the politicians who hold the cards.

Once participants, formats, venues and rules have been signed-off, then the production and technical challenges of staging a major election set-piece must be addressed. The production checklist is daunting: venue, camera positions, lighting, audio, clocks and timers; feeds, pooling, distribution; rehearsals, question selection, scripting the opening and closing; snap polling, on-screen text, fact-checking; facilities for post- and pre-event shows; make-up, hospitality, audience management, security, party liaison; budgeting, marketing, ad breaks, legal compliance, complaints procedure - I could go on and on.

If you are lucky enough to "own" a debate in a campaign, you will have branding issues to consider. This is a historic event in which the participants are rightly the focus. While you will probably want to exercise some self-imposed design restraint, you don't want an important branding opportunity wasted. Marketing and PR is a big consideration. A sophisticated promotion campaign is the minimum requirement. On-air, you should also consider building complementary coverage around the debate: preview programming, reaction programming, analysis and commentary, highlight specials and full reruns. I like to compare it to the pre-match and post-match coverage of a cup final in football or cricket. News channels are particularly suitable for this type of broadcasting because they can clear their schedules: on multi-genre channels, election debates are just slotted into the regular programming, limiting the scope for preview or post-event analysis.

Coverage in the rest of the media, including your broadcast competitors, is just as valuable in giving your debate impact. So facilitating the media by providing work areas with connectivity where they can view a feed of the debate, file stories, broadcast from their own live positions and interview party surrogates - in the so-called "spin room" - has become common practice. Indeed, many news channels anchor their post-debate programming from the spin rooms.

My advice to any news channel would always be - if you can get a foothold in the televised debate machinery and negotiations then you should take advantage of it. It may be expensive and you may not get everything you want, but it's no fun during an election campaign looking in from the outside when your broadcast rivals are having a say in shaping the democratic conversation. Be part of it.

(3) The Election Results Programming. This is the culmination of election coverage, the show-piece output, the ultimate test of production and story-telling skills and probably the most technically complex programme of the year. It is undoubtedly the product of months of planning and weeks of rehearsals. You will almost certainly have to take a studio, gallery and graphics suite from the live output team for much of the short campaign to allow for a set and technology build that will give you the capacity to handle all the incoming data and lines. And any new set-up will need to be exhaustively rehearsed with your production and presentation teams, while the channel is focusing on the final stages of the campaign. This period makes a prodigious demand on resources and is a test of the stamina of your teams: you are effectively running two operations simultaneously.

But the rewards on election night make it worth the effort. "It is like every single Shakespeare play put together," says Sky's Editor of On-Screen Information, Paul Bromley, who supervises how election data is displayed on the Sky News's election results programmes: "You get comedy, tragedy, history, rivalry, ambition. All together on one night. There's no script, so when the curtain goes up, you don't know how the play's going to end." Bromley's assessment certainly captures the raw drama of any UK parliamentary election night with its 650 separate counts carried out in town halls and council buildings across the British Isles - and it also points to an essential truth about results output: there will be many threads to the night's narrative, different storylines to follow, the winners and the wounded to chase down, implications of the vote to chew over. But, in the end for a news channel, there's only really one thing that matters

- people want to know what the outcome is, quickly and accurately.

While election night programmes on multi-genre channels often employ eye-catching graphical gimmicks, celebrity guests and exotic outside broadcasts, I believe that the successful news channel should be focusing on what I call information-rich output. I've been fascinated by the way CNN over the past decade has shunned the multiple outside broadcast, multiple guest, pundit-heavy election night formula, to instead concentrate its resources on producing the most powerful in-studio, data-driven, real-time results service. Anyone watching CNN over the past few election cycles will have been impressed by the clarity of its election-night storytelling: the wonkish anchor, John King, standing at the studio's touch-sensitive interactive electoral map, drilling down into the results in individual counties across the US to indicate the state of the race nationally.

Ironically, the CNN touch-screen was piloted in 2008, the year of the infamous "hologram". In contrast, this piece of technology, which was originally spotted by a CNN producer at a military intelligence trade show, has stood the electoral test of time. Now, all the US cable news networks have one. Donald Trump is said to be a fan of King's lengthy, information-packed routines that fill CNN's election night airtime, leaving little space for the overindulgent gizmos, pompous punditry and premature political reaction more typical of some results coverage.

You need only look up one of CNN's 2016 election screenshots online to see how much raw information is accessible to the viewer at any one moment. There's one of the state of play in Athens County, Ohio, with votes and percentage share for each presidential candidate; the county map coloured for the victorious party; the running totals for Clinton and Trump in Ohio, share and real number of votes; the percentage of votes counted in Ohio; the electoral college votes assigned to Ohio; the state of play, Trump v Clinton, in the electoral college nationally, in figures and projected onto a US map; and finally a countdown clock to the next round of poll closures. I make that at least 10 sets of data simultaneously displayed on screen. And at the swipe of his finger, King will instantly switch his focus to another county. Information-rich, indeed.

Of course, there are other building blocks to election results coverage. As I discussed earlier, an exit poll can provide the data backbone to a programme, particularly in the early stages of a broadcast. As soon as voting ends, the exit poll provides a forecast of the result. Then, as real votes are counted and announced, the number crunchers amalgamate them with the exit poll data and the "forecast" becomes a more statistically robust "projection". Which itself is superseded when the actual voting figures come in and the official result is announced. Studio guests, politicians and pundits feed off the inflow of data, both projected and real. Typically, in addition to a headline projection, the exit poll will break down voting by turnout, demographics, issues and regions, all of which can contribute granular content both for TV and online services, adding depth to on-air analysis. The exit-poll data can drive discussions involving contributors from parties' headquarters, counting venues, gatherings of voters - a dynamic, organic conversation that can make compelling viewing, albeit one that carries the large caveat that the exit poll might not be 100 per cent accurate.

And therein lies a dilemma for some broadcasters - a mature democracy can withstand a discrepancy between an exit poll and the real result: it's usually put down to sample weighting errors by the pollsters. I remember that happening in the Lok Sabha (House of the People) Indian parliamentary elections in 2004 when the exit polls vastly overestimated the strength of the ruling National Democratic Alliance at the expense of the United Progressive Alliance. But in less established electoral landscapes, if an exit poll predicts victory for one side, and the official results came down for the other side, then the exit poll can bring the legitimacy of the whole election into question. That's happened recently, for example, in Georgia, Peru, Serbia and Ukraine, where discrepancies between exit polls and the official vote result led to elections being challenged and successfully overturned. In these circumstances, the election night coverage needs to be chasing stories about vote rigging or voter suppression as much as conveying the official numbers. And even in the most self-assertive democracies, the verdict of the people can be delayed by days or weeks as counts are disputed, and the courts are called in to adjudicate. Remember Florida 2000 and the "hanging chads"?

In many senses, exit polls are themselves now part of the democratic process. If you commission an exit poll, you are not only creating content for your own platforms but contributing to the electoral narrative on which you are reporting. You may have to acknowledge that it could put you at loggerheads in certain territories with the authorities, a possibly uncomfortable position for your organisation. Which places an even bigger responsibility on you, as a commissioner and/or broadcaster of an exit poll, to make sure it is as rigorously conducted and as accurately interpreted as possible. If that means spending substantial resources on it, then so be it.

And it is in this arena of data-driven content where I believe the battle for eyeballs will increasingly be focused. The beauty of data is that it can be configured and curated effectively on multiple platforms: feeding on-screen graphical information or presenter-led analysis for a television viewer; or as a rich, drill-down source of on-demand information, available at the swipe of a finger on digital services and social media. Thus one highly complex data-set purchased by your news organisation can be repurposed for maximum reach and impact across all platforms.

Other Set-Piece Events

While I believe that elections are fundamentally a data and opinion-driven narrative, there are numerous other big set-piece events that are, at heart, stories deriving their potency from the pictures. The national ceremonial, the state celebration or funeral, the royal or celebrity wedding are all examples of when images tell the story and the emotions they stir carry immense cultural weight. They are tune-in moments for large audiences - and getting it right in content, breadth and tone is one of the biggest challenges that a news channel will face.

Indeed, it's not too far-fetched to say that the history of the mass communication industry has been shaped by the way people have consumed the most monumental TV events - from the Apollo 11 moon landing in 1969 to the wedding of Britain's Charles, Prince of Wales to Lady Diana Spencer in 1985. In America, more television sets are sold in January than any other month of the year because of the upcoming Superbowl. Major cricket matches have the same effect in India and Pakistan. The live coverage of the coronation of Queen Elizabeth II on June 2, 1953 is said to have cemented the future of television in the United Kingdom, or as the *Radio Times* magazine described it: "The moment television was instantly transformed from a primitive minority activity into a sophisticated mass medium." Within a year of the Coronation, the national broadcaster, the BBC, had launched its first daily television news bulletin.

More than six decades later, television executives were still gripped by the transformational potential of significant royal events in Britain. That's why Sky News took the commercial decision to spend £3 million (about US$4 million) on a single-day's ultra-high-definition coverage of the wedding of Prince Harry and Meghan Markle in May 2018, investing in more than 20 UHD cameras for the ceremony and kitting-out a UHD-capable outside broadcast truck and control room. The sumptuous royal wedding pictures from inside St George's Chapel at Windsor Castle were seen as the ideal opportunity for Sky to showcase 4K technology, already used for some of its sports events, in a news environment, and, in so doing, to push subscriptions to its latest UHD-compatible set-top box. Just as the Coronation was believed to have boosted the sale of television sets in the 1950s, so Sky believed that Harry and Meghan, thenceforth the Duke and Duchess of Sussex, could help accelerate UHD's take-up by consumers.

Delivering a picture-rich experience of a historic national ceremony requires similar levels of planning to that of an election coverage. And that's why so many news organisations invest a considerable amount of time and money in rehearsing and practising for these showcase events. For more than 50 years, the national broadcaster in the UK, the BBC, has been preparing how to deal with the death of the nation's Majesty, Queen Elizabeth II. As I write these words, she is 93 years old and the last time a reigning British monarch died was 67 years ago, when the release of the news of the death of King George VI was choreographed entirely with the print media in mind. Today, under the codename Operation London Bridge, detailed sets of plans and protocols have been agreed between broadcasters, other media outlets and Buckingham Palace covering in precise detail how the announcement of the Queen's death and its ceremonial aftermath will be handled, including how the funeral of arguably the most famous woman in the world will be transmitted to an audience expected to be in the billions. At least once a year, rehearsals are carried out in great secrecy, surrounded by the highest levels of security. They are intended to establish an appropriate tone for the coverage - from refining the scripts to deciding what anchors and reporters will wear - as well as testing the technology and newsgathering. It's already been decided that nine days after her death, the spectacle and ritual of the Queen's state funeral will take place in Westminster Abbey in London, and the world will watch those images just as they did others that are etched on our collective memories: John F. Kennedy's three-year-old son saluting his father's coffin; Neil Armstrong's "giant leap for mankind"; a frail Muhammad Ali lighting the Olympic Torch in 1996; and Nelson Mandela's walk to freedom on his release from prison in 1990.

For major occasions such as these, if the event is taking place in your own country, it's most likely that an individual news channel's involvement in the coverage will be on a pool basis, and that you will have access to a mixed feed of the whole event. If you are covering a big event outside your own territory, you will probably have a news agency feed available as the core of your coverage. Either way, there's an opportunity to add your own layer of production and embed your editorial values - in some senses to "own" it, even if your competitors are playing in the same market.

Let's take the example of a domestic event to which you are contributing to "the pool". If the event involves a street procession, you may be expected to contribute to the multiple camera requirements. These could include fixed cameras at the start or end of the procession and at key locations; jib or crane-mounted cameras along the route to provide sweeping shots of crowds; portable wireless cameras, mobile cameras on motorbikes or cars; and, potentially, helicopter and drone cameras for aerial footage. You can then add your own "unilaterals" - other outside broadcast cameras which capture the excitement in the crowds; or locations elsewhere in the country to reflect a national mood. At British royal weddings, for example, it's common to cover the colourful street parties and eccentric celebrations that coincide with the more formal ritual.

Your own team of commentators will be crucial in establishing an appropriate tone: respectful and restrained for a memorial service or funeral; celebratory for a royal wedding, even excitable for a celebrity event. It's about knowing when *not* to talk as much as providing an informative commentary - natural sound and picture can often be the most effective device. In the case of ceremonial commentators, the best may already have been signed-up to exclusive contracts before any death or wedding announcement. Make sure you, too, are in the game: experts on the history and pageantry of a royal occasion, fashionistas to deliver their verdict on *that* wedding dress; celebrity watchers to spot the famous and infamous among the guests - all could be required. Or maybe not. For the wedding of Prince Harry and Meghan Markle, Sky News introduced artificial intelligence technology to carry out the celebrity spotting function. As guests arrived for the wedding, they were identified by facial recognition software, which then automatically called-up background information as subtitles and graphics on the live stream. No longer would the minor royal, the foreign dignitary or the B-list celebrity go unnoticed!

And never forget the two biggest competitive advantages of a news channel - the opportunity to sub-brand your own distinctive coverage, and the capacity to exploit the air time you can devote to ancillary programming, such as preview shows to sample the atmosphere, fast-produced highlights programmes that cherry-pick the defining images, rapidly turned-around current affairs programmes to capture a national mood by assembling material from multiple sources. In 2012, on the day the United Kingdom celebrated the Diamond Jubilee of Queen Elizabeth's accession to the throne, I was impressed that Sky News put together an entire programme compiled solely from social media videos submitted by members of the public. Sky built a video upload facility into its mobile app to enable viewers to share their experiences of their local street parties, which were then turned into content for the TV channel - social, digital and television working seamlessly in sync. Later that night, full replays of the whole televised event gave viewers the opportunity to sit back and experience a day of history again.

Of course, not all events are of international or historic significance. Opportunities to mount special coverage, to "own a story", can present themselves in a range of events: for specialist business, or even mainstream news channels, regional trade shows are a good example. Take the highly successful Dubai Airshow or the India-based Auto Expo, one of the world's most important motor shows. Both are picture-rich, full of stories about innovation, technology and enterprise with deep relevance for people's lives because of their economic importance and their impact on the consumer experience.

A final thought on event coverage

A single image of St Peter's Square in the Vatican, showing the thousands gathered for the inauguration of Pope Francis in March 2013 tells us a great deal about how we now consume set-piece events. Almost everyone visible in the picture is their own newsgatherer and filmmaker - recording the historic event on smartphone or tablet held high above their head. Hours of that content, probably hundreds of hours, would have been uploaded to social media to be shared with millions at the click of a button or the swipe of a screen.

Few there on that day would have transmitted their images live, but there are now a multitude of apps that would enable any passing pilgrim to broadcast the ceremony live on the internet on numerous platforms. So, with all these do-it-yourself newsgatherers and content makers, what is the need for the sort of coverage that we have been discussing in this chapter, with all its associated costs and commercial risks? I believe that there are three reasons why television coverage of major events can help news organisations thrive in an era of ubiquitous user-generated content and social media supremacy.

Firstly, there's the enduring power of storytelling: put simply, a million individual clips don't make a narrative; a live hand-held image taken from a single vantage point can never reveal the whole story; context and history cannot be conveyed by the mumbled comments of whoever is making the video on their smartphone. Storytelling is a craft that news organisations have refined over decades. Of course, it needs to be adapted to changing tastes and technology, but it's an artistry that is still at the heart of broadcast journalism.

Secondly, there's the quality of the content, both aesthetically and technically. No amount of hand-held, poorly lit, out of focus, distantly filmed, wobble-vision can match the near-theatrical experience of a beautifully shot, multi-camera, ultra-high-definition outside broadcast with exquisite audio and measured commentary, watched on a television-size screen. One that you can sit back and enjoy - like lingering over a delicious and satisfying meal. The other is, at best, fast-food grabbed on your phone. Both have their place.

Finally, and I make no apology for going back to this, it's a question of trust. The reputation of a news organisation is built on a satisfied viewer experience. No type of coverage is more influential in building trust than the sort of set pieces we have discussed in this chapter. Reputation can slip away very quickly and is won back slowly, if at all. To earn trust, people must believe what you are showing them; they must accept that what you are saying is fair to everyone who has a stake in the story; and they must be confident that all your creative energy and technical resources are devoted to bringing them the outstanding experience of world-class output. Successfully meet all these tests and 24-hour news channels will thrive: the public will raise their eyes from their smartphones and embrace the enduring and compelling drama of television news.

12

GENERATION Z AND THE NEW DIGITAL ORDER

"Trust the young people; trust this generation's innovation."
Jack Ma

We live in a world in which more than two billion individuals belong to Generation Z, generally defined as those born from the mid-1990s to around 2012. They make up more than a quarter of the Earth's population, and will increase to about one-third by around 2020.

This generation, following on from Millennials (aka Generation Y, those born c.1981-1996) and Generation X (born c.1965-1980), is markedly different from its predecessors in many ways.

It is the first truly mobile generation, born into the era of smartphones, social media, instant interaction and always-on connection. Gen Zers communicate 24/7 with each other and the world through their favourite social media networks. They order their food online, they know what's being sold anywhere around the world, they live in a shared economy of Uber and Airbnb. They trade in cryptocurrencies and have replaced plastic money with digital payments, just as their predecessors supplemented cash with credit and debit cards. In a similar way, they've dumped desktop computers in favour of the PC in their pocket, their smartphone.

They are also hungry for content, watching and consuming it wherever they are, whether they're travelling, at the gym, at school or in a shop. Every 60 seconds on the internet, they're largely the ones responsible for more than half a million tweets, the viewing of 250,000 hours of videos on Netflix, and four million videos on YouTube. They are constantly checking social media sites and video source platforms such as Instagram, Snapchat, Vine, Facebook and YouTube for content that is engaging and entertaining. They regard as antiquated the idea of their going home to do this sitting down at a screen that's fixed in one place; a 2017 study revealed that while Millennials and Gen Xers spent more than an hour a day accessing the internet over a PC, Gen Zers spent just eight minutes.

They can't - won't - wait an hour, let alone a day or a week, to watch the next episode of their favourite show. So they binge watch. They want to be the first to know, the first to comment and the first to share. The days of people writing an email or - heaven forbid - a letter to the editor that may or may not then be published a day or so later are long gone. If you publish some news, you will get instant feedback. And they will tell you when they don't like it; members of Gen Z like to like things.

Generation Z is truly native to the Digital Age; technology is in their blood. While the generation before them is still acquiring these skills and trying to keep up with the break-neck speed of digital progress, this new demographic group is pushing the tech industry to constantly innovate. Gen Zers are at the heart of the world's digital transformation, and by the time these words are written, let alone read, they and it will have moved on.

Of course, each generation down the centuries has come with a different set of behaviours and posed a new set of challenges to their elders. But in today's increasingly fragmented ecosystem, the advent of Gen Z is causing profound social, economic and political changes to societies around the world, and disrupting the way in which businesses work. The demographic landscape of almost every market is rapidly changing, with many countries in the developing world - across Africa, the Middle East and Asia - having up to 70 per cent of their populations aged below 30. A staggering 41 per cent of Africans are aged under 15.

In America, Gen Z and Millennials now account for half of the population, and the ethnic composition of these two groups is more diverse than any seen before. As of early 2018, among these two generations, Hispanics, Blacks and Asians accounted for more than 40 per cent of the total. Generation Zers differ from Millennials in several significant ways. In a world of continuous updates, they process information faster and are better at multitasking due to the number of apps and sites they constantly interact with. They are generally more entrepreneurial - 72 per cent say they want to start a business some day - more independent, and more likely to opt out of the traditional routes of higher education and employment, and instead look at finishing school online, if at all. If they do work for someone else, they want flexible work hours, more freedom and less top-down direction.

Millennials were considered the first "global" generation with the development of the internet, but Generation Z has become even more internationalist and diverse in their thinking and relationships. Nearly two-thirds of adults worldwide aged over 35 agree that "kids today have more in common with their global peers than they do with adults in their own country".

This is a generation that was born into and grew up with technology; it is a crisis of major proportions for them to be without their smartphone or other devices, akin to an older person losing their wallet or handbag (or even a limb, so much has the phone become an extension of self). A US study shows that roughly four in 10 teenagers feel anxious if they leave home without their cell phone and more than half (56 per cent) associate the absence of their phone with at least one of three emotions: loneliness, being upset or feeling anxious. Gen Zers are 25 per cent more likely than Millennials to say that they are hooked on their digital devices, with 40 per cent self-identifying as digital-device addicts.

What does all this mean to someone seeking to create relevant and popular news-based channels? Here are some of my thoughts, in no particular order and almost certainly not comprehensive.

It is unlikely that any of the businesses we start will be sustainable in the medium- to long-term unless they satisfy the wants and needs of Gen Zers, and deliver that when and how they want it. If this generation is constantly on a phone or mobile device and not watching as much or any traditional TV, we will experience a massive shift in advertising methods and marketing messages, the like of which has already begun.

The traditional media's control of the agenda and timings of news and information is over, for ever. The digital transformation has made it possible for one and all to create content, much to the hand-wringing of legacy journalists. Not only can anyone make their own content, but they can publish it on the internet and share it instantaneously with the whole world. This has completely flipped the model of mainstream media.

A teenager in Kerala, Kazakhstan or Kentucky doesn't need a newspaper reporter to come and interview her if she is at the centre of a story. She can just tell her narrative herself and post it online. Take the real-life example of Rahaf Mohammed al-Qunun, an 18-year-old who fled from her allegedly abusive Saudi family in January 2019, and sent out a series of tweets from detention in Bangkok, pleading for help to stop her being deported home. Within 24 hours, the hashtag #SaveRahaf had been circulated in more than half a million tweets and the unknown teenager went from having 24 followers to more than 27,000. On the back of the campaign, she was given asylum by Canada.

Whether one likes it or not, telling stories and breaking news is no longer in the hands of big media. People are in control of their own stories. And this has led to what has been the single largest shift in the public sphere: the so-called democratisation of media. Crowdsourced content creation means people share their experiences of singing, cooking, travelling, teaching, DIY projects or make-up tips. This has given rise to the blogger, tweeter, influencer, vlogger and YouTuber. As Kevin Allocca says in *Videocracy*, his book about YouTube, "It's a culture shaped by all of us."

As these content creators have attracted more viewers, these viewers have attracted advertisers, monetising new media and platforms. For instance, one million views on YouTube guarantees between US$15 and $2,500 in revenue to the creator. As people realised they could earn significant sums from YouTube, professional content creators started joining in. As with Holly-wood celebrities, there is now a new breed of social media millionaires and celebrities who are rated solely on the size of their online followers/subscribers: stars such as DanTDM (professional gamer and author); Zoella (fashion and beauty vlogger); Lilly Singh (one-woman show involving comedy and singing); Tyler Oakley (an activist who talks about issues such as discrimination against LGBTQ people, bullying, and eating disorders); and Huda Kattan (make-up trends, reviews and how-tos).

So we media entrepreneurs need to think and act radically differently. In the old days, we would first concentrate on starting a TV channel, and spend almost all our time on its creation. Once that was all but complete, we might put a bit of effort into planning our digital or online presence; it would be an afterthought, a secondary consideration, a sideshow to the main

event. Small wonder that these associated websites were generally mediocre, under-resourced and under-funded, and staffed by
the least-able people. They were the poor step-child.

That has changed over the years, and broadcasters are today
largely aware of the absolute importance of having a robust
online presence, not just on their own websites but on social
media platforms, too. The trickier part has been fulfilling that:
despite good intentions about revamping themselves for the new
age, few established channels have properly made the transition
to being truly digital. As with newspapers, many of which
continue with a print-dominant mindset and approach while
paying lip-service to digital, TV owners and managers have
struggled to rid themselves of their belief in the superiority of
"television".

But the beauty of what we are contemplating here with this
book is a completely clean slate. We can now be a startup, unhin-
dered by old, entrenched thinking or out-of-date working practices, and unencumbered by dyed-in-the-wool staff who've
always done things the way they've done them, and just want to
continue doing that till they retire or die, thanks very much.

So let's take that clean slate and write a few words on it to
help us focus on what is needed and wanted today.

We might start with: "Let's not fall into the trap of creating
yesterday's TV station."

Followed by: "Digital has changed the game forever. The
consumer is at the centre of the picture, and is motivated by
instant gratification, which means we must provide the best user
experience for him and her."

And then: "So we'll give our target audience the relevant
news and information they want, when they want it, and how
they want it - on the screen of their choice. The pre-internet
generation (40+) may still turn on the TV set for news. The
digital generation will turn to their phones."

The demographic of "television" viewership and audiences

has altered entirely, and a culture of on-demand viewing has been created with the introduction of fast broadband internet speeds, near-universal access to WiFi, and powerful smartphones. This will only accelerate with the arrival of 5G networks over the next few years.

Traditional television channels and their websites are being left behind because news now breaks on social media. Young people have also developed an aversion to television culture and brands, partly because their attention spans are shorter, and partly because of a generational perception that big media, with some exceptions, is generally out of touch and untrustworthy. They would rather go to their peers online on social media to find out what is happening.

Another major reason is Gen Z's belief that mainstream major media outlets do not cover their lives and issues. They are bypassing traditional television and websites as irrelevant. You can see the inversion: television channels now report what they see on social media as news, rather than being the outlet that breaks news that then disseminates on social media. The future lies in harnessing digital properties and inverting the television pyramid.

So, as you contemplate starting a "television" news channel, don't think about one platform, but many. Don't consider how your content will look on a big screen in the corner of the living room, but about how it will appear on a mobile phone screen being watched on a bus. Audiences are not just sitting in front of the television any more. If a brand wants to be relevant, it has to be where the eyeballs are, and go to where they have moved. This not only means websites but other digital platforms. Of course, some of these platforms are beyond our control, and each has its own model to make money. Sometimes they tweak their algorithms in a way that's detrimental to us. But we have to live with them and work with them.

Don't think of a newsroom staffed with television reporters, producers and presenters, but one packed with multi-skilled individuals who are as adept at shooting and presenting a video news clip as they are at writing a 600-word article or a 280-character tweet. Of course, you will still want and need some specialists, who are the best in the field at one or other skill, whether it be presenting, breaking exclusive stories, writing beautiful, long-form news features, or shooting and editing compelling video. But in a multi-platform, always-on world, you need multi-skilled, always-on journalists, ready to respond 24/7.

The real success comes when these skilled individuals - be they reporters, TV editors, online website editors, producers or social media experts - work together in the best interests of the audience. It follows when they realise that they exist to serve the consumer, not to engage in petty squabbles over which role in the newsroom is most important, or who does what, when.

Collectively breaking news or creating compelling and credible journalism is much better than flitting around like lone rangers, ploughing the same old furrow. The journalist is never bigger than the media brand, whatever he or she would like to think. In the world of a converged newsroom, the beauty is that everyone gets credit on all platforms. The more they cross-share, the stronger they become. And the stronger they become, the stronger your brand, and the stronger your business.

This is the converged newsroom of which most established media companies, whether in the Global North or Global South, can still only dream. Traditionally, journalists are a prickly, ego-ridden lot. Too many print journalists continue to look down on their "ephemeral, clickbait-obsessed" online counterparts. Digital journalists reciprocate by dismissing the "dying dinosaurs" on the papers. Television journalists look sneeringly down on everyone: they are the stars of the screen, after all, with charisma, glamour and mass appeal.

While many of these perceptions have begun to alter in the past five years or so, suspicions and self-interests have survived even as the existing media model has been smashed and a new order has emerged. They're fighting yesterday's battles, with yesterday's technology. They're the cavalry on horseback charging the Gen Zers in their tanks. The world has moved on, folks.

Forget the legacy labels of print, radio, TV, digital: these old demarcations, those old turf wars are gone. What matters is serving the customer as best you can, with the most compelling journalism/stories/content that you have. If you produce it on all your platforms, then you have nothing to worry about in the long run. The focus must be on becoming - and remaining - a trustworthy source of reliable, useful, actionable information about the world. That beats unverified social media posts and what people share in their personal capacity any day. Journalists doing their jobs well is the not-so-secret secret. Which is why - as I said earlier - you need to employ the best, most talented people you can.

The digital world gives so much more for us as news providers. It allows us to supply a superior service to consumers over any solitary traditional platform, and helps power our businesses. Such as:

Providing searchable on-demand information

Once a piece of news has been aired on a traditional TV bulletin, it disappears from the airwaves, at least until the following hour's bulletin. Today, it's available to view 24/7, not just at a time when we say to the viewer that he or she must watch. Ultimately, in the bigger picture, as it were, this serves society, ensuring that information/knowledge is always accessible.

Being a source of revenue

Delivering our content on different platforms allows us to earn more money. News bulletins can be streamed live on one's own website, on YouTube and elsewhere, allowing us to earn revenue from the number of subscribers or eyeballs. Facebook and Twitter and, to some extent, WhatsApp are all experimenting with monetisation models for content providers. Social media teams can work with the marketing and advertising departments to obtain sponsored or paid content to push on to Instagram accounts and elsewhere.

Engaging with audiences

The greatest advantage of having digital properties, given how technology works now, is engagement with one's audience. Every single digital platform that a media house has is a vehicle or mechanism by which to engage in a two-way communication with its viewers, helping to cement loyalty and build revenue streams. Before these, it was largely a one-way street.

There are, of course, different approaches and techniques required when it comes to producing content for different mediums. While there are crossovers in audiences, each platform has a slightly different set of viewers, who want and expect varying things. What works for one platform, or one audience, won't necessarily work for another. A 400-word story for print might just about be OK for a website, but might it be more compelling online if it were converted into a "listicle"-style article, such as "Five Reasons why X is the new Y", or a series of charts that illustrate better than words why the housing market is in crisis. And, of course, none of those approaches will work well in video, without relevant footage, graphics, an interesting script that talks to the pictures, and a good voiceover. And if it is to be converted for a radio-style bulletin or a podcast, it will probably need reworking again.

Here are some differences between TV and digital that are worth considering:

- Television screens have their own visual vocabulary. But a digital presence cannot look exactly the same as that. Setting up a website for a video-based channel requires a design team that not only understands the brand and aesthetic of the channel but knows how to tweak it to become appropriate for an online audience.

- Pick the right font - is serif or sans serif best? Serif tends to give a website the feel of a newspaper or magazine, depending on how strong it is. Sans serif, which is what traditional television channel news sites often pick for their websites, is considered clean and modern. But it is worth surveying what the entire industry is doing and considering if one wants to go the same route or be slightly different.

- Consult the developers/architects. Design choices have to be made in conjunction with the web developers who will erect the scaffolding at the back end of a website or app. Designers can often create front-end designs that weigh the pages down, and make them slow. There is hardly any point in having a pretty page if it takes aeons to load.

- Keep a flexible brand colour palette. The assumption is often made that media organisations will want to branch out into different digital properties, create verticals, grow and experiment. If the core logo colour signifies one value, then spin-offs have to adhere to that philosophy. But designers and the web and social media teams must work together to ensure that the palette choices are made collaboratively and in a way that suits the content. It is perfectly acceptable to take risks (Bloomberg's website, for example, went with a startlingly vibrant blue reminiscent of ink) but the content must match or be complementary. There is also no need to reinvent the wheel. Sports can be colour coded yellow or green, as it often is in the old world.

- Do not design without first understanding the sort of content you will be dealing with. Ask yourself these questions: who is filing the main content? In what form is the main content coming (eg, text stories, scripts, video footage, photos, audio, compressed WhatsApp videos, graphs, vertical photos, horizontal photos, degraded photos, tickers, wire copy, reporter copy)? How often is content coming in?

- The nature of stories and videos and other information elements should inform design and not the other way around. Designers too often concoct "sexy" section pages and story pages without understanding the audience's psychology and preferences as well as how the newsroom produces material. Beautiful designs look amazing on the website but they are useless if they do not serve the user. People absorb news in certain ways. They also navigate and browse in certain ways. The design must be attractive but practical enough to keep them on the website, the app, the screen.

- Keep flexible story formats. Stories can be told in many different ways. While it is fashionable to claim that no one really reads any more, beware of trendy conventional wisdom. Not all stories merit video treatment. Not all news has footage. You should design for all storytelling formats and keep room for innovation.

- Live, breathe and design mobile first. While desktop viewing of websites and platforms and TV livestreams still forms a large proportion of the viewing mode, we've discussed how Gen Z has turned its back on this. Mobile is increasingly the major lens through which media content is viewed. Design for mobile phone screens first and then move on to desktop. Keep in mind that loading time is important. Mobile also involves creating what are known as amp pages (Accelerated Mobile Pages), for example, so the web developers should inform the designers of the different formats in which mobile phones can present material and how different platforms configure it. For example, Twitter likes square video, Instagram's IGTV likes vertical.

- Figure out your existing and future audiences. The design process should take place only after the online audience is understood and areas of growth are determined. Analytics will tell you what people like but that is still contingent on what you provide them. So you can create future audiences with new content and see growth. For example, one Pakistani television channel found its audience to be overwhelmingly 25- to 35-year-old males in two cities. With some small investment into pro-women and pro-youth content, it was able to start attracting those audiences, too, without alienating its core audience.

Technology is key to achieving the converged newsroom; multi-skilled journalists need the tools that allow them to do an array of things seamlessly, such as to produce videos, create visually appealing graphs, source still photographs, write scripts, stories and podcasts, and to record them. In the past, each medium had its bespoke software of choice, developed to do only what that medium required. Television stations had their own software, such as Octopus or ENPS, to manage their scripts, footage and photos. Newspapers would use content management systems for their stories and photos, such as Adobe or Atex or Méthode. Their digital spin-offs, both in TV and papers, would almost inevitably use some different CMS (content management system), one which probably didn't "speak" to the other. Today's systems have to cater for all of the needs of different platforms, providing a simple solution that all types of journalists are comfortable using.

It is extremely likely that many young people will have been reading this chapter with a smug, self-satisfied smile on their faces, thinking: "I know all of this already, what the heck is Siddiqi banging on about?" As paid-up, card-carrying members of Generation Z, they are probably of the mind that they need no lectures on what they and their colleagues want from life or from a news channel.

I would simply say this to them: take a look around you. See those babies in their prams and pushchairs, and those toddlers having fun in the play-park? Say hello to your nemeses: Generation Alpha is on its way, my friends, and it's coming to do to you what you've done to the Millennials and the Gen Xers. So heed the inherent lessons contained here, don't stop changing and learning, and good luck with keeping one step ahead in the never-ending alphabet soup of generational change.

13

'YOU MAY SAY I'M A STREAMER... BUT I'M NOT THE ONLY ONE'

"We keep moving forward, opening new doors, and doing new things, because we're curious and curiosity keeps leading us down new paths."
Walt Disney

The digital age has made launching a news channel faster, easier and markedly less expensive than it used to be. The result is that dozens of new entrants are coming to market, streaming their output directly to consumers over the internet, while existing media companies operating in the traditional TV space scramble to play catch up, and big new players such as Apple and Amazon jump on the bandwagon.

Internet broadcasting - described variously as OTT, or over-the-top, in industry parlance - is increasingly the focal point for the future plans of all these businesses, big or small. Some are relying on a free-to-air model in which advertising is the major revenue. Others believe that subscription is the way forward, while some - particularly established businesses - are hedging

their bets and trying a mixture of approaches. As Michael
Morris, a media and entertainment analyst, told *The Hollywood
Reporter* in 2017: "It's not going to be sufficient to say, 'I only
do streaming', or 'I only do broadcasting'. You want to be a pay-
TV network and an ad-supported streaming business."

It has been estimated that around one million households
across the world start subscribing to streaming services every
week, lured by both their content and their convenience. And
almost every week brings word of some new initiative or channel. As I write, a quick glance at the headlines on industry news
websites reveals the scale of the revolution. One states that new
direct-to-consumer services will grow the American subscriptions market by 53 million within four years, a 25 per cent
increase that would generate up to US$3.6 billion in incremental
revenue. Another proclaims how, in Britain, the BBC and ITV
intend to launch a rival to Netflix (dubbed, inevitably, Britflix,
but actually called BritBox). A third declares that ESPN+, the
OTT American sports service, now has two million paid
subscribers, double the number it had just five months before. A
fourth tells how All Access and Showtime, CBS's OTT offerings, have reached eight million subscribers, up from five
million six months earlier, while another asserts that Netflix's
acclaimed movie *Roma* was deliberately snubbed from being
awarded the Oscar for Best Picture because of what it calls "Hollywood's Streaming Anxiety".

And, finally, under the title of *A Tale of Two Streamers*, a
report reveals that the US entertainment giants Disney and
Viacom are massively gearing up their OTT efforts, and, help-
fully, makes the play on words from *Imagine,* John Lennon's
best-selling 1971 song, that has provided me with the headline
for this chapter (thanks to you, reporter Stuart Thomson of Digi-
talTVEurope.com).

It's not at all clear where all this will end. Might the vast
array of such offerings - from Netflix to BritBox through

Disney+ to Amazon Prime - lead to consumer confusion and resistance? How much will people actually be willing (or able to afford) to spend on multiple streaming video services, each requiring separate subscriptions, passwords and apps? Some market research suggests that the average number of subscriptions to video services that American consumers are willing to pay for is three, and Europeans just two. Which brands will be successful in cutting through the competitive clutter and capturing attention? Might a super-aggregator emerge that can provide the sort of ease of access, convenient payment method and discovery of universal content that many consumers probably crave?

Most of this battle will be fought on the lucrative fields of entertainment and sport, but news is far from immune to the winds of change sweeping through the industry, as existing and new providers pop up to take advantage of the new technology.

Iflix, a free and subscription internet TV service that started in 2014 and originally focused on entertainment for emerging markets such as Malaysia, Thailand, Indonesia, Sri Lanka, Pakistan, Saudi Arabia and Egypt, last year launched a 24-hour service aggregating live news streams, clips, and linear feeds from international, regional and local news channels. In America, Fox has set up a subscription streaming service (partly to counter the rise of two rival conservative news OTT channels - One America News Network, or OANN, which launched in 2013, and NewsMaxTV, which began in 2014) while the traditional TV broadcaster Sinclair has launched STIRR, a free streaming service with local news and sports.

One of the most eagerly awaited new streaming services is the brainchild of Jeffrey Katzenberg, a leading Hollywood producer, who has raised US$1 billion to fund a new subscription mobile video streaming service, called Quibi, which is due to launch by early 2020. Among its investors are every major Hollywood studio - including Disney, 21st Century Fox, Entertainment One, NBCUniversal and Sony Pictures Entertainment. Each one of them anxious to join the streaming party as they warily observe the likes of Netflix, Amazon, Apple and others, in the words of one Hollywood reporter, "all trying to drink their milkshake".

Quibi's focus will be on creating bite-sized chunks of video - serialised at around 10 minutes long - designed for people to watch on their phones, on the move. Katzenberg is forecasting that Quibi - short for Quick Bites - will attract subscribers numbering anywhere between 11 million and 70 million within five years, each paying some US$5-$8 a month.

Quibi's pitch is that it can bring Netflix-level talent and programming to mobile screens, and has lined up well-known filmmakers such as Guillermo del Toro and Jason Blum to make exclusive programmes. Significantly, it is also going to cover news - though exactly how and in what manner remains unclear.

Despite all these potential new threats to its territory, CNN, the global and enormously successful American news network now owned by AT&T, has loftily proclaimed itself to be relatively unconcerned by the OTT phenomenon. Speaking at the Mobile World Congress in Barcelona in 2018, its worldwide president, Jeff Zucker, said news channels like his were in general "somewhat immune" from the rise of OTT giants like Netflix.

"CNN has never been more relevant," he said. "The way people consume live news has made us more immune... from OTT... and dwindling cable audiences." While the likes of Amazon, Facebook and others were competing with CNN in some areas such as documentaries, Zucker said that the news cycle, which deals in "immediately perishable" programming, made it "harder for platforms like that to compete with what we do".

Hmmn. Why does that remind me of the dismissive comments made by the CBS news president when CNN itself launched in 1980? And some of the younger entrants into the news business, who are using the internet to reach their (primarily young) audiences, certainly take issue with Mr Zucker's self-confident views. In writing this chapter, I sought the insights of several of them to gain their perspective on what's happening in the industry and to clean a closer understanding of what they are trying to achieve. I hope you will find their thoughts, experience and advice useful. I certainly have.

Newsy.com, which is aimed predominantly at millennials and bills itself as the fastest growing news network in America, believes it can take advantage of today's technological advances to compete with the likes of CNN, Fox and MSNBC. It had a staff of more than 100 people in early 2019, with rapid expansion plans in place.

Newsy began in 2008 as a syndication business, selling video news to digital content sites such as AOL and Microsoft. It has evolved into a fully fledged news channel, streaming 50 to 70 video reports across 14 hours of live news every day - delivering what it calls unbiased video news and analysis on the most important stories from around the world, free of the hype and slant common to many news sources.

"I can't see our business as it stands right now being successful without the technological advances that have come about in the past three to five years," Newsy's CEO, Blake Sabatinelli, explains. "They have actually been one of the biggest catalysts for our growth. The business has changed significantly over the past 10 years, but variable bit-rate streaming has given us the capability of delivering video anywhere to any device, in a high-def capacity with no latency. Giving people the opportunity to see the content is step number one."

Newsy is distributed across the internet through platforms such as Apple TV, Amazon Fire, and Google Chromecast, and reaches 36 million homes in the US via a cable deal it struck a couple of years ago. It had annual revenues of $25m in 2018 (up 200 per cent from the previous year) and while that may make it a minnow compared to the CNNs of the world, it has lofty ambitions. "We've doubled revenue year over year for the past three years," Sabatinelli says. "We've been able to ride the tidal wave that's currently pushing behind us so things are fantastic. It's been incredibly exciting to see the OTT ecosystem start to blossom and it's been advantageous for us to be first movers in that space.

"Cable has also been a real catalyst for us. Here in America, cable news and broadcast newscasts are still regarded as the gold standard, as legitimate sources of information. OTT's still growing so there is scepticism in some cases as to whether or not its news is legitimate, so cable for us has been a great opportunity for our channel to be directly placed next to our competitive set, which is CNN, Fox, MSNBC and Headline news, and help us grow and legitimise our brand."

Newsy, which operates on a free-to-watch, largely advertising-funded basis, was bought for $35 million in 2013 by E.W. Scripps, a media company formed in 1878 which owns traditional TV stations and daily newspapers across America. At the time of its purchase, the chairman of Scripps declared: "Newsy adds an important dimension to our video news strategy. It's a next-generation news network designed and built exclusively for digital audiences. Newsy's uncommon approach to curation and storytelling has helped it build a strong national brand, which fits well with both our current media assets and our ambitions to further develop digital media businesses."

So should the CNNs and the MSNBCs be worried?

"The CEO in me says they should be very worried," Sabatinelli says with a chuckle. "The reality, however, is that there's a lot of room for a lot of players in this space so we've been fortunate enough to be incubated within a larger company which has allowed us to experiment and find our way onto a platform - OTT - that has allowed us to have a first-mover advantage in that space.

"That doesn't mean the legacy players aren't well funded enough to come play catch up, which they will, but we have started our movement there quickly and it does give us a good position. And as we move onto their turf, there's an opportunity for us to take share and viewership away from them. There's a long road ahead of us in terms of building the business that we know we can build and building the audience that we know we're going to build, but there's a lot of room for all of us. I think each of us brings something new and different to the table and as much as we are competitive with each other, we also try to work together at the same time. We are well positioned to take audience and share, but I think there's a future for all of us as we look ahead."

Sabatinelli believes that the key to securing a successful financial future for Newsy and other ad-funded news channels lies in the ability to capture rich data on their customers in the same way a Facebook or a Google can - to know everything about them, not just who they are, but their likes and dislikes, their family status, their spending habits.

"That's really been a huge catalyst for us," he says, "and has made monetisation on OTT platforms go from something that was kind of a novelty into what we have all been hoping for for some time, which is truly addressable TV advertising.

"The industry is starting to get there. There's a huge push to understand what the data graph looks like in the television ecosystem. There are DMPs [data management platforms] that are really trying to rival what you can do with a Google or a Facebook data set. AT&T is trying to combine all the data from their handsets, TV sets and the digital data from all the Turner properties, but they still have a long way to go. We're not quite at the point where we can say with specificity exactly who we're targeting but we're getting to the point where there's a far more granular view of the viewer."

Having such detailed knowledge allows a channel to start charging advertisers up to eight times more. "It moves it from a $5-$6 cable CPM [cost per thousand] to a $20-$40 addressable CPM. In some cases, we've heard that platforms like Direct TV can charge upwards of $100 CPM, depending on who they are targeting and what they are targeting. There's an exponential yield on that viewer. It really comes down to us using the technology that's available to us and then starting to transact on it.

"As subscribership [to cable] and viewership continues to dwindle, TV channels are going to move from a one-to-all model to a one-to-one model."

Does Sabatinelli have any advice for would-be new channels thinking of joining the fray?

"There's a lower cost of entry with OTT, which is appealing, but there is still quite a significant cost associated with producing 16 hours of news that gets distributed across a number of platforms. It still costs a lot of money, but the reality is that you can produce a product that is on par with your competitive set for a tenth of the cost, if you think about things the right way, and that's the business model that we've taken.

"Don't try to replicate what everyone else is doing. Just because you can do something the same but cheaper, doesn't mean you should be doing it. The way that you're going to take audience and take share from your competitors is by providing a different solution, and that's the premise we've taken. We have one chair on our set and it's the chair for our host to help guide people through the news. We don't bring on opinion makers, it's just not our business model, and that's how we differentiate ourselves from the rest of the industry.

"Find your niche and produce it well. Don't expect that if you do something that's exactly the same but costs a little bit less, that you're going to be successful.

What are the biggest challenges for Newsy and other small players?

"Every startup comes into the market dealing with an incumbent of some sort. We're playing on a playing field where our competitors are incredibly well funded. They have large, entrenched audiences and taking audience away from Fox, for example, is challenging. You are talking about a company that generates $2.5 billion in annual revenues and something like $800 million in cash so they can thwart any opposing effort coming at them by spinning out new products or doubling down on investment in certain areas. The same holds true with MSNBC and CNN - these guys generate large amounts of cash. They can invest very quickly and strategically as needed, so we have to remain in front and maintain our advantage, especially in ad technology, in order to make sure we are delivering a better product to more people in a more rapid manner than they are.

"It's critical that Newsy and other entrants are authoritative and can be trusted. Huge numbers of people have become news refugees. These are people who have no place to call home any more. They feel like they have been burned by the traditional providers. There's no one out there doing news in what you might call the old-fashioned way: here are the facts and context that you need; any opinion you need to seek out on that, you're on your own. In order to achieve that, you have to make investments in very challenging places. We have made significant investment in investigative reporting, for instance, which was a crucial thing for us, a very important part of our strategy.

"It's incredibly expensive, and it's challenging and hard, and investigative reporters are hard to find. You don't just stumble across those sorts of stories and turn them out in a week. But we believe that part of our business is going to be a key differentiator for us, so we invest in it. It's not something that happens overnight.

"We have been fortunate to be acquired and then incubated

within an organisation that has allowed us to methodically build up and grow. You can't have hockey-stick growth forever. You can have a couple of years of exponential growth and then it levels out and you have reasonable growth. That doesn't always meet the venture-funded view of how a business should go.

"There's an argument right now as to whether we're still in the golden age of television, or whether that golden age is over or it's just now starting, but there's definitely a ton of growth happening right now and we're part of that growth and it's an exciting place to be in. It's never been more important for our society to have strong journalism than right now.

"News, just like any other business, is a customer-service business. It's a business like any other. We have to treat people well, we have to treat our viewers like they are customers buying something, and that's the mantra I preach day in, day out to my teams, whether you are dealing with a vendor, with a co-worker or with a viewer, you treat them well."

Technology has also been key for **Africanews**, a pan-African TV news channel that launched in 2016, broadcasting across the internet in English and French. Although initially started and funded by Euronews, its sister channel, it bills itself as the continent's first truly independent news service, free of any political slant.

Headquartered in the Republic of the Congo, Africanews has a staff of 85 and adheres to an editorial charter based on freedom of expression and editorial independence "limited only by respect for the facts". It streams over the internet and goes out on satellite across sub-Saharan Africa. After two years of broadcasting, the station says it is gaining greater awareness across the continent than the BBC or CNN.

"We're very proud of what we have achieved," explains Michael Peters, who is CEO of Euronews and Africanews. "We couldn't have started Africanews without the technological advancements we have had recently. It would have been impossible five to 10 years ago."

He initially thought that he might launch Euronews Africa, but quickly decided that would simply be doing what other big players, such as the BBC, CNN and France 24, had done. "Their headquarters are in Paris or London, not in Africa. With us, from day one, it has been important that this is a channel in Africa, run by Africans, for Africans.

"Africa is a land of opportunities. It is a continent which is rising. But why can't we hear what the Africans have to say, not only on African affairs, but on world affairs, too? The demand for unbiased news is unmet.

"I had this absolute conviction that I was not here to spread the European or the American perspective to the African people. I was there only to give my know-how about how to produce the quality journalism for a small amount of money.

"My promise from day one was that the team had total editorial freedom, without any interference from anyone. From the Editor in Chief to the most junior person in the newsroom, they are all Africans, giving an African perspective of African and world news.

"We are increasing. We have not yet fulfilled all our different targets. The biggest problem has been that there was no real pan-African advertising market; regional, yes, but nothing continent wide. We have had to create this market and as a result we have growth in revenue of 50 per cent a year. We are not yet profitable, but we knew we wouldn't achieve that until year five or six, so we are on track with our plans."

As with Sabatinelli, Peters is convinced that offering something different - and being trustworthy - is critical for news brands. "We are in a very, very challenging and hyper-competitive industry," he says. "The key to thriving in this market is the trust that consumers have in your brand. Trust will be the number one criteria which will make people choose one brand over another. Unbiased news. This is why we speak about African news, by Africans and we don't speak about Euronews Africa.

"Having a USP is important - there are so many brands out there. A channel really needs to make the consumer understand what is unique, what makes it different from the others and to stick to this DNA."

Not all new startups will be profitable or succeed, of course. After much hype, many millennial-focused digital news companies, backed by venture capitalists seduced by rising user figures and the prospect of a good return on their money, have struggled to meet the somewhat unrealistic expectations of their investors in the past few years. Once-hot new brands like Buzzfeed, Vice, Huffington Post - some of which were valued in the hundreds of millions of dollars - have been forced into shedding staff and cutting costs in order to survive. It can be a brutal experience. As one founder of a venture-funded startup described it: "It was like playing a game of double-or-nothing. It's euphoric when things are going your way - and suffocating when they're not."

Some of them sink and fail, and there are important lessons that can be learned from them. Cory Haik was the publisher of an American internet and media company called **Mic** that was formed in New York in 2011 to deliver cutting-edge storytelling to millennials, raised US$60 million of investment, and briefly had a valuation measured in the hundreds of millions. After various iterations, the final straw for Mic came in late 2018 after Facebook cancelled a deal to publish a news video series. Most of Mic's 60-plus staff - including Haik - left and the business was sold for just US$5 million.

Despite this bruising episode, she remains a passionate believer in the quest to deliver news in a different and more appealing way for younger generations. "I fundamentally believe the vision and the opportunity is important and still real and needed, but [at Mic] the execution against that need or opportunity in the market was kind of fraught for a number of reasons," she says. "To be very reductionist about it, we had an over-reliance on Facebook. That's not to blame Facebook in any way; it was a symbiotic relationship in many ways, it's developing its own business. But those organisations who built very big audiences off the virality of that network and assumed that revenue would follow to match the money they raised, had a sort of naivety about the idea that these audiences were in some way their audiences, when they're not. When they are finding you on Facebook, that doesn't mean they know who you are, or have a connection with your brand. So when traffic goes away, when algorithms change, you lose an important part of your value proposition, which is commanding a big audience."

The proliferation of new news organisations - taking advantage of digital's far cheaper start-up costs - has caused a glut, an oversupply of stories, each desperately competing for attention, according to Haik.

"I firmly believe that getting the journalism right is important - content is king, right? - but I also know we've been making an oversupply of stuff, which is part of the problem," she says. "A lot of it is junk - there's just too much of it in the universe. So many outfits are playing the scale game: the more content you can make, the more advertising opportunities there are, the more eyeballs, and quality has just gone down. To support a meaningful, high quality, high standard news organisation, the question is out as to how you monetise that.

"It is very expensive, particularly video. If you do high-quality video, it costs a lot of money. The more niche you go, the more quality you go, generally it's a smaller audience, and then that becomes a problem with monetisation. There is no silver bullet solution to that - it's going to be a mixture of revenues, from subscriptions, events, advertising, it's going to be hustle. All of these venture-backed digital media ventures formed over the past five to 10 years are now like, 'Whoah, you've taken all our money and it's not the scenario we thought it was going to be in terms of returns'."

Being heard amid all the noise is difficult, Haik contends. "I think Buzzfeed News is doing an absolutely killer job in terms of journalism, but it's fraught from a financial point of view. Buzzfeed writ large has taken on a lot of money, so where they go from here is a real question. Can Buzzfeed News find an audience? It's certainly competing with the big guys in terms of scoops and its investigative pieces, but is it sustainable financially without some kind of subscription model or real audience connection? I just don't think the person on the street knows Buzzfeed is a serious news player. For now, they have some runway, but how sustainable that is in the long term I don't know."

Such difficulties in making news pay have led some US organisations to go down a non-profit route, funding their journalism via endowments or philanthropic foundations, such as the Emerson Collective run by Laurene Powell Jobs, the widow of Apple founder Steve Jobs and the sixth-richest woman on the planet. The organisation has also provided support to several non-profit journalism outlets, including the Marshall Project and ProPublica, and has purchased a majority stake in *The Atlantic*, a 160-year-old American magazine that's morphed into a strong digital brand.

So what is Haik's advice to those crazy enough to be thinking of launching a new for-profit news channel? Despite the challenges and the gloom, there's cause to be hopeful: optimism, she believes, is required.

"There's definitely a need out there. There's a young demographic that doesn't watch television, which doesn't get a newspaper - it's not that they don't care about news - but you're competing with every single thing on their phone. They are ready to consume, but the way you produce it, the accessibility, the interestingness, is all going to be really, really important. Can

The New York Times or the CNNs make that jump? I don't know. It is almost incumbent on some new entrants to figure out what the right format and cadence and topics will be for these young people.

"*The New York Times* is still structured fundamentally around the sections of a newspaper, which, by the way, were created for advertising purposes. New entrants like Buzzfeed and Mic set up our beats around affinity groups that connected on the internet, audiences that were interested in social justice. Those are all new. I do think there's a need, there's a market, an opportunity to create some kind of real connection with new audiences that primarily live online on their phone, but it's going to be very hard. The old firms might figure it out some time, or they're in big trouble. It's just going to be a long, hard road.

"You look at someone like *The New York Times*, they're on top of their game. They have over four million subscribers and they want to get to 10 million subscribers in the next handful of years. [But] it's so expensive what they're doing - over 2,000 journalists. It would be very, very hard to create something like that. Anyone new is kind of playing at the fringes. What stories are they [*The NY Times*] missing? What mediums and platforms are they not paying attention to? Where are the holes?

"I do believe that there is going to be a real place for some kind of visual storytelling. We consume so much information but how much of it do we remember? Very little, actually. Even great pieces of journalism - you read them, you think about them at the moment, then they kind of go away and six months later you forget you even read it. And maybe that's OK but, journalistically, if you are looking to make an impact, you have to reveal something to them and it has to stick in some way."

The new way of storytelling might resemble more of a documentary-style than a traditional two-minute news bulletin. "More of these are being produced and consumed, and I fundamentally believe people are consuming them because they are searching for something real, for truth.

"What news is, is changing. Ask a 15-year-old what they think news is and it's a very different answer to if you ask a 40-year-old. If you look at some of the new services coming on line, Jeffrey Katzenberg's Quibi, for example, is really interesting. His thesis is that short-form video, 10 minutes is optimal, built for mobile is the future, and he is going to be doing news in that way. You have to think there is going to be some emergence of short-form, fact-based documentary, narrative-style journalism that is produced and consumed and is important and becomes a piece of the report in a way that it's not right now. I do think that will exist and I don't think it will be the CNNs producing that; they are too tied to their talk format which works for them, and *The New York Times* is too tied to its paper. They might try their hand at it, but I think the opportunity lies with the new entrants to do this work."

Her other guidance is to keep costs down - especially in the launch phase - to be flexible and not be wedded to one way of doing things, and to be prepared for more change.

"We are in a period of massive transition in media and it's not clear where it's going. Whatever you're doing right now, you may not be doing in six months. This is all a moving target. You can have a thesis about something but you have to be pretty open to that shaping up differently. If you want to be successful journalistically and you want to build something for the long term, you are going to have to be committed to the fact you want to do journalism because trying to find a sustainable revenue opportunity can lead you down a path you weren't planning and so you have to be very mindful of that. Be ready for anything, and be vigilant of your journalistic integrity and be creative around that."

Haik cited Cheddar, the New York streaming station that aims to be the business channel for millennials, as a good example of how to start small, but think big. "It's been really smart about the strategy of landing deals early, and getting in position. It didn't start with a very expensive operation and execution; more like two people sitting at a desk in front of the Nasdaq [stock exchange] and just interviewing people and reading headlines." After ensuring it got off to a solid, financially sound start, Cheddar has now hired a renowned news veteran, Jim Roberts, who previously headed up NYTimes.com and Mashable, to move them on to a new level. "He's a well-known, serious journalist and he will turn it into something important news-wise," Haik says. "It's a smart strategy."

Roberts himself is firmly convinced that Cheddar is forging new ground. When he joined the station as Editor in Chief in December 2017, he explained his reasoning: "For those of us who've worked in digital journalism for the past decade or more, you experience a series of epiphanies as new techniques arise or new platforms are developed that allow you to communicate better, more immediately and more intimately with your audience. I had one of those flashes when I learned about what was happening at Cheddar. The team is using the techniques of traditional television, but shaping the content and delivering it in a radical way that is naturally accessible and meaningful to younger audiences. I truly believe that Cheddar holds the key to the future of live video news."

14

GAZING INTO MY CRYSTAL BALL

"If there is any period one would desire to be born in,
is it not the age of Revolution... when the historic
glories of the old can be compensated by the rich possibilities of
the new era?"
Ralph Waldo Emerson

Predicting the future is a mug's game. Just ask Darryl F. Zanuck, the co-founder of 20th Century Fox, who in 1946 opined on the future of television: "People will soon get tired of staring at a plywood box every night." Or the US bank president in 1903 who advised Henry Ford's lawyer not to invest in his client's business because: "The horse is here to stay, but the automobile is only a novelty - a fad." Or Microsoft's CEO Steve Ballmer, who maintained in 2007: "There's no chance that the iPhone is going to get any significant market share. No chance." A year later, Ballmer went on to cement a claim to being one of the modern world's leading prophets when asked about the future of apps, he stated: "Let's look at the facts. Nobody uses those things..."

As the old saying goes, "Predicting the future is easy... getting it right is the hard part." That adage may be even more true when it comes to how technology will play out over the coming years. The pace of change and the innovation that accompanies it make it almost impossible to be certain what lies around the corner. So while I do not intend to proffer some hard-and-fast predictions here, I hope I do not err too much towards Nostradamus, the 16th-century French seer - his prophecies were so vague that they can be, and have been, applied to anything and everything, from the rise of Hitler to the assassination of US President John F. Kennedy.

It is fashionable these days for many large corporations around the world to employ people as futurists, or foresight professionals, as they prefer to be known. These are not latter-day soothsayers who have some supernatural ability to perceive events in the future, but rather they are smart, well-informed people who, armed with a lot of research, brainpower and strategic thinking, can advise what is *likely* to impact their sector or business five, 10, 20, even 50 years out, and how best to prepare for and manage that change.

These are less firm predictions than highly educated guesses, based on understanding history, interpreting data and trends, and engaging in some blue-sky prognostication. I, too, am a firm believer in utilising statistical inference. By looking at patterns across the world, the kind of developments that have shaped TV in the past, and where we are in the "present", we can start to understand what tomorrow might look like. It can give us the tools to predict with some reliability the changes that are likely to take place.

Let me stress at the outset that while this sort of scenario planning and forecasting is important, there's only so much that can be achieved through such an approach. In my experience, other indicators - such as listening to one's instincts, hard work, luck - play as important a part in launching, building and sustaining businesses.

As those who have read the earlier chapters know, after qualifying as a chartered accountant, I spent many years as a partner for KPMG in the Middle East. But as my four children were growing up, I wanted them to know where they originated from and belonged, so I decided that we would move back to Pakistan. It was not an easy decision because I had been told I was next in line to head the Middle East operation. But, at times, you need to go the way your heart tells you. It was the best decision of my life; my children have grown up to always remember that part of their lives, and to feel a deep connection to their homeland, irrespective of where they now live.

This was the first time I had worked in my home country. I set up a consultancy wing of KPMG, which was a great learning curve. I was lucky enough to produce a monthly economic and business review of the country based on statistical data, and also started to write on economic affairs for a leading national newspaper. This enabled me to develop some strategic insights into what was happening in different business sectors in the region - which eventually led me to start my TV production company, hoping to be part of the great changes that were happening in that industry at the time.

Did I use a futurist to tell me that this sector was going to open up to private firms as the state's monopolistic control of television ended? Or did I consult a palmist to tell me my future path after I had been blessed with a successful career at KPMG? The answer, of course, is "No". For me, it was just sensing a potential opportunity, doing some research, and having the passion, dedication and determination to try to make it work.

I want to relate this because I contend that success in life is 65 per cent luck, with the balance made up of hard work and having belief in yourself. Being in the right place at the right time is an important element. Does that mean you should forget doing the exercise of looking at trends, assessing the data, and trying to work out what the future holds? Of course not. If you have the good fortune to realise, or discover, what the next big thing will be, go for it. I would say that such insight, such certainty, is rare, and it is a great gift which, quite frankly, I have never possessed. Whatever path this guides you down, follow it. For me, it was just simply hard work, luck and being sensible in my planning process.

So let's take a look at the TV news business over the past 40 years or so, using those three "tools" of the futurist: a bit of historical analysis; insights into the relevant data; and some educated guesswork.

It's probably hard for anyone under the age of 50 to believe today, but the number of television channels available in most countries could be counted on the fingers of one hand until the 1980s (and until the mid-1960s, they broadcast only in black and white). Britain had just three stations before the launch of Channel 4 in 1982. Today, the BBC alone has nine, and there are some 400-plus others to choose from in that country. American television was dominated by three big networks for decades until HBO launched on satellite in 1975. Today, America has so many channels that no one is quite sure what the exact number is, though it is certainly more than 1,700. Pakistan (where television only began in 1964) had just two channels until the year 2000, when the government opened up broadcast media to the private sector, ending the monopoly of the state-run Pakistan Television Corporation (PTV). Though it should be pointed out that PTV continues to retain control of free-to-air terrestrial broadcasting - private channels can only operate on satellite, cable or over the internet. The result is that viewers in Pakistan now have more than 100 stations to choose from.

The manner of television-watching back then was as limiting

as the choice. Until the 1980s, viewers not only had just a few channels to pick from, they were forced to watch a programme at the exact time that it was aired. If you missed it for any reason, that was that. What mattered from a business perspective for TV executives was the size of the audience that the programmes could attract - they weren't selling the programmes, as such, but the audience for the programmes. The bigger the audience, the more money the networks could charge advertisers. So the programmes they put on were largely, and deliberately, inoffensive and bland; anything that might scare viewers away was to be avoided at all costs. In such an oligopoly, the TV viewing public had to put up with what they were given, when they were given it.

This first television epoch began to be overturned in earnest in the 1980s, as a second revolution got under way, resulting in a far greater number of channels and greater choices in the ways of watching for consumers.

The introduction of the home videocassette recorder allowed people to start recording and collecting movies and television shows, and to watch them when they pleased. By 1985, more than 20 per cent of American homes had a VCR, twice the number from the previous year. That same year, the first Blockbuster Video store opened, in Dallas, Texas, allowing people to rent from a range of thousands of movies and TV shows. Alongside this development, new technology - cable and satellite transmission - allowed the number of channels to exponentially increase. In America, so often the leader in our business, the sports channel ESPN launched in 1979, CNN in 1980, the music channel MTV in 1981, and CNBC, the American business news channel that was later to play such a large part in my life, began in 1989. Similar expansions swept across Europe and, later, the developing world. The viewer was starting to have multiple choices, and to gain control over what they saw, when.

A new economic model arose that was no longer solely dependent on advertising. Cable operators charged subscribers a monthly fee for access to a bundle of channels (whether or not they wanted them all or just a few of them), and in turn paid fees to the channels based on the overall number of subscribers. (For example, cable operators pay CNN a fee of around 60 cents a month for each of the millions of homes they reach, even if only one household in a hundred actually watches CNN.) Audience sizes were no longer king; even with small ratings, a CNN or an ESPN could bank billions in revenues before they even aired an advert.

Now that model itself is being challenged by TV 3.0, the industry's third incarnation. The technological advances that allow a TV station to circumvent traditional delivery methods and stream directly over the internet to global audiences has changed the business - and the audience experience - more in a few years than cable and satellite did over a few decades. And we have yet to see its full potential. Technology is dramatically altering how we experience entertainment and news.

Fast forward the TV viewers from the 1970s into today's world, and they would be amazed by the choice available at their fingertips. Hundreds of channels. Tens of thousands of shows. Billions of hours of programming, on almost any genre and subject you care to name. And all available on a variety of screens, in your home, on the move or sitting on the beach. Streaming services like Netflix and Amazon Prime have changed the game irreversibly; since there are no advertisers, it doesn't really matter how popular a particular programme is, so long as viewers are happy to continue to pay their $8 a month subscription. Contrary to the 1970s, the audience is no longer the product - the customer is. The consumer has gone from being badly served advertising fodder to calling the shots in fewer than 50 years.

We need only lift our eyes up from one of our screens to see the immense changes that this revolution is starting to have. The old ad-supported TV ecosystem is, in its current form at least, probably in slow but mortal decline. Linear television ratings will continue to fall as streaming consumption proceeds on its astronomic rise to become the dominant method of viewing. Consumption on mobiles will similarly keep expanding.

As with all revolutions, it is messy. As hundreds of new stations take advantage of the dramatically lower costs of entry to the TV market, consumers are being confronted by a confusing jumble of individual on-demand subscription channels that, added up, can cost more and often offer less than the old cable bundles. Yes, there are lots of great shows and movies being made, and new news sources springing up, but finding them and identifying the ones we might like sometimes feels harder than ever.

For the time being, however, the public's appetite for more channels and more choices seems insatiable. Viewers like having unlimited access to a wide range of programmes for a monthly flat rate, and being able to decide when and where to watch a particular show, and to binge watch six of them in a row if they wish.

All the trends point onwards and upwards for subscription video on-demand channels (known as SVODs in the industry). To look at a couple of areas of the world with which I am most familiar and have had the good fortune of building a working experience, SVOD subscriber numbers in the Middle East and North Africa are forecast to jump from 11 million in 2018 to 26.5 million by 2024, and from three million to 10 million in sub-Saharan Africa. Over the same period, annual revenues from such services are forecast to reach US$2.3 billion in the Middle East and North Africa (up from $0.6 billion in 2018), and to rise to US$1 billion in sub-Saharan Africa (up from $223 million in 2018).

While Netflix is expected to continue its global dominance (it's forecast to increase subscribers in the Middle East and North Africa from 3.1 million in 2018 to 7.7 million in 2024, and from 1.4 million to four million in sub-Saharan Africa), other players will also experience phenomenal growth. In the Middle East, Starz Play is forecast to grow subscribers from one million in 2018 to three million in 2024, while Shahid Plus will show six-fold growth to 1.8 million subscribers. In Africa, Showmax and iROKOtv are predicted to exhibit similar levels of growth.

On-demand channels that prefer to make their money from advertising (known as advertising video on-demand channels, or AVODs, in industry parlance) and be free for consumers to watch, are forecast to show a similar, if slightly less spectacular, growth. Much of their future will depend on the ability to understand their audiences down to the same sort of granular level as a Facebook and Google, and what happens more generally to the advertising market, aspects of which I shall touch on a little later.

As Joseph Dimmock, a technology analyst at GlobalData, puts it: "Video-on-demand has established itself as a serious challenger to traditional broadcasters and their competition has made SVOD and AVOD platforms a crucial part of any broadcaster's current and future product portfolio."

So this, as I write in mid 2019, is where we stand: in the midst of a burgeoning new revolution with no predictable outcome. When I think about the possibilities, I feel a bit like the Chinese premier Zhou Enlai who, in 1972, was asked about the impact of the French Revolution. "Too early to say," he replied, cautiously. Given that the French Revolution had occurred nearly 200 years before, Zhou seemed to be expressing a particularly long and extremely circumspect view of history. (Sadly, it later transpired that he had been referring to the student "revolution" in the Paris of 1968, rather than the original 1789 version.)

Before I make my stabs in the dark about the future, I thought it might be interesting to hear the views of someone who works in the business of forecasting. Not one of those futurists we talked about earlier, but someone engaged in a slightly older profession - that of clairvoyants and astrologists. Claire Petu-lengro is a UK clairvoyant and astrologer, who writes for various publications and the VH1 pop network. She's been reading palms since the age of six and comes from one of the most well-known clairvoyant Romany families in Britain. Her grandmother was a Romany gypsy, who established her name in the 1950s as a palmist and clairvoyant on Brighton Pier on England's South Coast.

Will her forecasts for the future be any better than yours or mine? Perhaps only time will tell, but let's see. I asked her four questions.

What will news presentation on TV look like in 2030?

In astrology, we are currently being hugely affected by the age of Aquarius, which is all about moving forward with technology and about spirituality also. This means we feel as if we, as a planet, are moving two steps forward and one step back; that with each advancement in technology there are also lessons to learn and setbacks to experience. Mercury also plays a huge part in us having to communicate as nations and so I predict and see that harsh lessons will mean the countries in the world will be forced to work together more in years to come.

I predict that in the next 20 years, events will happen which will prove to us that other nations have more advanced tech-nology than we knew existed and will be forced to share this with us. It will be an eclectic mix of events that makes us have to view the world as an umbrella, to protect and not to abuse. However, as I am sure you are aware, there will always be cruel people in the world and we may choose the wrong leaders, so mistakes will happen, but the positive in all this, is that for once the world learns from its lessons.

Will we have robotic, AI-driven news presenters or human beings presenting?

It is inevitable that we will have Artificial Intelligence news-casters in the future, but with the mood in the next 50 years also being about heartfelt emotion, there will always be a human touch needed, as that is what we need to nurture and grow.

I feel that the method you are talking about is only a doorway into a whole different dimension of the mind, on how we will be able to view things. I feel that there will be experiences on a day-to-day basis to touch, smell and hear as well as view the day-to-day things in our life which are before us technically as never before.

There will also be a discovery, towards the end of the time you asked me to study, where we shall find out that previous generations, from many thousands of years ago, had made more advancement in some areas than we have in our lifetimes. This will cause feelings of excitement and fear, and is what will lead to the world choosing to try to work harder together, as one planet united for the greater good of all.

So, TV will probably have the ability to let us smell the rain falling in a film, and to smell the cakes coming out of an oven on a cooking show. By way of major advancements, I see more a sense of technology for our senses, to heighten them.

Rather than robots being our friends, it will be more a case of robotic parts being able to give longer life spans to those with health problems and issues which could otherwise impede, or end, their lives. I pick up clairvoyantly that there will be a very famous person in the media, that we will all know, who will turn out to be half human and half machine and who will make the most incredible advancements of our time.

Will viewers have special spectacles to put on to watch news in Virtual Reality?

I see an abundance of ways in which people will view films, music, information etc. This is linked to the fact that I see transport becoming far more out of man's hands and into the hands of robots, thus allowing us to do more with our time for ourselves when we are travelling.

The biggest insight is that there will be a huge advancement in flying and people will be able to travel faster and more easily, but the stress and worry for their safety taken out of their hands.

How do you see the majority of viewers watching/following news - on a TV, a mobile, a laptop, or a combination?

Mobiles - I see will have to be used in a different manner to the way they are used today, and that is due to health problems that the future shows they will create. Headsets, more than contact immediately to our ears, will be the way forward. The need to filter such sounds is important to our future. It will be a more balanced, technological and spiritual future.

I did a television programme in my twenties for ITV, where experts including myself, other clairvoyants and astrologers and experts in various fields, including sports, politics etc, had our predictions locked in the vault for a year in the Bank of England and I came out on top. The future is easy for me to see to help people, it's often helping them get over the past which is hard to do.

Some food for thought there - and who's to say she may not be right in at least some aspects?

So at the risk of being upstaged by Clairvoyant Claire or

becoming a rival for Mr Ballmer's crown, here, with my best thumb in sucking mode, are my thoughts about the next five to 10 years, confined (mostly) to what will (probably) occur in the TV news space:

1. The growth in the number of channels - some supported by advertising, some by subscription, and some via both - will continue, as will proliferation of choice for the viewer. As the costs of starting a video/TV channel drop, so we'll see more and more new players come into the market. These will be a dizzying kaleidoscope of channels: some covering niche subjects and aimed at small audiences; some started by brands hoping to promote their products (such as Playmobil, the German toy manufacturer, setting up a channel to show animated videos of its figures in multiple languages); and others launched by pressure groups or political parties to bypass traditional news outlets and push their own agenda (such as *Real News Update,* the weekly show launched on Facebook, Twitter and YouTube in 2017 to support Donald Trump's 2020 presidential campaign).

2. This increase in the number of channels will lead to further declines in average audience ratings per programme, but the fragmentation will not be a symptom of declining popularity in TV, but rather a badge of its success; it will be better serving the diverse needs and wants of the public.

3. Some of the new upstart entrants that the established players in the industry dismiss today will come to supplant them if they don't take their threat seriously. There's a long and undistinguished history of this

hubris. In the 1990s, newspapers initially dismissed, then utterly misunderstood, the internet. Back in the 1970s, the dominant big three US car manufacturers - General Motors, Ford and Chrysler - laughed off the "dinky cars" being produced by Japanese entrants such as Toyota; Blockbuster ignored Netflix; Kodak ignored digital film.

4. As a way of averting this fate, the big traditional TV news players (think the CNNs, the Foxes, the MSNBCs) will arm themselves with their cheque books and their billions, and seek to buy their way out of trouble by acquiring the best bets among the new entrants. We've seen that, in a small way, with E.W. Scripps (est 1878) buying Newsy, the millennial-focused AVOD we looked at in Chapter 13, for US$35 million in 2015, and Viacom (dating back to 1927) paying US$340 million in January 2019 for the California-based Pluto TV - an AVOD that launched in 2013. Some will get it right, some won't (see Disney's gamble on Vice, for example).

5. Other big non-media players are likely to join the party, sometimes for reasons of diversification, sometimes as a complementary move for their existing businesses, and sometimes simply for the fun of it. For example, Walmart, the American retail conglomerate that generates around $17 billion in cash annually, has been considering launching a subscription streaming video service to compete with Netflix and Amazon Prime.

6. The distinction between TV and online video and the internet/linear/cable/satellite will blur to the point of being meaningless. As will the debates over what device a person is watching "TV" on.

7. Super high-definition TV screens (probably taking

over one entire wall) in the living room will remain popular with viewers - particularly for live events, sport, dramas and movies - and will probably be operated by voice. No more fights over the remote; just battles over who can shout the loudest, perhaps. All watchable devices will become more personalised and smarter, suggesting an intelligently curated, personalised playlist of content that is better suited and ever-more relevant to the user.

8. The concept of a programming schedule will fade to irrelevance, except as an internal guide for staff to know what they need to produce by when. All shows will become available on demand.

9. Subscription services will expand, as it becomes even clearer that it will be perfectly possible to grow successful enterprises around a business model that includes little or no revenue from commercials.

10. Advertising will change markedly as businesses wake up to the amount of money they are currently wasting, and the fact that there is a growing audience of younger people that marketers can no longer reach on linear TV. (I wonder, incidentally, what would companies pay to reach the millennials binge-watching shows on Netflix?) TV and online video planning and measurement will merge. Antiquated, generalised adverts will become replaced by smart, focused ones driven by the rich data that TV businesses will amass and know about each viewer or household. TV firms will know as much, if not more, about their customers than the Facebooks and Googles know about theirs. Not just information about what shows they like to watch, but such insights as their current and future spending habits, their interests, their intentions. The idea that

companies once spent millions delivering one general advert to all viewers, rather than one specific advert targeted to just one viewer will come to be regarded with derision by future generations. For example, a family with young children thinking of buying a car will receive an advert from a car manufacturer for a people-carrier, while the childless couple next door watching the same programme will see an ad for a sporty hatchback. It will be more measurable for marketers, and more pleasurable and relevant for viewers.

11. TV news will deliver more interactivity, and more viewer involvement. People will no longer just "watch" the news, but participate in it. Digitally streamed news that has VR immersive capacity will deliver unique and compelling experiences, letting viewers be transported from their living rooms into war zones, or into stadiums to watch a player score a winning goal. The social media divisions of news stations will be full of buzz and activity. Costs will dramatically reduce on the delivery portion courtesy of 5G (and, in about 15 years, 6G), but will increase on talent, content, presentation, technology, social media and digital. Revenues on the digital side will rise to compensate for all this.

12. The quality of content, its trustworthiness, its relevance, will remain the crucial factors and determinants of success or failure for existing and new players.

I could be hopelessly wrong on most, if not all, of these predictions. Who knows? What I am certain of is that this is a wonderful time to be alive and to be involved in our industry. It may be scary, the outcome may be uncertain, but isn't it exciting? It's not every day you get to take part in a revolution. It comes without an instruction manual - but I hope that perhaps this book will be something of a guidebook as you navigate the years ahead. Good luck, and please tell me about your journey by messaging me at my website, TVnews3-0.com.

SELECTED BIBLIOGRAPHY

This Business of Television, Howard J. Blumenthal & Oliver R. Goodenough, Billboard Books, 2006

The Television History Book, ed. Michele Hilmes, British Film Institute, 2003

Broadcast Journalism, Peter Stewart & Ray Alexander, Routledge, 2016

The Television News Handbook, Vin Ray, Macmillan, 2003

Television Production, Jim Owens, Focal Press, 2016

Now the News: The Story of Broadcast Journalism, Edward Bliss, Columbia University Press, 1991

How to Watch TV News, Neil Postman & Steve Powers, Penguin, 2008

Niche News: The Politics of News Choice, Natalie Jomini Stroud, Oxford University Press, 2011

Talking Politics: Choosing the President in the Television Age, Liz Cunningham, Praeger, 1995

Television News: A Handbook for Reporting, Writing, Shooting, Editing, & Producing, Teresa Keller, Routledge, 2019

Television News and the 24-Hour News Cycle, Kristin Thiel, Cavendish Square Publishing, 2019

INDEX

VISIT TVNEWS3-0.COM

I hope you have enjoyed my book. Please visit my website - www.TVnews3-0.com - to let me know what you think of it. You can also sign up to receive my occasional newsletter, designed to keep you up to date with developments in the world of TV news.

Thanks for reading.

Best wishes, Zafar

NOTES